PENGUIN BOOKS

THE GRIZZLY BEAR

Thomas McNamee was born in Memphis in 1947 and grew up there. He graduated from Yale University in 1969 and since then has lived in New York City and Montana. He is the author of *Nature First: Keeping Our Wild Places and Wild Creatures Wild* (1987) and *A Story of Deep Delight* (1990). He has been president of the Greater Yellowstone Coalition and remains a member of its board of directors.

THE
GRIZZLY
▾BEAR▾

BY

THOMAS McNAMEE

With drawings by

Gordon Allen

PENGUIN BOOKS

PENGUIN BOOKS
Published by the Penguin Group
Viking Penguin, a division of Penguin Books USA Inc.,
375 Hudson Street, New York, New York 10014, U.S.A.
Penguin Books Ltd, 27 Wrights Lane,
London W8 5TZ, England
Penguin Books Australia Ltd, Ringwood,
Victoria, Australia
Penguin Books Canada Ltd, 2801 John Street,
Markham, Ontario, Canada L3R 1B4
Penguin Books (N.Z.) Ltd, 182–190 Wairau Road,
Auckland 10, New Zealand

Penguin Books Ltd, Registered Offices:
Harmondsworth, Middlesex, England

First published in the United States of America by
Alfred A. Knopf, Inc., 1984
This edition with a new afterword published in Penguin Books 1990

1 3 5 7 9 10 8 6 4 2

Portions of this work appeared in *Audubon* magazine in different form.

LIBRARY OF CONGRESS CATALOGING IN PUBLICATION DATA
McNamee, Thomas, 1947–
The grizzly bear/by Thomas McNamee; with drawings by Gordon Allen.
p. cm.
Reprint. Originally published: New York: Knopf, 1984.
Includes bibliographical references.
ISBN 0 14 01.2812 3
1. Grizzly bear. I. Title.
[QL737.C27M36 1990]
599.74'446—dc20 90–7024

Printed in the United States of America

ACKNOWLEDGMENTS

ON the long road that has led to my first book I have been sustained, year after year, with unfaltering faith in my career, with scrupulous and always gracious criticism, with steadfast material and spiritual beneficence, and with love, by my wife, Louise.

Whatever understanding of the grizzly bear this narrative may claim has relied as much on talk as on the written word. Long, wide-ranging conversations with people who have devoted years to the bear have illuminated for me such questions as how what is known about grizzlies has been learned, how that knowledge fits into the larger realms of ecology, government, and civilization, and what, in those realms, the grizzly bear may mean. In a profession as busy and as specialized as the study of grizzly bears, only a generous sacrifice of time and a willingness to wander afield can make that sort of conversation possible, and it has been my good fortune to have benefited from just such generosity and good will on the part of a number of biologists, to five of whom I wish to express particular thanks here: Charles Jonkel, of the Border Grizzly Project, whose deep understanding of the nature of the grizzly bear and of why such an intractable wild creature *matters* in a civilized society has been the lodestar of this book's point of view; Richard R. Knight, of the Yellowstone Interagency Grizzly Bear Study Team, whose clear-headed realism has elucidated for me the significance of the difficulties now impinging on the grizzly's precarious existence in Yellowstone and elsewhere; Stephen P. Mealey, of the U.S. Forest Service, whose faith in the possibility of the bear's survival has given me what weak hope I have, and whose role in the United States government's all-important behavior is helping to strengthen that possibility; Larry J. Roop, of the interagency study team and the Wyoming Game and Fish Department, who has hiked with me into grizzly country and taken me grizzly-tracking in the air and grizzly-trapping on the ground and spent long hours with me in grizzly talk, and who is as good a friend as the grizzly could hope for; and Christopher Servheen, of the U.S. Fish and Wildlife Service, whose perspicacity and courage have already dozens of times sliced through the bureaucratic imbroglios in which the grizzly so frequently becomes ensnarled, and whose fine-tuned objectivity and sense of fairness have made him dozens of times for me a decisive authority.

I also owe thanks for valuable conversations to Gary Brown, of the National Park Service; Alan Christensen, of the U.S. Forest Service; John J. Craighead, of the Wildlife-Wildlands Institute; Mary Meagher, of the National Park Service; Bart Schleyer of the Yellowstone interagency study; and Paul Schullery.

Of the written sources of this narrative, none has been more important than the work of Frank and John Craighead and their associates, which forms the very basis of contemporary science's knowledge of grizzly bears. Virtually every assertion I have made about the biology of the grizzly draws in some way on their findings, and I owe them an inexpressible gratitude.

All the people mentioned above have reviewed all or a major part of this work in manuscript, and, although there remain disagreements on certain questions, the finished product incorporates hundreds of their suggestions. Without their meticulous scrutiny, this book would have been inestimably poorer.

I might never have found my way to this project unless Roxanna Sayre and Les Line of *Audubon* magazine had underwritten and published my piece "Breath-holding in Grizzly Country," bits of which crop up throughout this narrative. It was my agent, Jeanne Drewsen, who first encouraged me to turn that piece into a book, and I am deeply grateful to her. The many kindnesses of my wife's colleague Mindy Lesser also call for special thanks.

When I began this undertaking, I did not quite know what it is that book editors usually do, and now that I have finished I'm still not sure—for my lucky case must certainly be exceptional, so prodigious have my editor's contributions been. If there is to be credit at all for this book's creation, Barbara Bristol must share it.

THE GRIZZLY BEAR

APRIL

STILLNESS. Utter stillness. Miles on snowy miles of it, of nothing moving, not a bird, not a deer, not a wind-quivered willow shoot—no wind—no one. Only stillness. A world dead beneath six months of snow, dead blinding absolute white. Above, fierce mid-April sun, and empty midday sky. Beyond, a black and white horizon, crags of ice and stone. Below, an ice-encrusted forest pocked with buried meadows. Here, a few black rocks, a clump of whitebark pine, a single ancient gnarled subalpine fir; a steep blank slope of snow.

There appears in that whiteness a darkness, a hole. There appears in the hole a wet black nose. Sniffing.

And with a sudden snow-explosion, where there was nothing there is all at once a lot of something. A grizzly bear. Three hundred fifty pounds thereof.

Sniffing, sniffing. It is still winter here at nine thousand feet, but, on a zephyr too faint to feel, the bear can smell spring from far down-mountain, and the tang of putrescent meat. Yet although she has eaten nothing for half a year, the bear is still not hungry. What she is is still sleepy. With a grunt, a long yawn, and a last dim squint at the lifeless winterscape she turns, and goes back through the hole in the snow beneath the snaggled roots of the old fir tree.

A week goes by. Snow falls, the den again disappears, and again the snow explodes to disclose a sudden outburst of bear. For several minutes she just stands there as if dazed, blinking, slowly waving her big head back and forth, sniffing the breeze; then she sits down. Hind legs splayed out on the snow, long-clawed forepaws limp in her lap, she sits up on her rear like a man, luxuriating in this lush beatitude of sun. She scratches her belly, even after six months' fasting still a stately pot. Now, turning toward the darkness of the den, she voices a soft *whuff*.

And out into the dazzling white world tumble two more grizzly bears, rather smaller than the first, perhaps five pounds apiece. They are every bit as cute and fuzzy as your great-aunt Alice could please, rollicking frolicking teddies, clumsy and goofy and gay.

They are hard to picture now as the terror of the wilderness. Indeed it is hard to picture even their mother as such. Still half in hibernation, she barely moves. Her gait, when she does, is drunken,

3

unsteady, slow. If there were trouble now, her reaction might well be slow and clumsy. This posthibernation lethargy is one good reason why grizzly bears tend to choose such blizzard-blasted and remote places for their dens, and why for the next several days the family will not roam farther than a few seconds' travel from the safety of the den. The cubs are still unsteady on their feet, moreover, and the mother bear is still not hungry. Give her a week or so to shake this grogginess, though, and then watch out.

The cubs settle in for their first outdoor meal, of milk exceeded in richness only by that of coldwater marine mammals such as whales, seals, and walruses—grizzly milk being twenty-five to thirty-three percent fat, compared to three percent for cow or human milk. There are six nipples for the cubs to choose from, although grizzlies never bear that many young: litters are typically one, two, or three cubs, depending mainly on the nutritional status of the mother; litters of two are by far the commonest.

For almost three months now, nursing and napping have been the cubs' whole life. Their mother stirred and woke from her deep torpor from time to time—most notably near the end of January, to bring them into the world, eat the placenta, and clean them up a little —but the state of her consciousness even then was uncertain. The cubs, encircled in that massive furred insensibility, themselves not hibernating, have had nothing to do but grope and suckle and grow till their début today.

Pretty soon, though, they are going to be busy. Success in life for every grizzly bear depends on what that individual bear has learned in his cubhood; in the extent to which they rely on individual instruction, grizzlies are surpassed probably only by man and the great apes. Animals whose behavior is determined principally by their genetic inheritance tend naturally to be much alike; instinct is among the greatest of equalizers. Animals educated by their mothers, themselves the products of generations of individual instruction, tend to be individualists. Of the latter form there can hardly be a better representative than the grizzly bear. At least a year, more often two, and sometimes even three or more years of a grizzly's youth are spent in school. And in grizzly school the discipline is rigorous, and the lessons are many and hard. The mother grizzly is—must be—an exacting teacher.

Still a few days' respite remains, for the mother bear's hibernation wears off slowly. Basking, snoozing, nursing, frisking, all within

a moment's dash of the den, the cubs pass a lazy homebound week in sweet far niente. Even in such seeming indolence, however, a crucial process is under way—the inculcation of the three fundamental rules of grizzly bear cubhood: follow mother; obey mother; have, within those constraints, as good a time as possible. They learn to see, they learn to walk. When, gaily wrestling, the cubs tumble downslope in the snow farther than that all-important moment's dash from the den, the big bear gently takes each cub's whole head in her jaws and carries him, dangling limp, back within the safety zone. When they bite too hard at her teats, they get a prompt flat-pawed boxing of ears. When she calls to them with a soft peremptory *woof* (they quickly learn), they by God come. They dig in the snow, they sniff at the multivariously aromatic breeze, they learn to keep their balance and run. They nurse, they grow. They play.

Meanwhile, as the last woozy sluggishness of posthibernation lethargy wanes, the mother bear is getting seriously hungry. Up here it is still winter, and there is nothing to eat. It is time to sally forth into spring.

With frequent stops for nursing, somersaulting, climbing, cavorting, and every manner of exercise of the cubs' ebullient curiosity, the three make their way desultorily down to death-redolent elk winter range. The snowpack is deep this spring, and the elk—and deer and moose and bighorn sheep—who have wintered in these sheltered valleys are down to the woodiest stubs of browse, and there is not enough of even that to go around. Many are dying, many are dead.

The mother grizzly follows a scent to the edge of a seething snowmelt creek, and there finds a carcass. Ravens squawk in the treetops. A coyote leaps from his covert and skulks into the forest to await his chance to return. With a single slice of a single claw, the big bear neatly opens the elk's abdomen. She clips the esophagus with a yank of her teeth and pulls away the bulging rumen; this first of the elk's four stomachs is full, despite the fact that this animal did starve to death—so unnutritious are the winter's-end species of browse represented here. She lays the rumen aside. The cubs sniff fascinated at her every motion and its consequence: when she lifts her head to sniff for evidence of disturbance, their eyes are on her, and they, without the least idea what they are doing or why, wave their heads back and forth and sniff too; one waves his head so hard he falls over.

Although the elk may have died weeks ago, the body is barely thawed, and the liver, while she would not especially care if it were not, is still fresh. The mother bear lifts it out and presents it to the cubs to try their needly new teeth on. Clumsily they mouth at the liver, tugging and growling fiercely. Even in play, even with such a superabundance of food, the cubs make of every situation a contest.

The grizzly rips great chunks of flesh from the haunch and, hardly chewing, half choking, wolfs them down. The cubs, not quite ready yet for meat and already bored, want to play, and they hurl themselves merrily at her head. With a gourmand's single-minded snarl she bats them aside. She puts away an easy twenty pounds.

Done at last, licking her chops, she sits on her haunches and lazily scratches an ear and yawns. At such moments her winter torpor still threatens to reassert itself, but she cannot let it. There is work to do. She excavates a shallow elk-sized hole and maneuvers the carcass in. She shovels dirt, duff, mud, snow, sticks, rocks, whatever is handy, to cover her property and warn off any interlopers; this covering will be known to all as the signature of a grizzly bear, to be gainsaid only at great peril. She even drags a good-sized tree trunk out of a logjam downstream and heaves that over too.

There is a dense grove of Engelmann spruce and lodgepole pine nearby, in a particularly dense part of which the mother bear scoops out a cozy bowl just big enough for her and the cubs. She rips down green spruce boughs and lines the depression to form a springy, heat-trapping mattress. Curled up here, concealed to perfection within defensive-charging distance of their meat cache, the bear and her young may sleep their breakfast off in watchful security. For the next several days and nights, as she gradually consumes the elk and teaches butchery to the cubs, this nest will be home.

Upstream, along ten feet of bank, a little seeping spring has melted through the snow, and there, thus warmed and sunny, the black alluvial soil has yielded tender shoots of sedge, the season's first green succulence. After their midday nap, the mother grizzly leads the cubs there to graze. Although she esteems no food more highly than meat—for there is none more nutritious—the grizzly bear instinctively seeks out a balanced diet. After the die-off of starving prey in early spring and then the stress of calving season, there will be progressively less meat available: the weakest ungulates (hoofed animals) and their most vulnerable young will already have died, and their survivors will be too fleet of foot to catch. Until fall, when prey and carrion again become available, the bears' livelihood will be progressively more dependent on their ability to recognize and harvest the most nourishing food plants.

In some springs less lucky than this one—when, for example, the winter kill of ungulates is low, perhaps because the snows have been light and hence more browse has been available—grizzly bears must subsist almost entirely on vegetation. Yet even in the best of springs, in the high, cold country where most grizzlies live, much of their range is still under snow, or still so frigid that nothing is growing yet, and what meager plants there are are few and far between. And then in late summer and on into fall, as the countryside dries up and the nights grow cold again, many plant species mature and wither and die. At these times, especially in dry years, a grizzly bear's knowledge of when to seek and where to find such superficially insignificant microclimates as that of this sedge-fringed seep may spell the difference between life and death.

Spring is unquestionably the hardest time of year for grizzlies to find food, and in a naturally regulated population the nutritional deficits of spring are believed to be the principal cause of grizzly mortality—and, because spring nutrition directly affects fertility and cub survival, it is a major agent limiting their reproductive success as well. (A "naturally regulated population," by the way, is more a theoretical ideal than an observed reality, since grizzly populations everywhere but in the remotest Arctic tend to be at least partially regulated by human factors such as killing or habitat destruction.)

A well-educated and experienced grizzly bear's knowledge of his home range is astoundingly comprehensive and precise. Our mother bear remembers not only where she found good things to eat last year but also where, six years ago, in a summer of drought, a low moist spot in an otherwise sere expanse of sun-parched timothy still held a pocket of lush bluegrass. She remembers which slopes and ridgetops are the first to be blown free of snow in spring. She remembers, even before their aerial parts appear, where the richest starchy roots and tubers may be dug. She knows the buried whereabouts of pocket gopher populations. She remembers where, each fall, the squirrels have harvested and hidden their hoards of pine nuts. She knows the locations of all the avalanche chutes in her range, where the frequent snowslides have limited the vegetation to that which can withstand all that cascading snow—the grasses, supple-stemmed shrubs, and forbs (soft-stemmed plants that die down to the ground in winter, most of which are familiar as wildflowers)—and she re-

8

members which of those avalanche chutes, facing south, are first to catch the sun and therefore first to green up. Even now, as they learn to grasp the blades of sedge in their back molars and roll their heads to snap it off, the cubs are storing up essential memories.

This is the first of many lessons to come in botany, which will be the major subject of their primary education. Because grizzlies retain, albeit in modified form, the short gut of their more carnivorous distant ancestors, and lack the cellulose-digesting ability of the ruminants (cud-chewing, four-stomached animals like elk and deer and cows) with whom they share their habitat, they must make the most of the scant proteins which almost all their food plants contain in usable form for only a short time—in the preflowering phase, when the plants' reserves of solar energy and mineral nutrients are concentrated in the stem and leaves in preparation for the manufacture of flowers and seeds. The cubs will learn to recognize this stage in the lives of hundreds of species of plants, and they will learn precisely where to go to find these items at their peak of succulence at every time of the year, under a wide range of climatic conditions, and throughout a great variety of habitat types. To a greater extent than any other factor, this process, of following their food plants' phenology, determines how and where grizzly bears live their lives.

And it may seem strange, but that is how the awesome grizzly, widely known as "the largest terrestrial carnivore," actually spends most of his waking time—placidly munching on grass and flowers.

The vegetarian life is nevertheless a precarious one. At least until high summer brings the berry crops, the caloric value of most grizzly bear plant foods, although substantially higher than that of the plants they do *not* eat, is quite low in relation to the plants' weight and bulk. The bear's digestive efficiency is also low, so every grizzly bear is constantly on the lookout for a quick shot of easily digestible, high-protein, high-calorie goodness—in other words, meat. The discovery of a network of pocket gopher or ground squirrel tunnels will often send a grizzly into a perfect frenzy of excavation. So great sometimes is a grizzly bear's lust for meat that he will expend far more energy in its pursuit than could possibly be gained; one ten-pound marmot, more often than not never caught, can account for the furious hurling downhill of two tons of talus. Digging, by the way—more than ripping open a moose's belly or your sleeping bag—seems to be what the grizzly bear's prodigious front claws have evolved for.

Grizzly bear food habits can be fairly neatly summed up in one word: opportunism. They will eat some of the lowliest crud in the world, but they still know a square meal when it comes along, and they will let little stand between it and themselves. Watch.

A week has passed. Nibbling daintily at the streamside sedge again, the cubs spot a field mouse zipping across the snow. They are instantly after it, all vegetarian thoughts instantly banished. Such pursuit they do not need to be taught: grizzly bears instinctively chase things that flee from them—which accounts for the puncture wounds in the fenders of some park rangers' trucks, as well as certain other more serious disfigurements. But the mouse is too quick for these still clumsy babies, down its burrow in a flash. Dig then they must, and impressively do. Sod-clods fly between their little back bow legs. But their coordination is not yet sufficient, and the mouse has escaped—until their mother moves in. She cocks an ear groundward, hears the faint rustle of the subterranean quarry, and with a single scoop of her paw brings up a hunk of turf from which squirts the mouse, straight into her jaws. Crunch, gulp, and it is gone. The cubs look on, dazzled, one lesson closer to competence.

These are perhaps exceptionally lucky grizzly bear cubs, born in the prime of a conscientious and experienced mother's life, in a good year for food, in a relatively safe and undisturbed home range. Many another young grizzly these days is not so blessed. Indeed their own mother's youth was not nearly this easeful, and for years her very survival was in question. She was not born proficient in the art of motherhood; it has taken some hard learning.

She is not native to these parts, and her own early education was cruelly cut short, so it has taken her an exceptionally long and hard time to learn her way around and develop a modicum of adult grizzly skills. She was born well to the west, in the heart of the national park, where the countryside and the grizzly bears' way of life were substantially different from those here. Grizzlies there, including her mother and her grandmother and her ancestors for generations reaching back before the turn of the century, had commonly made a large part of their living every summer by rooting through the plentiful high-energy garbage of the park, particularly in the large open dumps. Our bear spent the better part of the first year of her life at one of these dumps. But then early the next summer, when the yearling bear and her brother and their mother returned, they found the dump closed—bulldozed, buried, and devoid of food.

This was quite a shock. Even the yearlings' mother had scarcely learned the intricacies of maintaining an adequate natural diet, and their accustomed home range, once the dump was closed, was grossly insufficient in natural foods. They had also fed on unsecured garbage in campgrounds, but there was not enough of that. Still considering peanut butter sandwiches, hot dogs, and cookies to be supreme among grizzly bear comestibles, the family (and dozens of other grizzlies) sought such items where they might be found. That meant a sustained assault on the campgrounds.

And it often also meant a terrific lot of trouble to get at the goodies—chasing off campers, ripping up tents, bashing in ice chests, running from rangers, and so forth. Finally one night the rangers trapped the yearling and her mother (the other yearling, her brother, got away), and the mother got an accidental overdose of immobilizing drug, and died. The little female yearling awoke, some hours later, exiled by helicopter to these unfamiliar mountains, orphaned and ignorant.

Without her mother's milk to drink or garbage to eat or picnic hampers to raid, the young bear nearly starved. But bit by bit she learned enough to get along in her new home range. In spring and summer, she found the meadows, seeps, and other moist sites, with succulent herbs rich in protein and roots still richer in starch. In late summer and fall, she sought out the berry patches. In late fall, she made her way to the ridgetop whitebark pinewoods with their oily nuts. She grew rangy and tall that first year, but stayed skinny. Her fur was scruffy and lustreless. Nevertheless she made it, barely, to fall.

She dug her winter den in a windy mountainside where the snow often blew away—thus exposing the door of the den—and only the luck of an extraordinarily temperate winter kept her from freezing to death. The following spring there was a late hard frost, which meant no berry crop in midsummer. The fall was dry, the pine nut crop was poor, and again she nearly starved to death.

But as the years of her youth went by, she slowly grew in competence and resourcefulness. She learned to rifle garbage cans along the highway to the south without getting caught. She learned that on a cattle ranch to the northeast there could be found, in spring, the thawing carcasses of winterkilled cows. She learned where deep-drawn springs fed beds of succulent grasses even in the aridest September. And somehow, untutored though she was, she survived.

Some female grizzlies approaching adulthood enter a sort of incomplete estrus (period of sexual readiness) in their fourth summer, and may also mate, but these subadults almost never conceive. Because of her always tenuous nutritional status and her retarded physical development, sex at such a tender age was out of the question for our bear. Indeed, even the following June, when she was four and a half years old, passed without a sign of estrus. The majority of grizzlies do reach sexual maturity at that age, but a large minority do not reproduce until they are older. Some grizzly bears, both male and female, do not mate successfully until the age of eight or even nine.

Finally, in her sixth summer, she mated and conceived, and in the following January her first litter was born—a male sandy blond all over and a female chocolate brown with a creamy ring around her chest and upper back. The new mother, like all mother bears, was utterly devoted to her cubs, and she tried never to let them out of her sight, but solicitous and vigilant as she meant to be, she was inexperienced—orphaned as young as she had been, and herself a first cub of an inexperienced mother—and sometimes her attention wandered.

One foggy windless morning in late May, she and those first cubs had found the carcass of a bighorn sheep. Food had been scarce ever since they had emerged from the den in mid-April, and the cubs had gorged themselves; now they were snoozing in the brush nearby. The mother bear was feeding so hungrily on the meat that she did not hear the approach of another grizzly, a large old male. She knew he was there only when she saw his shimmering bulk materialize out of the mist and advance on her and the carcass.

A cub is a precious thing. Even the longest-lived and best-fed female grizzly bears can contribute only a few cubs to the population in the course of their lives. Their reproductive rate is one of the lowest known for mammals: where our bear lives, litters average only 1.9 cubs each, and the average interval between litters is three years. It is very much to the species' advantage, therefore, for mother grizzlies to defend their young with the utmost possible ferocity. And that is a quality of which mother grizzlies possess an awesome store. The male was triple the young mother's size, but when she burst out at him from the cover of a rock, he instantly recognized big trouble and took flight. The scent of the decaying sheep, however, continued to drift his way, and before long his resolve returned.

This time he approached still more quietly, and this time he came close enough for his nose to confirm what his judgment had, on the basis of the female's behavior, assumed: cubs. Again the mother bear charged him, and he withdrew, but now he stopped sooner and egged her on. Then he counter-charged, and she responded in kind, and he drew her a little farther on. At last, with a feint downhill toward the carcass, he dodged the other way and threw the female off balance and bore down on the terrified cubs. Before the mother bear could recover her equilibrium, the old male had snatched up the brown cub in his jaws and bounded to the top of the hill. In apocalyptic rage the mother bear raced after him, but the remaining, male cub was wailing in terror behind her and it chimed through her blood that she must not leave him. The big male grizzly was too far ahead anyway. With the abducted little one flopping limp from his muzzle, her neck broken, he ran on for several miles before stopping at last to devour her.

Not many days thereafter, the mother grizzly and her surviving cub struck up an acquaintance with another, older female and her three cubs. This proved to be one of the luckiest breaks of the younger mother's life, for as their informal association deepened into a working partnership, at the older bear's side she was to learn the locations of some of the area's best and remotest feeding sites, and by her too, that fall, she would be led to a new denning mountain far away, safe from all possibility of disturbance, where, on the leeward side, the snowpack would be heavy, thus insulating and concealing the den all winter long. What was most important, she had ample opportunity to observe in this painstakingly judicious mother an exemplar of balance between harsh discipline and carefully directed encouragement of their cubs' reckless enthusiasms. The older bear, in turn, found in her new companion a much-needed babysitter and a significant addition to her line of cub defense—for protecting three cubs from predatory males and other hazards is a much taller order than looking out for only one or two. The two families lived together all that summer and fall, and that winter they denned within a hundred yards of each other.

This kind of cooperation among individual grizzlies, biologists believe, is neither common nor rare. It is commonest, of course, where it is most useful: between family groups, and between recently weaned, inexperienced subadults, usually siblings. But it is not unknown to occur between solitary, unrelated adults—sometimes, though very infrequently, even in male-female pairings outside of mating season. The one permutation that has never been observed, presumably owing to unseemly gourmandise of the sort recently illustrated here, is that of an adult male and a female with cubs. In all cases, it seems to be a temporary state of affairs, since mating (with its attendant every-bear-for-himself convention) must eventually intervene in every possible combination of cooperating partners.

With the coming of spring, the two mother bears and their families still stayed together, but hormonal urges had begun to stir in the older grizzly, and she began to show less of maternal patience with her cubs and more of selfish restlessness; it seemed that estrus was on its way. Since her cubs were still not even a year and a half old, this was early to return to sexual readiness, but not unheard of. Two of her yearlings were in any case quite ready to have a go at life on their own: they were both precocious, substantially bigger than their littermate, independent-spirited, already inclined to wander off together on all-night rambles. Frequently, in play, they would team up against the runt, and when food was short he was always the one who went without. This little male, like our own bear's yearling, was shy and clumsy and still much too impulsive. He had, for instance, nearly been gored when, apparently for the sheer hell of it, he chose to charge an enormous bull bison head-on.

When the older bear went into heat that June, the last of her motherly solicitude went swiftly down the drain. No longer the all-enduring playmate, she would belt and bite and bully her cubs until they were sufficiently bewildered to leave off trying to come near her. It took only a few days of this shock treatment for their filial affections to undergo a distinct decline, and for the two larger yearlings it was all the urging they needed to sever their maternal ties and flee somewhere far out of their bafflingly changed mother's reach. The sad-eyed runt, who undoubtedly could never have made it on his own, was adopted by the younger mother grizzly, and for another year she cared for both her own cub and his new stepbrother.

Thus they were two and a half, and she was eight and a half, when the family separated. She did not breed until the following year, however, so it was not until she was ten years old that her second litter was born—two strapping and aggressive males, both reddish brown with funny snub-nosed white-silver faces and ears the same shade. They grew up fast, and they seemed to have an unerring knack for running into trouble with people. This was probably due at least in part to the fact that both their first two springs had been unusually cold in the high country, and the mother bear both years had brought them to the ranch, at a lower, warmer, elevation, on the fringe of her customary home range, where cattle carcasses could be pawed out of snowdrifts at first thaw. There was also a small residential development just down the road, and that meant that garbage could sometimes be got at. By late May of their third year, the young bears had learned to kill calves, and the whole family were confirmed beef eaters. And the two-year-olds, having grown up amidst the outraged shouts and rich food aromas of man and even his occasional gunfire, had lost all fear of him.

The mother grizzly may have sensed that this was an untoward turn of events, for she never grew as bold as her young, but she, just as surely as they, had fallen victim to the tragic flaw of the omnivorous, opportunistic feeding strategy of her species. During the millennia of grizzlies' evolution, they lacked natural enemies altogether, and they developed a proclivity to exploit the highest-quality foods available, without any consideration of possible dangerous consequences—because there weren't any. Most modern grizzlies seem to know that certain kinds of behavior are dangerous—such as getting too pushy around people—but there are all too many occasions when instinct overwhelms knowledge and they forget. High-energy food is as addicting and as blinding to a grizzly bear as heroin is to a human. By this time of year, the family should have been tending back into the high mountains and the security of deep wilderness, but it was hard to think of that when the backcountry alternatives to this ranchland certainty of beef and garbage were grass and at best a chance of wild carrion.

One afternoon the mother grizzly and one of her two-year-olds curled up in their day beds at the timber's edge while the other young bear went off prowling on his own. She had not been asleep an hour when she was awakened by a terrible concatenation of riflefire. She whirled to check her cubs' day beds, and there was the one, wild-eyed. And, sure enough, there, out in the pasture, in broad daylight, there lay the other, his paws quivering, his skull blown apart, his teeth still sunk in the thigh of a freshly killed calf.

She and the surviving two-year-old lit out that night for the high country. Mating season was just around the corner, and it was now time for them to separate. She would not let him feed anywhere near her. If he tried to curl up with her, she slapped him in the face. In general, she was suddenly acting as unmotherly as imaginable. Under such wretched conditions, the young bear quickly set off on his own.

The mother grizzly then had what seemed to be a normal mating season. But no young were born to her the following winter. Probably because of all that stress in May, combined with a severe food shortage brought on by a late killing frost, she had failed in June to conceive.

The next year's mating season was rather more successful. The bear had been hanging around the site of a small-town garbage dump which had been closed for several years but which she continued to check out every summer. Because grizzlies will return year after year to places where they remember having found food in the past, and their memories are long, the neighborhood was fairly crawling with bears—some of them bold enough to be scrounging at the edge of town upsetting garbage cans, breaking into a cabin or two, eating dog food off people's porches (not to mention the occasional dog), and generally scaring the daylights out of the citizenry. The people were quite certain there had never been so many grizzlies in these mountains, but in fact the backcountry was virtually empty of bears, for most of them had come to town. The countryside nearby was excellent grizzly habitat in its own right, and the bonus of bacon, Alpo, spoiled sardines, and other such delicacies made it unbeatable. And the dump, though itself no longer a banquet hall, continued to function as a sort of grizzly bear community center and all-purpose rendezvous. So when the bear went into heat and began broadcasting the hot delicious scent of her readiness, there were plenty of male grizzlies within sniffing distance, and she did not lack for suitors.

They would sidle up behind her as she grazed on an open hillside, themselves seeming only to be feeding too but all the while working slowly closer. She usually fed with her head uphill, but now from time to time she would face the other way, and the male thus favored, clearly taking her having turned toward him as encouragement, would mosey closer still, slowly waving his head and, because a direct stare is grizzly bear language for a challenge to fight, avoiding her eyes. Sometimes she would turn away and flee a short distance, and then wait until the male moved close again. Then she might swat him roughly away, or bluff-charge him and send him skedaddling back downhill. As his ardor grew through the course of an hour of such coy lure-and-refusal, the male bear's tongue would begin to lap slowly in and out. The female's own growing readiness was shown by a marked swelling and purpling of her vulva. Eventually, she and the male would pace back and forth, back and forth, with the clock-work regularity of caged tigers, perfectly synchronized and at a perfectly kept distance apart. If the male tried too soon to move closer, she would withdraw to the ritual distance, and again they would pace together, back and forth, back and forth.

Throughout these decorous ceremonies, the female grizzly's estrogen level was rising toward the point where ovulation would take place. In some animals, ovulation is induced automatically by copulation; in others, it does not need to be induced, but simply occurs on a preprogramed schedule, with the female then immediately receptive to males; in bears, it is thought, an elaborate sequence of behaviors —foreplay, if you like—is required to set the endocrine stage for ovulation.

Finally permitted to come near her, the male grizzly would nuzzle her flanks and snuffle in her ear, groaning and panting. She responded with a peevish cold shoulder at first, and then with cool aggrieved tolerance, and finally with unimpressed indulgence of his slobbering gallantries. All these saucy vicissitudes can almost certainly be understood simply as expressions of fluctuating hormone levels, but to an observer accustomed to thinking of such antics in terms of a presumably more sophisticated species' presumably greater emotional and intellectual complexity, their familiarity can be poignantly comical.

At length, one young male, who had gained her acceptance with an elaborate display of salivating and urinating all over himself (some pheromonal communication probably going on in the latter), got as far as mounting the female and starting to hump delightedly away, when she invoked the universal distaff privilege of changing her mind. The victim of this unmannerly and naturally unsettling rebuff was then so busy plotting a second attempt that he failed altogether to notice the advent of a much greater problem, in the form of eight hundred pounds' worth of magisterial grizzly great-grandfather— who wasted no time in giving the oblivious young swain his most definitively chilling bellow of challenge.

The old male approached with a strange, slow gait—his steps heavy and deliberate; his knees locked, his ankles stiff, his massive head low, his silver hackles erect and rippling in the wind, his half-shut eyes burning a ragged hole in the resolve of his obviously impressed young rival. But impressed or not, the smaller grizzly wanted what he wanted, and badly. He stood up on his hind legs, shivering a little, and sort of half-roared half-croaked back. Perhaps simply in astonishment at such impertinence, the old male stood up too, some eight and a half feet tall thus—a stature it had taken him twenty-two years to achieve. But you never know. Sometimes these old brutes aren't as tough as they look. A bear this big might be starting to get feeble. So, at least, went what must pass for the young bear's reasoning, for without stopping to consider the odds he flew at the old one's throat and sank his savage canines in and pulled away a highly gratifying gobbet of bearhide.

This was most unwise. Twenty-two is by no means yet the age of senescence. With the strength of, say, several heavyweight champions of the world combined, in a single blow the raging great-grandfather laid the young bear flat, and then fell flat on top of him, belly to belly, jaw locked on jaw, ten four-inch foreclaws raking stripes in his half-conscious challenger's face. The old bear's roars and the young one's terrified caterwauling echoed loud off mountainsides miles away.

The female clearly found this victory gloriously exciting (male combat seems to heighten the amorousness of grizzlies of both sexes), for the kind of preliminaries she had put her earlier petitioners through were now greatly foreshortened, and it was not long after the bawling loser had fled woozily for cover that she was presenting her purple-centered hindquarters to the victor, who sniffed at her vulva with unmistakable relish.

For the first twelve minutes of their coupling, the two bears barely moved. Then for the next eight minutes, the female, no longer the demure tease, squirmed and wriggled her hips against the male. For a sudden ten seconds, then, he was thrusting wildly, and then for three minutes they were still again. A series of vibrations began to travel up the old male's spine, and the fur rippled visibly all up his back—just a few seconds each time, eleven times in all, spread out over ten minutes. For ten more minutes, the bears simply stayed coupled, as the female slowly padded along, sometimes grazing a little, sometimes falling softly forward when her front legs seemed to collapse. After a total of three quarters of an hour, the couple uncoupled, nuzzled each other's face, and began cropping grass side by side. The vanquished young daredevil grizzly, meanwhile, skulked to a tangle of deadfall deep in the woods and lay down and bled.

Day after day, the big old male stayed close to the female grizzly's side. In the nest of leaves and branches that was their day bed, he would lie with a protective and possessive paw across her shoulder. When other male grizzlies came near—their caution low, their hormonal alarms set a-clang by the female's redolent receptivity—the old bear would strut his slow-stepping low-headed stiff-legged stuff, and the merest grunt would usually suffice to send any would-be contender off to consideration of more profitable pursuits. Most of these male bears knew the old one already; indeed many wore the marks of earlier, less circumspect encounters with his wrath. Only once, with a longtime adversary even older than himself though rather smaller, was the great-grandfather obliged to stand and face the prospect of actual physical conflict, a threat which, after much brave roaring and feinting, was dissipated in the aggressor's taking a moment to recalculate his chances and then prudently turning tail for the next creek drainage.

The grizzly couple spent two weeks almost constantly together. To stay so long with one mate was not the old bear's custom, nor any grizzly's particular preference, but females were less plentiful these days than in his youth. In highly concentrated grizzly populations, where more potential mates are available, promiscuity is usual for both males and females; where grizzlies are scarcer, pair-bonding more commonly occurs, and sometimes lasts even after the mating season. Our grizzly couple's situation conformed to neither norm: the local grizzly subpopulation was temporarily highly concentrated—because of the human food sources associated with the nearby town —but the proportion of available females was exceptionally low.

There was nevertheless one young female, coal black with silver ears, with whom the big male did manage to mate one afternoon— during which his putative mate also indulged in a hurried assignation, with one of her earlier young supplicants. Otherwise, both were the very picture of monogamy the whole two weeks. When the female grizzly went out of heat, however, it was suddenly as though the bears had never known each other, and they parted without a backward glance.

After a solitary and uneventful nine days, the female came into heat again: a mature grizzly's estrus is often split like this into two episodes; some biologists believe that the second estrus occurs only if the first has not resulted in fertilization. Once again, upwards of a

dozen one-track-minded males traveled miles to come calling on the source of that eloquent aroma. There were other females in the area now, and her earlier mate was, for that reason, no longer so proprietary, so the days that followed were rather a merry-go-round. In a little over a week, she mated thirty times, with seven or eight different partners—including the old great-grandfather again, whose dominance over all the other males was no longer even challenged.

Sometimes the bear and her mate of the moment would seem completely lost in their rapture, the male groaning, panting, gnawing at the back of her neck, and she in turn, eyes blind, clawing up the turf. At other times she seemed distracted, only half there, sometimes even strolling idly along looking for food while her thrusting swain struggled to stay aboard.

Again, from the moment when the flow of her sexual hormones and their attendant pheromones ceased, the male bears at once lost all interest in her, and she in them. And from that day forward, until the birth of this present litter, her third, the female had no interaction at all with other grizzly bears except scrupulous avoidance.

On the day of their birth in January, the cubs were hardly recognizable as bears. They were then decidedly uncute and unfuzzy: blind, all but bald, toothless, helpless, less than a pound in weight apiece, and ugly as rats. The extremely small size of newborn grizzly cubs—hardly bigger than newborn black bears, whom they will soon tower over—reflects the mother grizzly's very limited and very efficiently managed energy budget, and a wonderfully economical reproductive strategy.

Reaching so rudimentary a stage of development requires a mere six to ten weeks of gestation. Yet, as we have just seen, the mother bear mated last June—seven *months* before giving birth. The apparent contradiction is resolved in the extraordinary phenomenon known as delayed implantation. How it works in bears is still not understood, but this is what is thought to happen. After the mother grizzly's two eggs were fertilized in June—perhaps by different males —the resulting zygotes divided and grew only briefly. These two tiny blastocysts did not, as is usual in mammals, attach themselves to the wall of her uterus, but continued to float free in the womb—not growing, but held in mysteriously suspended animation—until November, about the time the mother bear had entered her den. Thus freed all summer and fall from what would typically be high nutritional demands from growing fetuses, she was able to devote her food-gathering season entirely to her own maintenance, insuring a maximum of fat storage for the long winter to come. Finally, triggered by the onset of deep hibernation and able now to take full advantage of her late-season fat reserves, the blastocysts attached themselves to the uterine wall, and growth began anew. It seems almost miraculously right as an adaptation to the feast-and-famine cycle of the grizzly bear year.

The bear and her cubs will need every adaptive advantage they can get, and none will prove more essential than the behavioral flexibility and the sheer intelligence their kind has developed over the millennia. The mother grizzly sitting on the snow at the door of her den placidly nursing her third pair of cubs this fine April morning is a wiser mother grizzly than once she was; these cubs' upbringing, because she has learned so much, will be the strictest and most cautious she has yet superintended. Her hard-gained wisdom is to prove most fortunate, for she brings these cubs into a world that grows less livable for grizzly bears with every passing year.

The evolution of her species has produced in North America a magnificently, singularly *wild* wild animal; and it is that very wildness that makes the grizzly so difficult an animal to accommodate in a world ever more crowded with people, and ever more tame.

The North American grizzly bear and the Eurasian brown bear are considered members of the same species, *Ursus arctos*, because they meet the standard biological criterion of being able to interbreed and produce fertile young. But when you get to know them, *Ursus arctos horribilis* (the grizzly) and *Ursus arctos arctos* (the Eurasian brown) are very different beasts. To understand why, we must go back in time a bit.

Evolutionary movement toward a mammal directly ancestral to modern bears began about twenty-five million years ago, in the Miocene epoch, when early bearlike animals began to branch off from the dog family. Our grizzly bear's first ancestor really identifiable as a bear was a European, the Auvergne bear, *Ursus minimus*, who first put in an appearance between three and eight million years ago, in the upper Pliocene epoch. These new creatures differed from the canids in a number of respects. They were substantially bigger, with much larger skulls. Their stance was plantigrade—that is, they walked, like man, on the whole foot, and not, like dogs, just on the toes. Their teeth were bigger, and much changed from those of the canids: the most significant evolution was in the molars and premolars, which in the dog family had been carnassial, or shearing, and which now in the bears were adapted to crushing—representing a change in diet from pure carnivorism to a substantial dependence on plant foods as well as meat. Related to the same adaptation to omnivorism was a lengthening of the gut—a response to the greater difficulty of digesting vegetation. As his name suggests, *U. minimus* was a small bear, anatomically similar to the modern North American black bear and probably, also like the black bear, adapted to a heavily forested environment.

By the lower Pleistocene or Villafranchian epoch—between one and three million years ago—the Auvergne bear had evolved into the Etruscan bear, *Ursus etruscus*, and within that species we then see a pattern of spectacular growth and change that culminated in an animal virtually indistinguishable from the one we know as the modern brown bear.

The early model of the Etruscan bear was a little fellow—probably, like his equally small Auvergne ancestor, adapted to the quiet woodland life and a diet of the nuts, berries, herbaceous vegetation, insects, and small mammals that abounded in the forest. He was almost certainly shy, reclusive, and partly arboreal.

But big change was on the way. With the coming of the middle Pleistocene, vast sheets of ice scoured the northern forests off the face of the land. When the glaciers retreated, they left behind immensities of treeless tundra, and in adapting to this radically changed, much colder environment, the Etruscan bear developed a much bigger body. (As body size goes up, body surface increases by the square, while body volume increases by the cube. Thus larger animals, with lower surface-to-volume ratios, stay warm more easily in cold environments, which is why Alaska moose are bigger than Wyoming moose, and why, as François Bourlière has observed, English house mice who live in cold storage plants are bigger than their confreres living in houses. There are exceptions, but the pattern is true enough to have become a familiar maxim of biology, known as Bergmann's Rule.) In response to the lack of forest cover with its easy escape routes, the Etruscan bear now also probably had a much more aggressive temperament.

U. etruscus eventually split into three lines of development. One led to the European cave bear, which went out of business about ten thousand years ago. Another, adapted exclusively to life in the deep forest, led to the Asiatic black bear and, thence, on to the North American black bear. The third line, of which the earliest fossils yet found have come from China, can be traced to the brown and grizzly bears, *Ursus arctos*.

The brown bear turned out to be a marvel of flexibility. His large size and aggressiveness made him king of the mountain wherever he roamed. His wide-ranging gustatory habits made almost any habitat a good place for food-finding at least some of the time, and his ease of movement enabled him to cover all the ground he might need to find food throughout the growing season. Most important, amidst the wrenching climatic vicissitudes of the Ice Age, the combination of his great size, his aggressiveness, and his omnivorous diet insured that he was equally at home in the forest and, with no need to fear exposure to predators, on the open ground left behind in interglacial periods.

The brown bear's remarkable adaptive success spread his kind throughout Europe and Asia. Fossil evidence has shown that brown bears throve even in the mountains of north Africa. In the dense forests of subglacial southern Europe, niche competition from brown bears probably was responsible for the extermination of the cave bear, and here brown bears recovered (or retained) many of the shy, vegetarian traits of their woodsier ancestors. In the semideserts of the Middle East, on the grasslands of central Asia, and across the Siberian taiga, their size and their aggressiveness grew still greater in response to those bitterly harsh environments.

It was presumably from among the big, ferocious brown bears of far northeastern Asia that the first emigrants were drawn toward North America, moving across the land bridge where today the Bering Strait separates America and Asia. This migration may have begun as long as fifty thousand years ago, and the Asian and Alaskan brown bear populations remained in contact until ten thousand years ago, when glacial recession parted the continents.

In these last ten thousand years of separation, Eurasian and North American brown bears have remained physiologically very similar, but there have been marked differences in their ecological roles and, in turn, in those traits, culturally rather than genetically transmitted, which develop in response to short-term changes in the environment.

With the end of the last major glaciation ten millennia ago, forests began to reclaim central and western Europe, and brown bears there developed a way of life similar to that of their southern cousins and to that of their own forefathers. Because these woodland bears were reclusive, and probably nocturnal, and, in the mast-rich deciduous forests, had no need to range over large areas in search of food, they adapted with relative ease to the explosive population growth of their first serious competitor—an expanding, tool-using, weapon-using human population. There must certainly have been occasional conflicts between brown bears and early man, but for the most part the environment was sufficiently rich, and the numbers of both species sufficiently limited, to sustain both bears and man in cautious mutual avoidance. Each, of course, was dangerous to the other, but when there were conflicts, the bear was more likely to be the victor. Probably only in rigorously organized hunting parties—which must have afforded serious danger to the participants—were the humans with their simple lances or arrows able to dispatch a bear. Along with the natural separation generally maintained by the differences in man's and bears' ecological niches (feeding regimes, habitat preferred, and so forth), these occasional hunting successes were probably significant enough that bears tended to avoid man except in cases of dire hunger, and even then, undoubtedly, the bears must have learned that a raid on provisions or livestock by night entailed far less risk than direct confrontation. Thus from the earliest times of association between brown bears and man, there have been selective pressures against ursine aggressiveness—because the bears who engaged in aggression against humans were those most likely to be killed—and there has also been, perhaps, a gradual growth of culturally transmitted knowledge that humans could be dangerous to bears.

As agriculture spread, Europe's brown bear habitat and population declined, but vast tracts of wilderness still remained, and even amidst farming of the low intensity typical of premodern times there was still plenty of room for bears. Some agriculture, such as the raising of domestic livestock or the cultivation of fruit, may even have enhanced the quality of bear habitat.

Along with agricultural civilization came rapid advances in weapons technology, and bear hunting now came within the realm of possibility, but it was dangerous enough—and the bears, no fools, hard enough to find—that it was at best a sometime thing, and not a serious drain on bear numbers. What was most crucial to the continuing viability of European brown bear populations was that man and bear entered the age of civilization at the same measured pace, each well acquainted with the other, and each therefore, given time, able to accommodate his way of life to that of the other. Not only did better weapons increase selective pressure against bear aggression, but also man and bear each learned, and profited from learning, to leave the other well alone. There was a kind of balance of power.

Even with the full flowering of European civilization—with the growth of cities and transportation, the cutting of forests, the ubiquity of agriculture, and the general triumph of man over nature—the bear hung on remarkably well, and it was not until the eighteenth century and the birth of modern firearms that brown bear populations in midcontinental Europe began to be extirpated.

It is instructive, and highly significant for our own efforts toward bear conservation, that the only brown bear populations wiped out before modern times were those of Denmark (about 3000 B.C.), Ireland (about A.D. 750), and England (about A.D. 1000)—two of them islands and the other virtually so, all three lacking buffer zones of low human density from which diminished bear numbers might be restored by immigration. Except for the immense uninhabited lands of the farthest North, this island situation is, unfortunately, precisely where nearly every bear sanctuary on earth today finds itself—lacking, just as surely as England and Ireland and Denmark did, adjacent populations from which immigrants may come.

It will come as no surprise that the rise of technology wrought havoc with European brown bear populations. Hounded and hunted, baited and hated, his forests cut down and plowed under, the bear was the very image of the wilderness that had come to represent to Europeans the darkness and mystery out of which, hungering for light and reason, they strove to climb. The bear was extinct in eastern Germany in 1770; in Switzerland, in 1904; in the French Alps, in 1937.

What may surprise is that so many of Europe's bears are still managing to hold on, even if sometimes by the merest thread. Kai Curry-Lindahl of the United Nations Educational, Scientific, and Cultural Organization (UNESCO) reported in 1970 that at least thirteen and perhaps even nineteen or twenty insular populations of brown bears remain in Europe. For some of these, however, the future is dark. In the Pyrenees, for example, Peter Röben of the University of Heidelberg has reported, the population has declined in the last forty years from two hundred bears to fewer than twenty, and given the relentless assault on their homeland fueled by the feverish French appetite for hydroelectric power and second homes in the mountains, not to mention that country's disgraceful overall record in wildlife conservation, the prospects for these survivors are extremely poor; although Spain can be as good a conservationist as France is bad, the Spanish portion of the Pyrenees alone cannot sustain a population. In the Dolomite Alps of northeastern Italy, the population is probably smaller than ten individuals, yet the poachers are still after them, and these bears are almost certainly doomed. In the rugged Abruzzi segment of the Apennines, in central Italy, there may be seventy to a hundred bears—perhaps, if poaching can be controlled, enough to sustain a breeding population. In Poland, Tadeusz Buchalczyk of the

Polish Academy of Sciences reported in 1977, there are two bear populations, but they total only about thirty bears in all; the prognosis here must also be considered poor.

Other European populations are doing better. There are about seventy brown bears in the Cantabrian Mountains of Spain. Ivar Mysterud of the University of Oslo has written that after reaching critically low numbers in the 1920s, several small bear populations in Norway have recovered nicely, and they may now total a hundred individuals or more. There are four hundred to six hundred bears, going strong, in central and northern Sweden. There are five hundred or more in Bulgaria, and healthy populations in Yugoslavia and Rumania. There is a small but probably stable population in northern Greece. In the vast interior of the Soviet Union, there are still thousands of brown bears.

Brown bears have adapted to an astonishing variety of habitats scattered across Asia—from lowland swamps to barren alpine zones. There are unknown numbers of brown bears, of unknown status, in Turkey, Iraq, Iran, and Syria, and a few may remain even in Lebanon. There are brown bears in Afghanistan, in Pakistan, in northern India, in Nepal, in Sikkim, in Bhutan. There are many brown bears in several parts of China—from Tibet to the headwaters of the Mekong River near the Laotian border, north across Kansu and the upper Yangtze and Yellow River drainages, through Shansi and on to the northwest into central Mongolia, and northeast into Manchuria and North Korea. Particularly ferocious brown bears also inhabit Japan's northernmost island of Hokkaido, where they claim several human victims a year. There are populations also on the U.S.S.R.'s Pacific possessions of Sakhalin, the Shantar Islands, and the Kuriles.

What seems most remarkable about these European and Asian bear populations is the tolerance many of them have shown for human activity, sometimes of quite high intensity, even in the heart of their range. We may probably safely assume that this harmony reflects a high degree of tolerance and restraint on the part of the people whose lives overlap those of the bears.

Which may, if Americans can ever learn to behave themselves in grizzly country, augur well for the sad few diminished and still declining grizzly populations of the western United States. Americans at least have the luxury of far lighter human population pressure than that which confronts many of the bear's European and Asian redoubts —and which will sooner or later doubtless vandalize the rosy portrait painted here of the Old World's genial coexistence of bears and men.

Of course, population pressure or the lack thereof be damned, America's thirst for resource exploitation—like, say, big mines and smelters smack-dab in the midst of grizzly populations already severely threatened (a true example, of which more later)—will settle for second place to nobody's. And anyway, as any old Wyoming mule-skinner could have told you if you had tried that happy-European-harmony bit on him, the *grizzly* is a whole nother kettle of bear.

In the first place, the American grizzly's ancestors were the biggest, meanest specimens Eurasia had to offer. They made at least part of their living out on the open tundra or in the wide rubble-strewn aprons of river deltas—without a tree to hide behind for miles—and there their size and their aggressiveness were their only defenses, and they learned to make the most of both. With the recession of the continental ice sheet ten thousand years ago, which seems to have blocked them from spreading south out of Alaska, those aggressive Siberian bruins' heirs began to work their way across postglacial North America, eventually reaching as far south as northern Mexico—where a scant few grizzlies may still remain—and east almost to the edge of the midwestern prairies.

Why they did not move still farther east, into the fertile bottom-land forests of the Mississippi Valley, is something of a mystery. The forest offered not only ample mast and berries of the sort the grizzly's European brethren fed on but also, especially after A.D. 1500, when the plains bison began to colonize the forest, a considerable complement of wild herbivores, and thus plentiful carrion and prey. Yet, aside from a few grizzly bones from widely scattered sites (which had probably made their way east via Indian trade or travel), there is no evidence that the grizzly bear ever lived in eastern North America. It may be that a diffusion in that direction might eventually have occurred had not the arrival of civilization intervened. Could an eastward movement have been under way when agriculture and the attendant destruction of bear habitat blocked it? Had grizzlies lived on the eastern prairies only a little while? A massive paleontological search might tell us, but so far nobody knows.

What is known is that ten thousand years ago, as they pushed into the West, grizzlies met with precious little resistance from the local indigenous fauna, which included not only their diffident cousins the black bears, who had slipped in ahead of the Ice Age and so had already been around for half a million years, but also not a few undoubtedly deeply impressed humans, who had settled the blissfully grizzly-free land some ten to twenty thousand years before.

The bear that had been forged in the crucible of the far northern ice was indeed an awesome creature. Up and down the glacier-free corridor that ran from northeast Asia across what is now the sea-bottom of the Bering Strait (the water then being tied up elsewhere, frozen) and into central Alaska and thence into the heart of the continent along the east front of the Rocky Mountains, there was under way, after long isolation, an extraordinary interchange of Asian and North American mammals. The climate of the temperate zone was fast growing warmer and drier. Stone age men were becoming better hunters, and they must still have been conquering regions where the animals had never before laid eyes on a human being; it is thought that a number of species may simply have been hunted into extinction. The gigantic old mammalian residents of North America—who had made it through most of the Pleistocene in innocent stability—suddenly found themselves under massive assault, not only from man and his weapons and from the changing climate but also from the strange new creatures arriving from the northwest with skills and traits and physiological characteristics often much better suited to the new environment than their own were. Within just a few thousand years, the mammoth, the saber-toothed tiger, the giant ground sloth, the horse, the camel, the giant bison, the tapir, the musk-ox, the dire-wolf, and the mastodon had all given way before this assault. One of the prime beneficiaries of the widespread conflict—already well acquainted with man and able to contend with his unpredictable vagaries, already sufficiently flexible to fit right into the new climate and the ecotypes associated with it, and already experienced in dominating the top of the food chain—was the grizzly bear.

The next several postglacial, premodern millennia were the great bear's golden age. His supremacy was so absolute, his freedom from danger so nearly total, that one of the lowest reproductive rates ever known for mammals was sufficient to sustain a population that may have exceeded one hundred thousand in what is now the western United States alone. The bear was quite long-lived—often reaching thirty years of age or more. Owing apparently to the extreme ferocity that had evolved in mother bears protecting their young in non-

forested habitat, infant mortality was comparatively low. Grizzly bears are also exceptionally healthy: parasites and microorganisms that readily fell other animals either do not infect the grizzly or simply live in the bear without causing illness.

Because (for all these reasons) the bearing of cubs was necessary so infrequently, and litters needed to be no larger than one to three cubs, time and attention on a scale unimaginable for most other mammals could be lavished on the young. This enabled the development of complex systems of behavior maintained by teaching and learning. Thus, unlike the limited repertoire of genetically programed and therefore extremely rigid responses in which most of their fellow mammals were imprisoned, the range of actions available to grizzly bears could be almost infinitely flexible. Growing ever less reflexive and ever more variously adaptable to the caprices of circumstance, the bear depended more and more on what amounts to decision making—or, if you will, thinking.

The culmination of this process was an animal so individualistic, so flexible, so proteanly responsive to what he—each single member of the species—has learned in his own experience (which might, of course, differ substantially from the experience of his peer living on the other side of the same mountain) that the grizzly bear was considered utterly unique by early man, more like man himself in fact than like the other animals.

In his food habits and in his domination of the environment—and, most of all, because of his great adaptability—the grizzly was man's most direct competitor. But because the bear was more dangerous to man, on the whole, than man was to him, there never had to be much confrontation. If a band of humans and a grizzly bear both had their eyes on the same berry patch, it is a safe bet that the people never even thought about contesting custody. To be sure, the odd party of brave youths must from time to time have felt compelled to assert their self-regard by going hunting for grizzly bears—smoking one out of his den, say, and then porcupining the poor half-asleep blighter with arrows (in 1983, Thomas Loy of the British Columbia Provincial Museum published a report of the first hard evidence of such occasions, which was grizzly blood on primitive stone tools between one thousand and six thousand years old, from the coasts and northern interior forests of Canada)—but killing grizzly bears in premodern settings can never have been common. Until the invention of the repeating rifle, it was just too dangerous.

31

Where the food supply permitted it, the grizzly grew to proportions that would have staggered the humble forest-dwelling brown bears he had left behind halfway around the globe. In the coastal mountains of California, for example, the oak savannas, basking in that winterless sun, yielded prodigious crops of acorns and clover and manzanita berries; along the coast, elephant seals, helpless ashore, came to breed, and dead whales and other marine mammals were continually washing up on the beach. In that environment, the grizzly bear sometimes attained stupendous size. The California grizzly, whose image still graces that state's flag, has been extinct since the 1920s, and proper records of his size were never kept, but the figure of fifteen hundred pounds for the occasional well-fed male is seen not infrequently, and there have remained enough pelts, claws, skulls, and newspaper accounts to give it some credibility. This bear—like the Siberian and other far northern brown bears, also the denizens of relatively open terrain—was noted for his testy disposition and his hearty willingness to take on any foe, and the Indian legends that have survived attest to the California grizzly's apparent conviction, at least as firm as that of any of his two-legged rivals to the contrary, that *he* was in charge around here and don't you forget it.

The Indian cultures of California were extraordinarily various —there were well over a hundred languages spoken, based on six linguistic groups, and these people's folkways and myths showed great diversity—but they seem to have been unanimous about one thing: they all feared and loathed the grizzly bear. He frequently raided their stores of grain, nuts, and meat. In times of scarcity, he preyed fearlessly on the people themselves, sometimes even breaking into their houses in the middle of the night to drag them screaming into the outer dark. Any Indian traveling in grizzly country considered himself to be in constant danger, and attacks were decidedly not rare. Moreover, grizzly densities in California were among the highest on earth, exceeded probably only by coastal Alaska; the population may have exceeded ten thousand. Early explorers and settlers occasionally reported seeing fifty or sixty bears in a single day, many of them feeding in actual herds.

The localities the grizzlies found most congenial were often those which first the Indians and then the pioneers also wanted for themselves. Of the tawny hills above Los Angeles, of the rugged headlands of Big Sur, of the Sacramento valley, the Napa valley, the

San Francisco peninsula, the grizzly bear was lord. When the Spanish missions came to these bear kingdoms, there was no surer way to gain the admiration and gratitude of the natives than to take a party of musketeers into the hills to slay the hated monarch. The Pomo, of the Russian River (whose salmon and steelhead runs made this valley a bear metropolis), believed that good men went after death to paradise, but the bad were kept on earth imprisoned in the bodies of grizzly bears, to be despised by all. In most cultures it was bad luck to dream of grizzlies. Many tribes' most puissant and most dreaded shaman was the bear-man, who would don a bear skin and take on the form and power of the bear, and lay waste to his own or his people's enemies. Among the Pomo, four such ritual murders were allowed each year. In other cultures there was no such regulation, and the bear-man was simply an odious spirit on the loose, robbing, raping, and murdering at will.

Some California Indians did kill grizzlies, usually in highly ceremonial circumstances—such as obtaining a robe for the bear-man— and always at great risk to themselves. When the Wintun, of the western Sacramento valley, killed a grizzly, the release of tension afterward was so great that the whole village would fall into fits of hilarity, pummeling one another with chunks of the meat. Anyone hit had to jump in the river. Most California Indians would not eat the flesh of the grizzly, however, believing that because he ate people —or, in some cases, that because his body actually housed a lost and evil human soul—to do so would be cannibalism.

They may have hated the bear, but they also recognized him as their closest nonhuman relative. Not just in California but throughout American grizzly country, the Indians addressed the bear directly, often as "great-grandfather." When a grizzly was to be killed— usually as an act of retribution for taking a human life—some formal speech, often an apology, would first be delivered to great-grandfather. Talking to grizzlies also undoubtedly forestalled some attacks, for a low, calm human voice can sometimes cool an irate grizzly's temper. The Shasta Indians believed that if a man would sit still long enough and not run away when a grizzly approached him, the bear would eventually speak to him.

On the Great Plains, another gigantic open-country grizzly bear, often pale yellow or reddish tan, made his home in the littoral cottonwood bottomlands or backwater marshes along the great prairie rivers. When the buffalo herds passed through, there were always some animals, usually the young or the old, who drowned in crossing, or else were sufficiently weakened that the bear could finish them off. On the prairies themselves, many plants provided food for the grizzly bear, but the skimpy cover and the grasslands' occasional extreme aridity probably kept grizzlies closely associated with the rivers. Because of the season-long abundance of succulent vegetation and the inevitable passing through of large prey animals in such areas, grizzlies everywhere depend significantly on riparian, or waterside, habitats. Human beings too, of course, are attracted to riparian settings, and it is often in these areas of conflict that modern grizzly bears are deprived of elements of food and cover that are essential to their survival.

It was also along the rivers of the plains that man and grizzly must first have disputed claim to meat or roots or sanctuary. The plains Indians, before the introduction of the horse from the Spanish settlements of Mexico, were few and primitive. Stone-age hunter-gatherers, they barely clung to subsistence, and their laborious way of life left little time for the sort of rich mythmaking and ceremony that characterized Indian cultures more blessed with leisure. Similarly, they could not afford much trouble with the likes of the grizzly bear, and they kept well out of his way. Yet man's and the bear's shared need for scarce riparian resources must have meant that the grizzly was an ever-present terror. These hardscrabble plainsmen, with a much humbler self-image than that of the well-fed Indians of California, dealt with their fear not by abominating but rather by revering the grizzly bear. The Cree called him Chief's Son; the Sauk, Old Man; the Menominee, Elder Brother. One of the Ute's most sacred rites was the bear dance, in honor of the grizzly's wisdom and his ancestral kinship with man, and after the introduction of the horse—which greatly enhanced the prairie peoples' leisure time and intertribal communication, and so made possible the blooming of a new plains Indian culture—the bear dance rapidly became a primary religious institution throughout the West. Bear-claw necklaces, jewelry made from teeth, ornamental daggers fashioned from the grizzly's baculum (the penis bone)—these, partly because they were so dangerous to obtain but also owing to a deepening pan-tribal cult of grizzly worship, came to be the most prestigious and symbolically most powerful of human ornaments.

The Blackfeet held the grizzly in particularly reverent esteem, and today their reservation, in northwest Montana just east of Glacier National Park, where the grassy highland plains abut the forested Rocky Mountain front, harbors a few of what may be the last of America's plains grizzlies. Blackfeet legends attribute many fine qualities to the great bear, including the ability to heal human wounds and to make favored warriors wise and brave.

In the Pacific Northwest, the dense, dark coastal rain forests, rich with berries and low-growing succulent vegetation, and the thundering rivers, up which steelhead trout and five species of salmon climbed to spawn, made possible large, easy-living populations of both grizzly bears and humans. Here too their actual relations were most uncordial, a fact sublimated in a variety of friendly legends. Probably the first European to see a grizzly here, a missionary named Claude Jean Allouez, wrote, in 1666, of an Indian tribe "who eat human beings, and live on raw fish; but these people, in turn, are eaten by bears of frightful size, all red, and with prodigiously long claws."

Nevertheless, when the Thompson Indians of British Columbia were visited by one of the greatest blessings that could come to a tribe, the birth of twins, the children were treated from birth like royalty, and called "grizzly bear children." They were considered to have within themselves the unique magic powers of the great bear— courage, healing powers, control over the weather. The grizzly bear children were raised in a house set apart from the rest of the village, constantly watched over and sung to and waited on hand and foot. They were considered too important to be allowed to associate with normal children. To a modern sensibility this seems perfectly frightful, but then American Indians continentwide in earlier days seem to have made something of a specialty of combining grotesque forms of torment with evidently persuasive assurance of what a big honor it was. In some tribes, inauguration as chief involved entering a grizzly den and chasing the bear out into a waiting hail of your constituency's arrows.

From northern California to the Alaska peninsula, the mild climate, easy fishing, and abundant wild foods of the Pacific coast enabled the development of extremely elaborate Indian cultures, filled with rituals of social hierarchy, obsessed with wealth and power, dependent on large numbers of slaves, and all characterized by an eerie, gloomy, rather Wagnerian mythology of terrifying dragons and sea monsters and grizzly bears. The elevation of the grizzly to mythic status is really no wonder when you consider what the appearance of a fearlessly misanthropic grizzly must have been like in those foggy shadow-forests where you can see no farther than a few feet ahead, and where a fisherman innocently hauling in his net, with the roar of water drowning out all other sound, might turn to face a rude expropriatory claim perhaps on his catch alone or perhaps on both fish and meat courses.

The white man got along with the grizzly bear even worse than the Indian did, and the grizzly to this day seems not to have gotten over his bewilderment at how well that pushy and querulous intruder has been able to back up his usurpation of the bear's ancient throne. For a while, anyway, the arrival of the Spanish in California and the Southwest must have seemed like a pretty good thing: all that food to steal, and cows that just stood there waiting for a grizzly bear to saunter up and smash them in the face. But the Spanish also lacked what we might call a highly developed philosophy of conservation of the native biota, especially concerning those components of it which insisted on burglarizing honest Christian granaries and eating up honest Christian livestock. The Spanish answer to ursine self-interest, in the voice of honest Christian firearms, was not readily apprehended by the California grizzly, unaccustomed as he was to actually getting hurt by mere people. Even after many bears had been slain, their survivors, if they chanced to find a pueblo lying along their chosen route, would stroll blithely down Main Street scattering indignant caballeros like pigeons.

Sometimes grizzly meat was the only thing that stood between the early Spanish settlers and starvation, and even in times of plenty they ate a lot of it. In *California Grizzly*—from which almost all of this narrative's information on the bears of California has come— Tracy Storer and Lloyd Tevis cite an expedition in 1772 from Monterey to a place called the Valley of the Bears, where the colonial governor and thirteen soldiers spent three months shooting bears, and from which they sent home some nine thousand pounds of grizzly bear meat! Later Spanish Californians, however, were devout beef eaters, and came to despise grizzly meat. Nevertheless they continued killing grizzly bears for the benefit of their livestock, as well as for their own peace of mind, and also to some extent for a rather low-profit trade in the shabby furs and smelly oil the carcasses yielded.

And still the grizzlies poured down from the mountains. By the early nineteenth century, cattle had become so numerous in California that there was no way to protect the herds from bear depredation, but the range was so good that the ranchers could afford massive losses. The cattlemen ate only the choicest cuts of beef, and left the rest to rot for guess who. In times of drought, cattle pastureland was seriously degraded by the almost unbelievably huge population of wild horses—herds of them sometimes twenty miles long—and thousands of horses were driven off cliffs or into the sea. When the Americans and the British established a thriving trade in cowhide and tallow with the Spanish Californians, tens of thousands of unsaleable cattle corpses lay littered across the landscape. The result of these rather hysterical pastoral practices, no surprise, was that by the 1860s there were apparently more grizzly bears in California than there had ever been before the advent of their putative enemies. And because the bears had now had to learn to cope with mounted men carrying firearms, they had also gained a stealth and deviousness rather foreign to their grand tradition but eminently effective.

The Californians played several games with the grizzly that were worthy of their bloody Spanish heritage. One of the boldest was to go out armed only with machete and reata, and lasso a bear—which only the crazier vaqueros dared try. The craziest of them all undertook to slay the grizzly with a light sword, and on foot.

The greatest of bear spectacles in California, with its roots far back in Iberian history, was the bear-and-bull fight. This is how it worked. First you go out into the country and shoot a cow on a moonlit night. When the bear comes to eat it, you lasso him, one reata per paw. Then you put him in a cart and take him to town, or if you don't have a cart just bundle him up and drag him behind your horses. Next, you obtain the worst-tempered wild bull you can find. Take a leather rope about twenty yards long, and attach one end to one of the bull's front hoofs, the other to one of the bear's back feet. Release the contestants into a suitable arena, and stand well back.

It's easy to picture the bloody rest. The bear usually won, by the way, at least the first go-round, but the resourceful citizens usually had several more long-horned bear-hating bulls in reserve, and the fun would continue until the grizzly finally packed it in. Occasionally that took a dozen or more bulls. Bull-and-bear fighting became Spanish California's most popular sport by far, a much bigger deal there, thanks to the plentiful supply of combatants, than it had ever been back home in Spain.

The first U.S. citizens to get acquainted with the grizzly bear were members of the Lewis and Clark expedition, in 1803–1805. They saw a lot of grizzlies, both on the plains and in the mountains, for these bears were fearless, never having known bullets. They were to know soon enough. Wrote Meriwether Lewis of one of the many grizzly bears they shot: "It was a most tremendious looking anamal, and extreemly hard to kill notwithstanding he had five balls through his lungs and five others in various parts he swam more than half the distance across the river to a sandbar, & it was at least twenty minutes before he died; he did not attempt to attack, but fled and made the most tremendous roaring from the moment he was shot."

With the opening of the West began the closing of the grizzly bear's glory days. There are a number of excellent accounts of this period. Particularly to be recommended are Andy Russell's *Grizzly Country*; Harold McCracken's *The Beast That Walks Like Man* (which also includes a lot of Indian grizzly lore); William H. Wright's *The Grizzly Bear*; Storer and Tevis's aforementioned *California Grizzly*; an anthology edited by Bessie Doak Haynes and Edgar Haynes called *The Grizzly Bear: Portraits from Life*; and the journals of the Lewis and Clark expedition.

The history of man and the grizzly in nineteenth-century America is full of rip-roaring yarns and reckless bravery and guys getting their abdomens ripped open and then crawling twenty miles to town —and there are even a few lighter touches here and there, like old James Capen "Grizzly" Adams promenading up and down the streets of San Francisco with his huge tame bear Ben Franklin on a leash— but the story of America's conquest of the grizzly suffers, ultimately, from a deadening sameness. Bang bang bang. How I kilt the bar that almost kilt me. Bang.

For with the American pioneer came the agent of the great bear's doom: the repeating rifle.

The big tawny grizzly of the plains was the first to go—his buffalo slaughtered, the roots and green prairie grass plowed under. At first the butchery of bison and the establishment of farms must have benefited the bear, as the Spanish waste in California had done, but wherever American agriculture came came also a squinty-eyed sharp-shooting son of a gun with a gun, who cared not at all to share his corn or pigs or children with a grizzly bear.

Although a tiny remnant population of the California grizzly made it into the twentieth century, mostly in the high wilderness of the Sierra Nevada, the fact that the bear's principal abode—the coastal hills, and the central valley—was also perfect for human habitation made his eventual extirpation inevitable. With the treaty that ended the Mexican War in 1848, California became United States territory, and the discovery of gold the next year touched off a flood of immigration from Europe and the eastern states. Few saw their dreams of splendor fulfilled, but there were plenty of other reasons for staying on, and word went out that California was the land of opportunity. Between 1850 and 1890, the population grew from ninety-three thousand people to a million two hundred thousand— and virtually all of those people were living in what had recently been grizzly habitat.

In the Rocky Mountain West, it was not human population pressure or grizzly habitat destruction that wrote the bear's death warrant. It was that squinty-eyed fellow with the rifle. Much of the country was either too arid or too high and cold to support a very great density of grizzly bears in the first place, and those few bears' crucial spring and fall foraging areas were concentrated in lower-elevation grasslands and fertile riparian zones—which just happened to be precisely where that fellow's cows or sheep were grazing at the same time of year. Bang.

What about all the wilderness still there today? Well, virtually all of it was soon ringed by ranchlands that had been a critical component of grizzly habitat. Bears continued to use it even after it had been settled, and still more were drawn down from the mountains by the availability of easy-to-get prey and carrion. And even in the few self-sufficient grizzly sanctuaries, the bears were pursued like the devil incarnate. The use of strychnine baits became widespread, and the steel-jawed bear trap was introduced. Cattle and sheep growers' associations and local and state governments all offered bounties for any bear killed at any time of year, and eventually most grizzly populations dropped below a density sufficient for the remaining bears simply to find one another and mate. The last old loners were often the object of romantic community campaigns into the wilderness, and jubilant stockmen would ride into town, yee-ha, brandishing the bullet-riddled, ratty pelt of Old Such-and-such, the last dagnabbed grizzly in them mountains and good riddance. Drinks all around, bartender.

Still a few somehow hung on. The grizzly was considered to have been exterminated in Colorado about 1950, but then in 1979 a bow-hunter in the San Juans put an arrow through the throat of a bear that turned out to be a female grizzly. A subsequent two-year search disclosed no sign of others, so she may have been Colorado's last grizzly bear. The hunter said she had jumped him.

The Canadians seem never to have harried their varmints with quite the same addled glee as the Americans, and settlement came later and was sparser, so good numbers of grizzlies have survived in the mountains of the western provinces and on the barren grounds of the far North. The immense wilderness of Alaska still supports, it is thought, about ten thousand grizzlies. But in the lower forty-eight United States, the grizzly has survived only where the mountains were too rugged and remote for agriculture and where the grizzly was actively protected before the trappers and poisoners and riflemen could get to him: in northwestern Montana and northern Idaho, contiguous to a much larger Canadian population; in the ecosystem that encompasses Glacier National Park and the Bob Marshall, Great Bear, and Scapegoat wildernesses, also connected to a Canadian population; perhaps in the Selway-Bitterroot Wilderness of central Idaho; and in five and a half million acres of country centering on the nation's oldest national park, Yellowstone.

It is here, at the fringe of timberline high in the remote peaks that divide Yellowstone National Park and the Absaroka-Beartooth Wilderness, that we left the mother grizzly and her infant cubs.

Another week has passed. As she gnaws the last of the meat from the bones of the elk carcass she found last week, a faint scent wafts the mother grizzly's way. With the cubs drawn close to her side, the bear moves silently into heavy timber and circles downwind, and now the scent is clear. It is meat on the hoof, and plenty of it: a bull moose. The moose has heard something now. He raises his goony head and swivels his ears and snorts, black hackles bristling. As she will with any prospective large prey, the grizzly assays a test. She charges, slashing the air with her terrible claws, but does not strike. If the moose, thus challenged, were healthy and strong, he would almost certainly stand his ground, bellowing in rage and kicking stiff-legged with his brutally sharp front hoofs; and, unless she were desperately hungry, the bear would let it go at that. A full-grown thousand-pound moose is not an adversary to be taken lightly, even by a grizzly bear. But this moose turns to flee.

And is limping. Last December, the moose slipped on an icy

precipice, took a nasty tumble, and broke a leg. The leg has healed badly, and a moment like this has been inevitable ever since. (If there were still wolves in Yellowstone, it would have come much sooner.) The moose's winter coat is falling out in shaggy patches, and through the poor regrowth can be discerned the taut-hided rib harp and jutting pelvis of the doomed. The moose and the bear face off, staring each other in the eye.

Time slows. An air of predestination suffuses the scene. The moose undertakes a slow, weak, blundering charge at the bear, but stumbles. The grizzly backs up a few easy steps and again stares the moose in the eye. Both lower their heads. The bear lunges, the moose shies away. They stare again. The bear chases the moose, neither of them moving very fast, through a thicket of huckleberry, and the starving moose is soon winded. He stands panting and passive as the bear circles, bounds onto his back from behind, and bites hard into the base of the neck, crushing two vertebrae and severing the spinal cord.

Such a superfluity of food so early in the spring is an extraordinary blessing. The grizzly family now need not roam far in quest of nourishment for another two weeks, and the cubs, in this most vulnerable period of their infancy, will be that much more secure. A treasure as precious as a moose, of course, warrants protecting, and the mother bear begins to fashion a vault for her riches. By day's end she has dug an eight-foot trench four feet wide and five feet deep, of preternaturally boxlike symmetry, in rocky, root-choked, still half-frozen ground. At evening, after several intermittent bouts of feeding on its choicest parts, she drags the half-ton corpse to the lip of the hole and, as the cubs look on, shoves it in. The moose lands on its back. In the moonlight she refills the excavation, and by morning all that remains visible of the carcass are the four spindly lower legs sticking weirdly straight out of a mound of fresh earth, for the dining pleasure of come what scavengers may. The rest of her prize is now thoroughly safe, from all creatures but larcenous other grizzly bears.

With their dietary needs so handily taken care of, the cubs have plenty of time for play, and in their play already may be seen abundant prefigurement of their lives to come. The male, a beautifully multicolored little bear—golden blond face, chocolate brown ears, silvery gold shoulder hump, reddish tan rump, tawny flanks shading down to blackish brown feet, and a little ivory spot on his chest—has begun already to gain a little in weight over his sister. She, a strawberry blonde with an almost platinum band around her neck, makes up for her stature with a rather more active and aggressive temperament. So far, which cub will be the dominant one is not decided, but their every playful encounter puts that question to the test.

Ethologists regard play among young animals as principally a kind of rehearsal for a whole repertoire of adult behaviors, such as aggressive competition for desirable mates, and in their heedless romping the cubs are trying out a wide range of actions from among which they will gradually select a smaller number of gestures and other signals as those actions prove to be of consistent value. They push each other to the ground; they suck each other's ears; they slap each other here and there; they snort; they moan; they roar; they bawl; they pop their teeth and lips together with a loud clack; they stick their upper lips out like monkeys; they paw the ground; they claw at trees; they contest possession of bits of meat; they roll in the mud; they turn and flee for cover, peering back and blowing in mock alarm as though some intruder were approaching; they bite and box and play hide-and-seek. Certain of their movements and vocalizations —which may mean no more now to the cubs themselves than the random googlings of human babies mean to the babies—will get consistent responses from their mother, and slowly, by this means, the cubs will develop a sort of vocabulary in common with hers. It is probably also true that certain other elements of grizzly bear language are genetically predetermined—such universal bear expressions as the teeth-clacking threat display, for instance—and these may require only incidental reinforcement from the mother, or maybe even none at all; it may be that at a programed stage in the cubs' development, certain behavior simply appears.

For all the functional illuminations of ethology, there remains a lot of play that is difficult to see as anything but plain fun. (Some scientists characterize the behavior in this catchall category as the working-off of excess energy. As you like.) Watch this, for instance.

A long, open slope still covered with hard-packed snow. At the bottom, a rushing creek. At the top of the hill, the mother grizzly and the cubs, sitting up on their hindquarters. They paddle madly at the snow and start to slide, feet first, faster and faster, ending with a mighty splash into the rapids. They race back up and do it again— and again, and again. They slide on their backs, they slide on their bellies. They roll and wrestle and play tag. They ride the rapids downstream spinning willy-nilly.

This sort of thing is pretty hard to incorporate in any meaningful repertoire of practical adult behaviors.

The subjectivity of the narrative voice in these pages probably calls for some discussion of that voice's provenance. You will already have inferred, no doubt, that the story of the mother bear and her two cubs is a work of imagination, but you must not think of it as invented. It is, rather, an assemblage, put together out of observations made, mostly in the last twenty years, by biologists specializing in the study of grizzly bears.

If science has supplied the bricks of this literary edifice, then imagination takes on not only the humble responsibility of providing mortar but also the more daunting challenge of architecture, and that is where the writer is most vulnerable to discredit. The bear family of this narrative is a composite of findings from a broad sampling of grizzly bears, and as such it should be true and typical, but many pitfalls lurk in this kind of composition. Foremost among them, perhaps, is the extraordinary range of variation in grizzly bears—among individuals, among populations, even among local "subcultures" within a population—which can make a mockery of any attempt to isolate what is typical. Another difficulty may have been introduced by the decision to focus on one particular grizzly population, that of the Yellowstone ecosystem, which has been extensively studied but which also has long been cut off from others and has been subject to an exceptionally high degree of human influence and manipulation.

A further, darker danger lies, paradoxically, in the very wealth of the information available. The grizzly is a much-studied wild animal—the University of Alaska's recently compiled *Brown Bear Bibliography* lists over four thousand titles—and he engages in a great deal of behavior that can readily be understood in human terms. We are both, after all, big, intelligent, omnivorous mammals, both at the top of our food chains, both highly dependent on learning; and neither has anything to fear among his fellow mammals except his occasionally murderous conspecific brethren and the other. The problem comes in knowing where to draw the line—where to stop applying interpretations derived from human experience to what we observe in the grizzly bear. This, of course, is precisely where imagination most threatens to get us into trouble with that horror of zoologists' horrors, anthropomorphism. Yet no biographer can be expected to do his job without a liberal exercising of his intuition. He knows the facts, but their interrelation must be the work of his wit—he must, if you will, create their meaning. And must not the biographer's intuition be grounded in an identification with his protagonist?

The gulf between the human species and another is a big leap to take, but for all the attendant risk of imprecision and also of downright foolishness, the rich abundance of hard knowledge at our disposal makes it seem worth the trying, for in moving toward an understanding of creatures truly *other*, and in granting them what has come to be called existence value, people may come to a more realistic definition of their species' place in the intricate mechanism of earthly life than that which the hubristic expansionism of modern history has so emptily promised.

(The underlying contention here is that the exponential growth of human population and technology has made possible a far greater human influence on the biosphere than is good for us; that what we have thought of as victories over nature are usually not; that through an operant though rarely expressed belief in mankind as independent of or superior to nature, we have entered on a deadening alienation and tragic arrogance; that there is a wisdom in the complex interdependencies of nature which we are capable of destroying but which we have only begun to appreciate; that heightening that appreciation will enhance the appropriateness of the biological niche we create for ourselves, the only species able consciously to *choose* its own biological role; and that enhancing the biological appropriateness of the human role will result both in a richer biosphere—in which, for example, grizzly bears can thrive—and in greater human happiness.)

The age of science has shown that many of our ancient ideas about the mysterious kinship between man and his fellow creatures have been wrong, most of all in their pervasive anthropocentrism; but ecology has demonstrated that our ancient *sense* of relation is correct, and the actual mechanisms of that relation are gradually being revealed. It turns out, happily, that there is no less glory in the facts than there ever was in our most heroic myths. We sacrifice only an egotism that was harmful in the first place.

In taking our leap between species, we must banish the fear that we may be wrong in some of our assumptions. Intuition will always make mistakes. Progress of the kind we are attempting is always made only by successive approximation, and we have enough certainty now at least to begin. Enough, the reader must believe, stands to be gained in an attempt at a whole portrait that the writer can afford to make some errors of detail. For example, it may have been wrong, in this chapter's treatment of the mating season, to combine observations made by Frank and John Craighead and their associates in Yellowstone National Park, of a grizzly population highly concentrated by the presence of a large garbage dump, with observations made by Stephen Herrero and David Hamer in Canada, of bears from a free-ranging, highly dispersed population. It may have been wrong as well to assume that our female grizzly's choice of a superior den site for her first winter with cubs and much of her other maternal conduct that year were directly attributable to the influence of the older bear with whom she had struck up partnership. Do grizzlies really wake up fully to give birth, and do they, like most nonhibernating mammals, clean and groom their newborn young? What might be the role of inherited recognition factors in grizzlies' learning what foods to select? Only further research can resolve such uncertainties. In the meantime—and with the strict proviso that whenever there is reasonable doubt, notice will be given—the grizzly bear's portraitist must ask you to grant him his occasional cautious reliance on intuition.

Let us return to the scene whence that windy divagation veered off, the three bears sledding.

Add another scene now, a mile away, downwind: the old eight-hundred-pound great-grandfather grizzly, who may be father to one or both of the cubs but who also would just as soon have one for lunch as chateaubriand; pawing at blood-colored budding aspen shoots, rising on his hind legs, sniffing, sniffing. . . .

Third scene: the three bears at creekside still playing; the ridge-top above first empty, a mere line of snow against the sky, and then, over it, straight down at them, a sudden avalanche of great-grand-father.

Before they have a glimmer of what's going on, the mother bear has slammed the cubs into a willow thicket and come thundering out of the brush like apocalypse, claws flailing, teeth gnashing, straight into the face of what might seem ruin. But look at him. This huge old bear has encountered mother grizzlies half his size before and lived to regret it—his left ear is missing a piece thanks to one. Four legs stiff, twenty long ivory claws digging in, snow flying, he skids to a stop and whirls to retreat. You may think of bears as big, sloppy, sort of *slow* old clowns, and if so get a load of these two. Up that forty-five-degree snowslope and over it down an escarpment onto jagged scree and into a maze of matchstick lodgepole timber, that sensible brute and the enraged mother grizzly snapping at his heels are covering very inhospitable ground at something in the neighborhood of thirty-five miles per hour.

That afternoon, the bear and her cubs dig up a little biscuitroot, and, in consideration of their recent experience, they sleep then not in their day bed in the spruce grove but sprawled vigilantly across the heap of earth that covers their moose.

MAY

IF this is supposed to be wilderness and protected, just what has been going on? Why is this hillside such a mess? Has some deranged developer been up here in the middle of nowhere excavating a motel foundation? Was it vandals on a dynamiting rampage? Hundred-pound half-buried boulders have been ripped from the soil and heaved aside, and the doodlebugs and centipedes that had lived beneath are scuttling through the crusting white entanglement of now sun-roasted underrock roots and fungus, groping for their shattered home darkness. Heaps of mud are slung against and oozing down the few undislodged stone outcroppings. Divots of sod stain snowbanks brown. When the cloudburst comes, thick muck sluices down new gullies, and in the creek below sculpins clinging to their normally clean-swept riffle-rocks choke on clouds of silt. Asphyxiated stoneflies tumble downstream past the gaping maws of cutthroat trout too flummoxed to snap them up.

Just yesterday, this scene of devastation was a tranquil meadow, newly green with thousands of shoots all of one delicate lance-leaved little plant with a stem of radish-red-and-white and tiny buds with a peppery watercresslike scent. They had burst from the sun-warmed soil with the first recession of the snow, viridian tips through even the crackling rime at its edge. Another few days and they would have bloomed, and the whole green-blanketed hillside would have been overlain with a mild pink stippling of five-petaled pinker-veined flowers. *Claytonia lanceolata:* the western spring beauty.

All gone now—unless, that is, you count the almost countless heaps of glutinous cress-smelling two-inch-thick four-inch-long greeny-brown cylinders littering the plowed-out mud, the victims' indigestible cellulose remains. In twenty-four hours and maybe less, the meadow's bounty has been transformed into a mighty multitude of big piles of excrement. And there can be no mistaking whose, for spring beauty—buds, leaves, stems, roots, and all, especially the sweet subsurface tuberous corm, from which the plant sends up its sudden vernal energy—is one of the favorite foods of the Yellowstone grizzly bear, and the unconditional surrender of this landscape has grizzly bear written all over it. It is, by no coincidence, a bear we know who has wrought this destruction, as her cubs rolled and raced in the mire. Windblown seeds and remnant corms will eventually replant the meadow, and there are other Claytonia beds nearby which she has left untouched, but it will be years before spring beauty blossoms in profusion here again. Yet such disturbances ultimately enhance productivity: many bear foods, including spring beauty, thrive in disturbed sites, and the bears' digging may in fact maintain this meadow as a bear garden.

Especially compared to other wild plants, emergent spring beauties are superbly nutritious food—thirty percent protein, eleven percent starch, nearly four calories for every gram of plant. And caught, as by our grizzly, at its succulent preflowering peak, it can be digested with superb efficiency: more than sixty percent of the protein and more than ninety percent of the starch are converted directly into bear. Because the plant in this phase has not yet begun to build the hard-walled cells necessary to the rigid reproductive structures of its flowering and seed-bearing stages, the proportion of indigestible material is at its lowest point in the annual cycle of the organism's life. Actively growing, or meristematic, tissues now predominate in all the plant's parts, and these are composed principally of digestible, juicy cell middle in amounts very large in relation to the presently low degree of thickness and rigidity in the dry and indigestible cell walls. Later in the year, those proportions will be the other way around, as growth slows and structural tissues come to preponderate. Converted solar energy will then flow not to meristematic tissues in the aboveground plant but straight to the roots and corm, to be ready for next spring. Once that phase is under way, the bears no longer bother the spring beauties, for there are always more and younger ones higher up as the season progresses and spring comes to the highest alpine zones—sometimes even as late as mid-August. (Which leaves all of about one week to call summer, since the first snowstorms of autumn often come to the high country later that same month.)

The following spring, if carrion and prey should be scarce, the grizzlies' amazing sense of smell will enable them to find spring beauty corms underground even before the first green appears—even under thick snow. In such bad springs, a diet of roots, corms, rhizomes, tubers, bulbs, and the first meager sedges and grass will keep a grizzly bear alive, but just barely; he may lose quite a lot of weight, even while eating constantly. When summer finally comes, it will be a struggle just to catch up before fall. It is in such springs, when carrion and prey availability is low, and especially when, perhaps because of drought, the previous summer's production of underground plant parts has been poor too, that grizzly reproduction begins to suffer. One of the body's first defenses against starvation is to cut production of sexual hormones and devote maximum energy to maintaining the existing bear, so a malnourished male grizzly's fancy in spring may simply never turn to thoughts of love, and a female may never enter estrus, or if she does she may not conceive. It is also in such springs that grizzlies may roam far from their familiar haunts in search of garbage or sheep or whatever other fondly remembered petite madeleine may stir them to boldness.

But never mind. This is a good spring. Meadowlarks just in from Mexico are trilling in the meadows, peepers peeping in the pines. The old pair of ospreys who have summered on the cliff above the river for fifteen years are back repairing winter's damage to their forebears' ancient nest. Frogs are ribbeting in the marshes, ducks quacking, beavers building. Water, which can sometimes be desperately scarce in the Rocky Mountain West, is here in Yellowstone in abundance this spring. Where a seep in a limestone bluff drip-drips through moss and fern into an emerald-algaed stagnant pool on a low shelf above a creek, the mother grizzly and her cubs are scarfing up the unfriendly-looking jointed stems of a strange and primitive plant growing at the rim of the pool. This is *Equisetum arvense*, or horsetail, and nothing but a grizzly bear can even keep the stuff down. Horsetail has long been known as "scouring rush," because its high silica content makes it useful as a kind of natural Brillo. Indeed, if you should try eating some you would find that your stomach reacted quite as if Brillo was what you had eaten. Some animals do occasionally eat it on purpose, in fact, as an emetic, but for grizzlies it is just plain food—one of their favorites. Like many of the grizzly bear's most important food plants, horsetail grows only in the moistest soils, often at the edge of streams or lakes. It is not particularly nutritious, and nobody knows why grizzlies like it so much, but they just eat the hell out of it.

Among the nice things about being an omnivore is that if, let's say, a muskrat should paddle by while one is munching on horsetail, one can swat it and pop it into one's mouth with none of the kind of energy expenditure which pure predators must ceaselessly invest in searching and stalking. It is just such opportunism that characterizes, and might even be said to govern, grizzly bear nutrition: feeding sites certainly are actively selected, remembered, and repeatedly sought out for their specific rewards (like this horsetail, say), but the bear's very manner, so obtrusive and disruptive, tends to stir up all kinds of serendipitous dividends (like the muskrat). This May evening, for example, after their customary afternoon nap, the grizzly and her cubs are moving lazily up the mountainside cropping tender preflowering bluebunch wheatgrass (*Agropyron spicatum*)—which is pretty good food as grass goes, three calories per gram and nearly fifty percent digestible, but which hardly packs the punch of the agreeable surprise its pursuit has in store—when the mother bear hears the scurrying rustle, beneath the turf, of a tunnel-colony of montane voles. All three bears set busily to digging. For the cubs this is still mainly play, although they do catch and eat a few, but for their mother this is really serious feeding now, an opportunity to put on some weight. Tiny as voles may be, there are hundreds of them here, and every mouthful of vole is seventy percent highly digestible protein. And again a smooth green meadow is churned up, turned over, and overnight a mess.

It would seem that she ought perhaps to have continued to pursue the voles wherever their tunnels led, but in fact the hillside has been dug into only along the edges of the meadow—for, despite their reputation for fearlessness, grizzlies are ever mindful of cover, and where, as here, thick forest borders open space, they tend to use only the margins, where concealment is but a few bounds away. Mothers with cubs are especially restrictive in their sense of how much exposure feels safe. Of course, there are kinds and kinds of cover. It need not be trees. Darkness alone can serve, and grizzlies do move out into the open more often in the middle of the night. Tonight, however, the moon has been full, the hoarfrosted meadow resplendent silver, and the bear and her cubs have kept to the shadows. Isolation too is a kind of cover, and grizzlies will readily use the open meadows above timberline as long as they know they have the place to themselves. (This isolation must be defined principally in terms of the absence—and the likelihood of the continued absence —of the two creatures whose presence always troubles the grizzly bear: man and other grizzly bears.) On the arctic tundra and in other largely treeless habitat, the grizzly's concern with cover must naturally be less, and in the low shrubfields and rolling open tundra of Alaska's Denali National Park and Preserve, for example, the grizzlies compensate for the lack of cover with heightened vigilance and a tendency to run at and investigate any disturbance—which has led to an impression of greater aggression, although grizzlies there generally retreat if the object of their investigation turns out to be human. Such compensation nevertheless is insufficient to cope with really significant intrusion—especially when, as is sadly so often the case these days, naïve grizzlies (that is, those unaccustomed to people) are given little time to adjust to radical changes in their world. In the grizzly country of the far North, where oil and gas exploration and pipeline construction in recent years have brought heedless work crews, bellowing heavy machinery, and endless low-flying aircraft to the flat unbroken arctic plains, the barren-ground grizzlies' lives have been grossly disrupted. In the alpine zones of Yellowstone and of northwestern Montana, recent huge increases in high-country recreation have also denied grizzlies use of essential habitat. A bear here or there, surprised, perhaps, far from cover, may resist—there are eloquent photographs of tundra grizzlies angrily shadowboxing at Piper Cubs a hundred feet overhead—but substantial human use of grizzly habitat ultimately means simply that bears will no longer enter the area, and in the end the same thing always happens: people come, bears go.

The fact that many European and Asian brown bear populations have learned over the centuries to tolerate a great deal of human activity in their midst as long as it has been gradual and predictable may indicate, as the biologist Charles Jonkel has hypothesized, that given enough time, and sufficient assurance that people are not necessarily deadly, the grizzly bear could eventually adjust here too. But in the North American experience so far, such time and such assurance have been conspicuously unoffered.

In pure biological terms, the grizzly bear is a wondrously flexible creature. With respect to what scientists call behavioral plasticity, he is without peer. The range of environments his style of life is suited to is exceedingly wide—tundra, forest, swampland, prairie, desert. He does not, contrary to the general view, absolutely require wilderness. All he needs is to be left alone, in big enough country to serve his food requirements and to sustain a breeding population of his wide-ranging fellows. As for accommodating human presence in such country, we must believe—and some evidence does at least suggest—that he is capable of it, as long as we in turn will tolerate him and his occasional high jinks . . . capable of it, that is, given time. But in the latter part of the twentieth century, human time has largely ceased to correspond to biological time. In the tick of one second on the evolutionary clock, whole worlds are destroyed.

Okay. It may be true that this grizzly's world is in danger, but she doesn't know it. For all the haze of species-foreignness and regulation and protection and human meddling that obscures her from our sight, her life is authentic, authentically wild, authentically faithful to the whole long history of her kind. She is no zoo animal. Her past has not been bred or bored out of her. She is herself, and nothing of ours.

That, anyway, is how we must see her if we are to have the full benefit of knowing her: free, a perfect image of freedom, wild, an avatar of wildness, natural, nature incarnate.

Shall we fear that knowing her too well may diminish those mysterious qualities? No. Indeed intimacy should heighten our sense of awe, if only because she is, more clearly the better we know her, so immitigably *other*. And there will always be plenty of her that will not yield to our craving to understand.

The mother grizzly continues up the mountainside where she has spent the night feeding, into a refulgent sunrise. She leads the cubs along at a briskly businesslike pace, now walking, now loping, never stopping, in an evidently purposeful straight line. They crest the mountaintop and cross a glittering snowfield, by now high above where any food might be growing, and below them the earth drops away in a thousand-foot precipice, at the foot of which a still frozen alpine lake glows white in the talus-rubbled cirque. The lip of the cliff has been blown free of snow, and the yellow-lichen-spattered rock is already warm with dawn. The bear goes straight to the edge with an air of intent, but there is nothing there—only a view of miles of countryside, and the morning sun. She sits back on her haunches and closes her eyes. The cubs scamper this way and that, playing peekaboo around a lightning-struck skeleton of whitebark pine. In a while they will tire and return to their mother to nurse. For the moment she has nothing whatever to do. She opens her eyes and gazes into the empty distance. An hour goes by, and all she does is sit, and stare. Why has she climbed up here—just to admire a pretty view? Surely grizzlies are not quite such esthetes as that. Who knows? We don't.

The landscape comprehended in the mother grizzly's view is an

intricate interweaving of lifeforms and landforms. Much of the broad, volcanically upthrust central plateau of Yellowstone is underlain with a granitelike volcanic rock known as rhyolite, and it has generated shallow and infertile soils which tend to be evenly blanketed with forests of a single tree species, lodgepole pine. These forests are a mosaic of stands each made up of trees all of identical age, spawn of the wildfires which periodically, on an average cycle of two hundred to four hundred years, have wiped out all the living trees of portions of the forest, usually that which is at or near its climax phase. Some of the lodgepole forest has also been massively infested by the mountain pine beetle, which has served the woodlands just as fire does, killing mature trees and allowing younger, more diverse plant communities to move in. In the national forests that ring the national park, logging has accomplished the same thing, and here too the suppression of natural fire by man has contributed to pine beetle abundance, which would otherwise have been occasionally decimated by fire. The lodgepole forest sometimes grows so dense that little sunlight penetrates the canopy, and there is so little understory vegetation that not much life of any kind is to be found either on the pine-needle mattress of the forest floor or in the gloomy treetops— only a few hardy patches of grass, some kinnikinnick and some mushrooms, jays and a few other birds, martens, rodents, and the occasional waddling porcupine. It is one of the most oppressively boring environments on earth, and much of it is also lousy grizzly habitat, good only for hiding in or traveling hidden through. Yet interspersed through much of the lodgepole forest, especially in the cooler, moister regions, there are many ecotypes more congenial to grizzly bears, through which, in high summer, the bear and her cubs will work their way generally upward: although some of these sites may be no bigger than a few square yards, such microsites as meadowland openings, seeps, springs, and creeksides can be significant sources of grasses, forbs, and roots; beneath the lodgepoles there are rotten logs teeming with ants to be clawed out; there are also zones of Engelmann spruce and subalpine fir woodland within the lodgepole forest, and here the understory shrubs produce bountiful harvests of fruit; and finally, as the bears near timberline, they will encounter interminglings of whitebark pine, whose nuts are one of the most nutritious of all Yellowstone grizzly foods.

Besides the relatively poor rhyolitic soils of the plateaus, there are also a few tracts of land visible from the cliff whose soils are derived from sedimentary rocks—built up when this whole region was under water ages ago and in more recent geological times by the action of Ice Age glaciers—and here a glorious diversity of life abounds. Many of the forested communities based on sedimentary soils are dominated by subalpine fir, in combination with important low-growing grizzly foods such as gooseberry, huckleberry, and grouse whortleberry; many of these ecotypes also produce succulent forbs in spring and summer. Other woodland communities may be dominated by spruce, by Douglas-fir, or (a very few) by limber pine, and each has goodies to offer.

There is also quite an array of nonforested countryside sustained by the sedimentary soils—riparian meadows and marshes, dry grasslands, low moist swales, alpine tundra, avalanche chutes, shrub steppes, old burned-out forest now revegetating, talus, scree. Botanists have classified these communities into dozens of types, and no doubt grizzlies have their system for it too, for each successful adult bear has filed away in his memory myriad data on when what grows where, to be consulted, edited, added to, and revised all season long, year after year.

Here in the Absaroka range, the homeland of our mother grizzly and her cubs, still another geologic past has determined the vegetation and in turn the distribution and abundance of the animal populations. These are andesitic (fine-grained volcanic) soils, derived chiefly from plagioclase and feldspar, and they are exceptionally fertile. The forests that grow here are mostly spruce and fir, and there are also extensive subalpine meadows, large ridgetop stands of whitebark pine, and much highly productive alpine tundra as well. This is lonely, beautiful, and very diverse countryside, rich in grizzly bear foods, and full of grizzly bears.

Along the major rivers to the west—the Lamar, the Yellowstone, the Madison, the Snake—there are broad flats and tablelands of transported soils, which, having eroded from the life-rich uppermost layers of all three of the major substrate soil types, are the most fertile of all. The warmer climate of the lower-elevation valleys supports forests often dominated by the magnificent Douglas-fir, and, as in Pelican Valley and along the upper Madison and Firehole rivers, there are also large, lush meadows, whose vegetative composition varies widely, according to rainfall, snowmelt, ground water, elevation, and temperature. These meadows nourish tremendous numbers of elk and many bison, and, except for the heavily human-used meadows near the river-following roads, they are also superlative grizzly habitat. Indeed, when night has fallen, and the fishermen and photographers and picnickers and all the rest of the human host are snug in their motels and campers and tents, grizzlies often have moved in unseen just behind, foraging even to the shoulders of the roads.

The great mosaic of land visible from the mother bear's clifftop takes in the domains of many grizzlies, but, because it is so diverse, the bears are not at all evenly distributed. There are about one thousand species of plants growing in this ecosystem, but of those at any given time only a few are available and of high nutritive value, and these few are concentrated only in certain vegetative communities. Some of the bits that compose the mosaic are exceedingly small, and some of these can be among the most crucial—like, for instance, the foot-wide strip of mushy mud along the border of a pond, which in a dry year will continue to produce succulent long-leaved pond-weed throughout the heat of August and the general desiccation of September. Even when good food is abundant, the distribution of certain critical plant community types will tell you pretty accurately where within this bewilderment of variety nearly all the grizzly bears of Yellowstone are likely to be found.

For all the outward vastness of this ecosystem, therefore, the ranges of individual grizzlies must substantially overlap, and there is no strict territoriality. (The biologist Lynn Rogers has found that where food resources are abundant and evenly distributed, adult female black bears establish quite a rigid system of territories; but other studies, notably one by Christopher Servheen of grizzly ecology in Montana's Mission Mountains, indicate that even in environments where food is relatively uniformly distributed, grizzlies are not territorial.) Even without territoriality, in any case, grizzlies as a rule do shun one another's company—except for mating, of course—and the sharing of resources takes place in an atmosphere of warily cordial mutual avoidance. Where food is exceptionally highly concentrated —as in the park garbage dumps of old, or along an Alaskan salmon stream, or as in the beached-whale-eating days of primeval California—grizzlies will work out a cautious social accommodation and live close together if not exactly cooperatively, and a hierarchy among individuals will form.

Living so close together exacts a price, however. In some places where grizzlies gather in groups larger than family units, some bi-ologists have found, the cannibalistic males wreak havoc, and cub mortality is high. It has been speculated that the killing of cubs may enhance the males' chances of individual reproductive success: despite the fact that males do not recognize their own offspring and therefore do occasionally kill them, the majority of their victims will inevitably be the progeny of rival males. To knock these cubs off, the theory goes, will be advantageous because a female whose cubs have been killed before mating season—with her hormonal status now altered by the cessation of nursing—may enter estrus that very spring. Kill-ing cubs anytime will result in a higher availability of breeding females at least by the following spring. The problem with this theory is that males are rarely able to kill more than one cub at a go—as we have seen, mother grizzlies are ferocious defenders of their young—and the females are therefore not made more likely to enter estrus early. If the object were reproductive success, wouldn't the males dispatch whole litters? Or is that precisely what they do try, and is it simply that the mothers are more successful in defending the surviving cubs? Or is the killing merely opportunistic predation? And how important is it? Some biologists argue that such killing is far rarer than is generally thought, and that threat behavior alone is the significant thing.

Whether backed up with real killing or not, such threatening of the young by adult males does seem to be ever present, even in dispersed populations, and it is probably mainly for this reason that the home ranges of females with young, despite their high nutritional needs, are usually smaller than those of solo females. Adult males, evidently to maintain acquaintance with as many females as possible and thus to maximize their chances of reproductive success, have the largest home ranges. Those of subadult males, subadult females, and adult females without cubs fall in between. It is the facts of social life, and not nutritional needs, which determine the *relative* sizes of grizzlies' home ranges. The *absolute* sizes are determined, at least in part, by the quality and availability of food. Thus, on Admiralty Island, Alaska, where the coastal rain forests' rich berry crops and the rivers' teeming salmon runs make possible a tremendous density of bears, one study found male home ranges to average forty-one square miles, while female home ranges averaged only sixteen. In another study area in northwestern Montana near Glacier National Park, where moist maritime air blows in from the Pacific and bear food plants are therefore relatively abundant, the average male grizzly's home range was found to be one hundred eighty-nine square miles, and the average female's seventy-two. In Yellowstone, with its more arid continental climate and therefore poorer habitat, adult male home ranges average three hundred eighteen square miles, and those of females average one hundred seventy-eight.

Averages can be misleading, however, especially in so individualistic a species. Those Yellowstone adult male home ranges that average out to three hundred eighteen square miles, for example, represent many individual bears, one of whom uses one hundred seventy-eight square miles and another of whom seems to need six hundred thirty-three! And the biggest home range is not necessarily that of the biggest bear. Nor are the smaller ranges closely correlated with higher-quality habitat. Nor can any other combination of known factors account for the variation. The average figures can be useful for comparing whole ecosystems, of course—and even then they should ideally be based on many years of observation, since food availability and mate availability may both vary substantially over time; but when it comes to predicting how much country "a" grizzly bear might require, the averages are all but worthless. The individual variation is just too great.

Not only the sizes but also the compositions of grizzly home ranges vary widely. Especially in an ecosystem like Yellowstone's, with its extensive lodgepole forest, much of any grizzly's home range amounts to little more than travel space among feeding sites and other important places. Hence a home range can be more accurately envisioned as a constellation of centers of activity, or biocenters, than as a uniform piece of real estate. There is some evidence that experienced adult bears develop a routine circuit of their biocenters, although of course the routine will vary according to season and forage conditions, and a grizzly who finds a dead elk today may naturally decide to forgo tomorrow's jaunt to the horsetail patch. Still, many grizzlies will leave a feeding site long before they have exhausted its food supply, and will then move on to another one, in some cases biologically identical. Such a circuit, in the best conservationist fashion, would tend to maximize year-to-year productivity of the whole home range. Nevertheless, the availability of high-quality feeding sites does not seem to correlate very meaningfully with home range size. Some grizzly bears just seem to like to cover a lot of ground. Others, even in apparently identical habitat, are homebodies. Some home ranges fluctuate widely from season to season and even from year to year. Almost all grizzlies make occasional long excursions far outside their home ranges, and then, as a rule, return. Nobody yet knows why.

You will have noted that even the smallest home ranges are still a great deal of country, and that is one of the bear's biggest problems. People, especially some of those in charge of managing grizzly habitat, seem to have trouble understanding land use on so big a scale—by anybody else but people, that is. To provide adequate food, cover, denning habitat, and other grizzlies to mate with, a grizzly bear's home range necessarily includes a lot of "dead space," but it has been shown time and time again that you cannot take away that dead space and still have grizzly bears. People naturally want to be loved, but the plain fact is that grizzly bears don't love people. As a matter of fact, most of them flee at the very sight of us. Which can hardly be surprising, since those who don't are customarily denied the opportunity even to live to regret it. Wherever intensive human use comes, right-thinking grizzly bears leave. Clear-cut the lodgepole timber in (or even near) the "dead space" in a grizzly bear's home range—or put in a ski lift, or set up an oil exploration camp, or run a new road through, or let the local youth stage their dirt-bike moto-crosses there—and even though you may think you have protected all the critical habitat components, the feeding sites, the denning areas, and so on, in fact you have disrupted the movement corridors that connect those components, and you no longer have a grizzly home range because you no longer have a bear. They need space. They need solitude. They need to be left alone.

To appreciate why the loss of even a little grizzly habitat, and the loss of even a few grizzlies, can be dangerous to the survival of whole populations, we need to understand grizzly bear population dynamics. Remember, foremost, that Yellowstone, like many another of our wild animal sanctuaries, is an ecological island. Losses to the grizzly population here cannot be made up by immigration of bears from adjacent populations, because there aren't any.

How many grizzlies are there in Yellowstone? Nobody really knows. Especially when you have to search five and a half million acres of wilderness looking for them, bears are hard to count. The question has nevertheless been furiously debated, and still is. It has been the focal point of the most famous wildlife-management battle of this century, which will be examined in the next chapter. In the meantime, we can probably be safe in assuming that there are a minimum of about two hundred. Is the population in decline? This too is the subject of some dispute. Almost everyone agrees that it did decline between 1960 and 1980, and present indications are that it is probably still dropping. Some argue that this may be a natural adjustment to changes in climate and habitat, others that it is directly attributable to insufficient protection and poor management.

Even if the Yellowstone population does not decline to extinction, there are long-term dangers inherent in its isolation. A population this small of any animal, over generations of inbreeding, becomes more prone to genetic defects, because the frequency of occurrence of recessive traits fluctuates wildly in small isolated gene pools. A technically temporary preponderance of maladaptive recessive characteristics, especially if their random combination comes up unlucky, might well be sufficient to reduce the population below a point from which it could recover—imagine the synergism of, say, lowered fertility and increased susceptibility to infection—and what was "technically" temporary would in the event be quite final. How soon the results of inbreeding may become significant for the Yellowstone grizzly is unknown, and there are enough threats much nearer at hand that not much thought has been given to it.

The ecologist Harold Picton has suggested that there may be a remnant biological link, allowing genetic flow along the Rocky Mountain chain across western Montana, between the Glacier and Yellowstone populations, for there continue to be sporadic sightings of grizzly bears in this supposedly unoccupied habitat. For such a link to be maintained, and enhanced, would certainly be in the long-term interest of the grizzly, but it would also entail a great deal more careful and restrictive land management than the likes of the U.S. Forest Service, the custodian of most of this bridge country, are inclined toward. There is also a lot of private ranchland linking the centers of potential grizzly occupancy along the bridge—and try talking to most Montana ranchers about enhancing grizzly habitat on their property.

In the foreseeable future, the grizzly population of Yellowstone is likely to remain uncounted. There was, briefly, in 1982, a proposal for a rather grandiose saturation-trapping program which would have resulted in a highly accurate estimate, but the costs would have been so high, and the side effects so disruptive (helicopters shattering the wilderness calm daily, stress on the bears due to repeated trapping of some individuals, and so forth) that the idea was dropped. Nevertheless, the people responsible for the grizzly's survival must have some idea of whether they are succeeding. For that, however, the absolute number is irrelevant. What matters is the *trend* of the population.

Grizzly bears are what is known in ecology as a K-selected species—long-lived animals with inherently low reproductive rates, able to maximize learning and to occupy stable habitat at a level near its carrying capacity, or K. The population trend of any K-selected species is determined by the survival and reproductive rate of the females. There are frighteningly few adult female grizzly bears still alive in Yellowstone, and that is why the welfare of the heroine of this narrative is so important. To determine the trend, a number of factors must be looked at in combination.

The first is the *age of recruitment*—the age at which an individual first reproduces, or is "recruited" into the adult population. Our bear's age of recruitment was six.

Another critical factor is the *reproductive rate* for breeding females, expressed as the average number of young born per year. In nine years (at the ages of six, ten, and thirteen), our grizzly bear has given birth to three litters of two cubs each. Divide six cubs by nine years, and we find that her reproductive rate is .67—which happens to be the current mean for Yellowstone grizzlies. Year-to-year comparisons of the mean reproductive rate of a sample of adult females will tell you how basic cub productivity is faring.

That figure will not be specially meaningful, however, unless you also know the rate of *cub survival*. Again, it is the survival to maturity of females which is the critical factor, since the population can continue to grow even with a considerable shortage of males. Data on cub survival are notoriously hard to get, but some studies have suggested that no more than twenty to fifty percent of cubs ever make it to the age of recruitment.

The rate of females' *adult survival* must also be known. Remember that in the first thirteen years of her life, our grizzly has given birth to only two female offspring, and the most optimistic odds, based on fifty percent cub survival, are that only one of them will survive long enough to have cubs of her own. Thus, at the age of thirteen, the mother grizzly *may* have managed to replace herself with another breeding female. If we take the possible low end of the survival rate—twenty percent—and assume average litters of two cubs, average intervals of three years between litters, and an equal sex ratio, and because she must live another year after the birth of her last cubs for them to have a chance of survival, she will have to live to the age of twenty-three just to replace herself.

Yet the oldest Yellowstone grizzly ever known to have borne cubs was twenty-six. Very few, of course, ever make it near that age, since the youngest bears are the most vulnerable. Obviously, the survival of the very few long-living females is critical, and you don't have to lose very many of them before the population trend takes a nosedive.

Age structure—the relative proportions of cubs-of-the-year, yearlings, subadults, and breeding-age adults—can also be an important indicator of the trend of a population. The Yellowstone grizzly enjoys total legal protection: only the occasional nuisance animal may be officially dispatched. Under those conditions, such a long-lived species should show a considerable preponderance of adults in the population. An increase in the proportion of juveniles would suggest that factors of greater magnitude than the usually small natural or "background" adult mortality were at work.

Sex ratio can also tell us something. At birth, the sex ratio of grizzly bears is roughly equal. Male and female vulnerability should remain equal while the cubs are still under their mothers' protection. After weaning, however, partly because males always have larger ranges and partly because the subadults looking for a place to settle tend to wander around somewhat haphazardly, and also because they are more inclined to fighting and other dangerous aggression than young females, subadult males are the most vulnerable segment in the whole sex-and-age structure. After they reach maturity, males continue to be slightly more vulnerable due both to range size and to their continuing tendency to fight. Thus, in a naturally regulated population, we would expect to see a rising preponderance of females in all age classes from subadulthood to senescence. Anything else, and we should suspect something fishy.

Now let's look and see how these factors work out in real life in the Yellowstone ecosystem. We do not know the real size of the grizzly population, but two hundred is probably a safe guess, so let's start with that.

Recent data tell us that forty percent of them will be above the age of recruitment—a rather drastically small proportion, the reasons for which we shall see in pages to come. So we have eighty adults. Of those, according to recent research, as few as thirty-eight percent may be female. That means only thirty adult females in all. (Some authorities argue that because of their smaller home ranges and perhaps also because they are more cautious, females have been under-represented in trapping efforts. For the moment, however, keeping that in mind, we must work with the existing data.)

The average interval between litters, or *reproductive cycle*, for adult female grizzlies in Yellowstone is three years, which makes ten females available for breeding per year. If we assume that all ten breed successfully, and we apply the latest figure of 1.9 for mean litter size, we get nineteen cubs born per year. If half of them are females, and half of *them* survive to the age of recruitment, we are getting only five likely new mothers a year. Some recent data suggest that the sex ratio of grizzly cubs in Yellowstone may, for unknown reasons, be skewed to males, in which case the number of likely new mother grizzlies per year may be only three or four.

It gets sticky fast, doesn't it? The inescapable inference is that this population is in a parlous state indeed. Clearly it cannot endure much mortality beyond natural background levels. Yet from 1970 through 1982, an average of *eighteen* of Yellowstone's grizzlies per year have been shot, poisoned, run over, or (the new sentence for some incorrigible nuisance bears) shipped to remote areas in Canada; and the majority of these losses to the population have been female. So while we are gaining three to five adult female grizzly bears a year, we are losing nine to eleven. Obviously, the preservation of every possible female is unequivocally essential to the Yellowstone grizzly population's survival. And even at that, recovery can only be long and slow.

Much has been made in recent years of the use of computer modeling in population biology. The general idea is to take current parameters (meaningful variables)—such as age structure, reproductive rate, and so on—and then project the long-term results of certain changes in them. The reason you need a computer is that the meaningful variables are so many and so, well, variable. The problem is that there is not much agreement about which variables are meaningful and how much weight to give them. There have been a number of computer analyses of Yellowstone grizzly bear data, and, unsurprisingly, a number of strikingly different conclusions.

On one conclusion, however, all the modelers have agreed—that the current level of man-caused female mortality is intolerable. One analyst, L. L. Eberhardt, has projected that a ninety-six percent survival rate for breeding-age female grizzlies in Yellowstone will result in a slow increase, but that a rate of ninety percent results in a steady decline. After thirty years of ninety percent female survival, Eberhart's model predicts, only ten females above the age of two and a half would be left alive, and from there the population drops rapidly to extinction. In 1981, the estimated survival rate of adult Yellowstone females—counting only man-caused mortality—was eighty-seven percent.

Some fancy mathematical footwork by biologist Mark Shaffer, in a paper entitled "Determining Minimum Viable Population Sizes for the Grizzly Bear," examines the effects of various changes in overall mortality, percentage of females reproducing, average litter size, adult population size, subadult population size, and total population size—all raising hell with one another in a fantastically complicated system of multiple feedback loops. Shaffer's model arrived at threshold values for various habitats in the form of population sizes below which no recovery would be possible no matter what the sex and age structure. Estimating the productivity of those habitats is crucial to Shaffer's work, but that is an extremely imprecise exercise, so the whole thing has to be taken with a grain or two of salt; but such is computer modeling. It can still be instructive.

Shaffer's most significant contribution is that his analysis takes into account not only the effects of *systematic pressures*, which are the regular and predictable events of classical ecology, but also the effects of *stochastic changes*, or random irruptions of catastrophic events, which may be unpredictable but are, over time, nonetheless inevitable—such as fire, flood, drought, disease epidemics, random changes in gene frequencies, variation in the habitat's carrying capacity, fluctuations of the populations of other species, and a few hundred other devastating possibilities. In any insular ecosystem— which Yellowstone is—stochastic events are vastly more significant than in ecosystems with a possibility of immigration from adjacent populations, and the smaller an isolated population is, the more severe are the impacts. In this rather scary light we can see the full importance of Harold Picton's idea about the possibility of maintaining a biological bridge between the Yellowstone grizzly bear's "island" and the populations of northwestern Montana and Canada.

Shaffer concludes that once a population falls below fifty to ninety bears (the wide range is due to the imprecision of some of the data he had to depend on as well as to variations in the productivity of various habitats), there is no hope of recovery, and the population will inevitably decline to extinction. What is most frightening about Shaffer's model is how long that last doomed population hangs on: without sophisticated analysis, even an experienced wildlife expert would not necessarily come intuitively to the belief that the population was in trouble until long after it was too late. So, rough and ragged and confusing as present computer simulations may be, they are indispensable for peering into the future, and worthy of continuing refinement; they have already made it indisputably clear that the reproductive capacity of the grizzly bear cannot possibly compensate for the Yellowstone population's present level of mortality.

Why, then, we may well ask, are Yellowstone's grizzlies—and others —still being killed at such a doom-defying clip?

Despite the clamor of simpleminded apostles of virtue thirsting for the blood of an easily identifiable villain, there is not a government conspiracy against the grizzly bear. It may less intemperately be argued nevertheless that there might as well be, for all the good they've done the bear. The problem with that argument, however, is that there is no unitary "they." Far from amounting to a conspiracy, the many state and federal agencies whose paths intersect that of the bear have done their greatest harm through *failure* to conspire. To this day some of them barely talk to each other.

What must be recognized is that all these agencies, while they tend to have certain stereotypical organizational personalities, are made up of individuals—and when it comes to grizzly bears, very individualistic individuals at that. The supervisor of this national forest over here may have made it his highest personal and professional priority to help save the grizzly, while that one over there, on the other side of the same mountains—whose forest is part of a different administrative region and who therefore has a different boss who may himself have ideas about grizzlies totally different from the other supervisor's boss's attitude—may merely pay lip service to grizzly recovery while privately feeling, or fearing that maybe his boss privately feels, that it's about time they finished off the son of a bitch so they can get on with their timber harvest.

Even as this is being written, however, things are changing—in most cases for better, though in some for worse. The evolving role of government and the laws will be treated in a later chapter. For the moment it will suffice us to keep in mind that, although the loss and degradation of habitat may be the greatest long-term problem, the most immediate danger to marginal grizzly populations like that of Yellowstone is illegal killing; that all the sophisticated management and habitat protection in the world will be futile if the killing is not stopped; and that the only people who can stop it are in government agencies.

There is no denying that in the past, many of these people and their agencies have let the grizzly down, sometimes through bureau-cratic inertia, sometimes because the laws and regulations or the funds to enforce them have been inadequate, sometimes through good old basic personal incompetence, and once in a while even out of malice or corruption. But you know how government employment is: for the most part, nobody ever gets fired. So we and the grizzly bear are stuck with these people, and we've got to make the best of it. Most of them really want to save the bear anyway. Others can be made to want to, if that's what the law lays down or their bosses tell them to want.

The agencies nevertheless harbor a few case-hardened enemies of the grizzly bear, and they do much harm. As for them, probably all we can hope is that our looking over their shoulders will at least keep them within the bounds of the law and their official responsibilities. Public activism on behalf of good conservationist causes is too often aimed, shotgun-style, at a monolithic villain called government, fail-ing to recognize its human diversity and failing therefore to focus the pressure where it can do some real good. The bear does have friends behind those gray walls. If the partisans of the grizzly, inside and outside of government, together put their minds to workable solutions—and perhaps also to rooting out those individuals in gov-ernment who prove utterly intractable—the agencies can save the grizzly bear. And they can start by getting the killing under control.

The sources of the killing are remarkably few, and for the most part they are easy to scotch.

Some grizzlies will unavoidably get run over on the roads, but that danger can be minimized by regularly removing carcasses and other attractants that draw bears to the roadside. This is already being done in some jurisdictions. In others, well, they just don't seem to have the time, or the money, or something. And of course it is essential to keep road building and traffic to a minimum, for a simple road is one of the worst things you can put in grizzly habitat. A grow-ing number of people, in fact, would like to see some existing roads plowed under and returned to God and the grizzly bear. They would have Yellowstone and Glacier and other parks closed to private traffic altogether, and let the visitors travel at a pace appropriate to the experience of wilderness, on foot or on horseback or in horse-drawn wagons, or maybe by slow jitney or light rail—an idea whose time may come, though probably not soon. It would certainly be good for grizzly bears, and people would probably come to like it too. Before we get that far toward paradise, however, there is an awful lot of government land in grizzly country, belonging to the Forest Service and the Bureau of Land Management and the states, which is in imminent danger of having new roads put in and old ones made faster. Some grizzly habitat in the national forests, even as you read this, is being crisscrossed with roads at a density, if you can imagine, comparable to New York City's. Roads bring people, and some of those people, inevitably, kill bears.

Some grizzlies, also unavoidably, will be executed for repeated commission of crimes against the ruling class. A truly addicted garbage bear is often a truly hopeless case, and a genuine danger. A grizzly who develops a taste for human children, although in a purely biological sense that might be said to be perfectly normal predator behavior, is obviously not going to be allowed to patrol the motel parking lots in West Glacier, Montana. It may well be that the standards developed for deciding who is and who isn't a certifiable nuisance bear do lean excessively toward human security and away from grizzly welfare, particularly when it comes to the precious breeding females; but in fact the application of those standards is agonized over in officialdom—even if only because bureaucrats quake in their boots when they think of the nasty stories that tend to appear in the newspapers when they shoot bears. No doubt that is why Yellowstone Park now likes to ship problem grizzlies to Canada rather than kill them outright, although it ends up amounting to the same thing—another loss to the population.

Because the national parks are so carefully protected, and firearms are forbidden, almost all the illegal killing of grizzly bears takes place outside their borders, on the national forests and private lands where guns are allowed and there are hunting seasons for a number of other species. These lands are by no means just some sort of fringe of grizzly habitat. Fully *half* the Yellowstone grizzly's range is outside the national park, and rife with rifle-toting hunters, stockmen, and others. Glacier National Park is critical as a refuge, but it is only a medium-sized chunk of northwest Montana's grizzly country. Most of the rest is fraught with armed danger.

The sources of the slaughter are remarkably few. Black bear hunters make mistakes, or claim to. Grizzlies raid hunting camps for game meat or provisions and are shot by outraged sportsmen or their outfitters. Domestic sheep are grazed in grizzly habitat, and the bears do what comes natural, and the sheepmen shoot them—old Western sheepherder tradition holding that you shoot any bear you see, black or grizzly, adult or cub, and only later, if at all, worry about whether or not the bear was actually killing sheep. Ranchers set out poisoned meat as coyote bait, and grizzlies eat it and die. Professional poachers get a minimum of two hundred fifty dollars for a single grizzly claw, and ten thousand for a good whole skin; there is even a market in the Orient for dried gall bladder, at about seven hundred dollars the ounce. And some folks, of course, kill grizzly bears just for the sheer rawhided hell of it.

And, as we will later see in detail, almost all of them get away with it scot-free.

The disadvantages of our bear and her cubs with respect to these human dangers are many. First of all, they're always hungry. In seven months they must make twelve months' worth of a living, for by the time they enter the den in October or November they must have put on enough fat to keep them going through five months of hibernation. The cubs must weigh at least seventy-five pounds apiece by midautumn, so their mother has a great deal of milk to produce in addition to serving her own nutritional needs. Although the cubs also forage for the same foods she eats, they will continue to nurse until next spring and perhaps for another year after that.

A mother with cubs usually maintains the smallest of grizzly home ranges, but her high energy demands require that she use that range intensively, ceaselessly traveling through its network of feeding sites and thus exposing herself and the cubs to a higher likelihood of contact with humans than bears even with larger home ranges might have. Because their metabolic demands are so great, grizzly bears have evolved an opportunistic feeding strategy that calls for them to take advantage of the highest-quality foods available, almost without considering the consequences—for during the thousands of years of this behavior's evolution, as we have seen, the risk associated with laying claim to whatever a grizzly wanted was small, even if the food belonged to man. Our bear remains a prisoner of that strategy. She knows that people are dangerous, but her fear, if she is hungry enough, can be overwhelmed by a powerful whiff of good food.

As spring moves toward summer, the availability of carrion and large prey wanes, and she is ever more dependent on low-energy vegetation. Under these circumstances, the temptation of human foods naturally grows still greater. Moreover, people are just about the only expanding resource in this ecosystem, and although a concerted effort is being made to educate them about keeping their food un-available to bears, some people will always be too dumb or too ornery to cooperate, and the increase in human numbers may be so large that the availability of their foods, even if at a lower rate, is increasing too. A single carelessly dropped peanut butter and jelly sandwich may seem an insignificant item in the diet of a creature as big as a grizzly bear, but it truly can be the first step down the path to her doom. Maybe the next time she smells peanut butter and jelly she will have to rifle somebody's unoccupied tent to get at it, and maybe the time after that the tent will be occupied, and maybe the occupant will be an elk hunter sleeping with his thirty-ought-six beside him.

A mother with cubs is by far the most aggressive of grizzly bears, the one least likely to flee from danger. One study has shown that in a population in which only seventeen percent of the grizzlies were mothers with cubs, they caused nearly eighty percent of the human injuries. A mother grizzly's "critical distance"—a perimeter, varying quite a bit from bear to individual bear, beyond which a tres-passer is more likely to be charged than to be fled from—is larger than that of any other grizzly. A charging bear, of course, is the bear most likely to die.

Because her nutritional demands are so high, a mother grizzly is very serious about defending her food. If a person, or another bear, happens to pass between her day bed and a carcass she has been feeding on, she may very well charge the interloper, again exposing herself to risk. In many cases such a charge may not be meant as a full-out attack, and another bear is likely to read it correctly, as merely a firm warning, and will then, with appropriate salaams ex-pressing apology and submission, peacefully withdraw. Most people, on the other hand, when confronted with a charging grizzly bear, tend to freak out and run, which is a big mistake, since grizzlies seem to be quite rigidly programed to chase—and catch—any creature that flees from them. Flight, after all, is the very signature of a weakened and therefore available large prey animal. Of course, standing your ground may not work either. But if you can't get up a tree (most grizzlies do not climb trees) before the grizzly reaches you, standing your ground—especially if you can figure out how to express your deep humility in bear language while doing so—remains the best of an admittedly poor selection of alternatives.

Especially for those grizzlies who spend all or most of their lives within the idyllic gunless confines of a national park, and who therefore have ceased (or never begun) to associate human beings with danger, violent responses to perceived threat or even to mere invasions of their privacy can easily become a habit, because at least at first they work so well. A grizzly discovers, let's say, that when he charges a person wearing a backpack, the person usually drops the backpack forthwith, and there is almost always something good to eat inside. It doesn't even have to pay off that often, for, as Pavlov showed and as many visitors to Las Vegas can testify, an infrequent and irregular reinforcement can be more powerfully addictive than a dependable one. A strategy like ambushing backpackers can rapidly become an ingrained habit, and it may work wonderfully, but it generally does so only for the short while before the authorities close in. The grizzly who finds violence useful is the grizzly most likely to come to a violent end.

Quite a number of experiments have been tried in the search for nonlethal ways to change the bad habits of grizzlies gone bad, or at least to survive them—chemical Mace, ear-shattering airhorns, trained bear-hating dogs, emetics, salt-loaded shotgun shells, electrified fences, you name it. One oddball technique that seemed to show promise as a measure against a grizzly in full charge was pointing a furled spring-loaded multicolored golf umbrella at him, pushing the little button, and having the thing burst into bloom with a *whomp*. Most bears they tried it on turned tail in astonishment. The problem was that old familiar grizzly specialty, individuality. Every once in a while, the golf umbrella trick made a charging grizzly even madder.

The bears' idiosyncratic personalities are really just a small part of the difficulty, however. The big one is the tenacity of their habituations. A grizzly bear will happily endure a whole chorus of boathorns, walk through fire, and climb a fence electrified with near-fatal voltage as long as doing so will get him something good to eat.

Grizzly bears are extremely inquisitive animals. This characteristic has evolved as an essential part of their opportunistic, omnivorous feeding strategy: *I wonder what's under that rock . . . might be something to eat . . . let's have a look.* But it isn't only cats that curiosity can kill: *Gosh, that smells good . . . now how might it be got at? . . . ah! all you have to do is smash through this door here . . . nothing to it*—until the old-timer's truck pulls up out front, and he sees the cabin door in smithereens and reaches to the rifle rack behind the seat.

Particularly in spring and fall, grizzlies' food habits take them to riparian zones. The earlier it is in spring and the later in fall, the lower the elevations are to which they must move to find succulent vegetation, for the likelier it is then that the highlands will be snow-covered or parched. Early spring and late fall are also, of course, the two periods most critical to their nutrition, postdenning and pre-, so the bears found at lower elevations during these times are likely to be under some stress and therefore in an especially touchy mood. And the farther downstream a bear has to go, the closer he probably comes to human settlement, and the likelier it is that he will encounter live-stock or people. National parks like Yellowstone and Glacier, both of which occupy mainly high mountains and plateaus, offer only limited spring and fall range, so even for grizzlies who spend most of their year in the safety of those refuges, movement to lower elevations may mean braving the illicit but (given the sorry state of law enforce-ment) perennial hazards presented by the trigger-happy few among the black bear hunters of spring and amidst the massive occu-pation of the backcountry that comes with the general big game season in fall.

There are still more disadvantages in being a grizzly bear facing modern manmade dangers. A grizzly is one of the biggest creatures out there, and one of the noisiest. Never having had to evolve any-thing like a deer's ability to slip as silently and invisibly through the woods as a ghost, he is easily seen and easily heard. As the fragmen-tation of grizzly habitat worsens, the likelihood of being seen or heard increases. More contact means more trouble.

There is more and more exploration for oil and gas in grizzly habitat, for both the Yellowstone and the northwest Montana popula-tions lie astride the famous Overthrust Belt, where the collision and folding of tectonic plates long ago buried huge deposits of ancient hydrocarbons far enough beneath the surface that they have not been accessible until the recent development of new extraction tech-nologies. On the East Front of the Rockies, where the Great Plains crash into the crumpled wall of the mountains of Glacier Park and the Bob Marshall Wilderness, grizzlies wander out on to the prairie as far as fifty miles from the security of broken terrain and heavy cover. These bears may be a remnant population of the plains grizzly, a sub-species or type which has been considered extinct for a hundred years. Because of their use of open habitat, these grizzlies are exceptionally vulnerable to disruption of their travel patterns. Yet today the East Front is being overrun with seismic exploration, oil wells, pipelines, and people. Most of the land is in private hands, so, with the exception of two crucial sites which have been purchased by the Nature Conservancy and set aside as grizzly range, little can be done to protect these grizzlies except to enforce the laws against killing them.

In many other parts of grizzly country, especially in Canada, logging and mining are displacing grizzly bears. Ranchers often dispose carelessly of their dead livestock, and so invite trouble with grizzlies. Ranches, resorts, second-home developments continue to take bites here and there out of grizzly habitat. Increasing recreational use of the backcountry causes more and more bears to flee their traditional sites of feeding or sanctuary, pushing them into areas where they are more likely to be exposed to danger. Garbage continues in many places to habituate grizzlies to the presence of man and thus to lead them into peril.

Anomalies in the population structure also contribute to the risk of confrontation with humans. As the proportion of males in the grizzly population rises, there is more fighting, and the spacing that is normally maintained between individuals grows less stable, and more bears are forced outside the realm of safety. As the proportion of subadults in the population rises, more bears are inexperienced and thus likelier to take stupid chances, and there are accordingly fewer of the peaceful, conservative, man-avoiding, successfully reproducing adults on whom the burden of the population's continuing vitality rests.

And yet, and yet. A grizzly bear also has a few advantages. Being the baddest mother in the woods is one. Where does a five-hundred-pound grizzly bear sit? *Wherever he damn well pleases.* The great size of grizzlies does entail the disadvantage of high visibility, but it also means they are awesomely strong and scary. The biggest known Yellowstone grizzly—albeit a habitué of the old garbage dumps, and doubtless a fatso—weighed in at over eleven hundred pounds. The huge bears of the Alaskan coast may once in a while weigh a ton. (These bears are sometimes popularly known as "Kodiak" bears, although they are found in a number of localities besides Kodiak Island. Some taxonomists consider them to be a separate subspecies of the brown bear, *Ursus arctos middendorffi.* Other biologists, however, point out that this coastal race seems to intergrade with the classic grizzly type of the interior—*Ursus arctos horribilis*—and that they are all one bear.) But in the American West, now that the gigantic bears of the California Coast Range are gone, grizzlies seldom weigh more than six hundred pounds. Their weights are often overestimated, even by old backwoods hands whose perceptions of other wildlife are usually accurate, partly because grizzlies' coats can be very thick and fluffy at certain times and partly also, no doubt, because the person doing the guessing is so flabbergasted at the sight of one.

Grizzly bears are fast, too. A twelve-year-old Yellowstone grizzly and her two-year-old cub were once observed to cover twenty-one miles of brutally rugged terrain in less than an hour. Gary Brown of the National Park Service once clocked a subadult Alaskan grizzly at thirty-six miles per hour. In *Grizzly County*, Andy Russell reported measuring the distance between tracks left in the snow by a grizzly at full gallop—seventeen feet. Their endurance is equally impressive. Grizzlies can easily travel all day and night without stopping to rest, moving along in their long-strided, rolling, rather comical shuffle at an unflagging six miles per hour or better.

They are built like the heavy-duty earth-moving machinery whose handiwork their own so often resembles. Their leg bones and shoulders are almost grotesquely massive. They have skulls like river rocks. The musculature that powers those terrifying jaws—a bulging knot the size and shape of a flattened football on each side of the head, often giving the scalp a distinct central crease—is quite sufficient for a full-grown grizzly to snap a six-inch-thick pine tree in two, or to crush a Hereford's skull like an eggshell. The large shoulder hump—the grizzly's most distinctive feature and the one which usually distinguishes his appearance from that of the black bear—is not, as some folklore holds, stored fat or water or any other kind of analogue to a camel's hump, but rather an enormous wad of muscle, the engine that powers the mighty digging and death-dealing machinery of the front legs.

For all their brute power, grizzlies possess remarkable dexterity. Both black and grizzly bears commonly use single digits just as people use their fingers, and, although bears lack an opposed thumb, they perform many feats that would seem to call for hands. In Yosemite National Park, for example, black bears have learned to open jars with screw tops. With their long, slim claws, grizzlies are able to "card" berries with impressive efficiency, managing to consume surprisingly little foliage or stem material. When a grizzly smashes open an anthill—a favorite summertime snack, low in food value but rich in formic acid, which may aid in digestion—the usual tactic is to thrust paw into swarm and then to lick up teeming ants one finger-tipful by one, like a child finishing off the last of the chocolate frosting.

Grizzlies' feet are big, and tough. Their flat-footed, or planti-grade, stance gives them a greatly enhanced ability to walk on snow: in terms of weight load per square unit of foot area, a grizzly's foot carries less than a fifth the load that ungulates or people do, so where man or moose would sink helplessly, the grizzly can bound lightly across the top. In the critical pre- and postdenning periods, when snow may be deep and grizzlies may be very dependent on predation, you can imagine the benefits.

The soles and toes are heavily padded, and covered with a thick horny leather that is not only soft and flexible but also virtually im-possible to cut. The claws of the front feet are very long—four to six inches in the average adult grizzly, although active diggers' claws may be worn down shorter. The color of the claws varies widely, both among individuals and among separate populations, with black, brown, amber, tan, yellowish, and ivory white all reported. Unlike the hooked claws of black bears, those of grizzlies are only slightly curved—the difference between adaptations to tree-climbing and to digging. Grizzlies keep their claws ever sharp by raking them vertically into tree bark, on the sweet cambium beneath which the bears also feed. Certain heavily gouged "bear trees" seem to be used for this purpose generation after generation. Some black bear research has suggested that bear trees may also, perhaps with the assistance of some kind of scent-marking, serve as a reminder to other bears that a certain individual is in an area; such communication would aid in spacing and in the sharing of resources.

The longer a grizzly bear lives, thanks to his excellent memory, the more advantages accrue to him. Good places to go, hazardous ones to avoid, effective tactics and bootless ones all accumulate. We probably go too far if we say that the bear employs actual reason and draws intelligent inferences from his experience, but at the same time there is no question that once grizzlies have reached a certain age, the rate at which they die drops off precipitously until senescence sets in.

Grizzly bears are models of health and fitness. They seem not to suffer from heart disease or cancer or diabetes or any of the other major diseases that bedevil humankind. A certain number of parasites —protozoans, liver flukes, tapeworms, nematodes, and the like—turn up in autopsies, but they are only rarely plentiful enough to have contributed significantly to mortality. Grizzlies' wounds heal fast, and are seldom infected: the natural secretions of their skin are extremely acid, and act as a kind of disinfectant and insecticide. Fleas, ticks, and lice do live on bears, but in far smaller numbers than might be expected. Only when grizzlies get old do health troubles finally mount up—arthritis, lost teeth, failing livers. Besides man, the principal sources of grizzly mortality seem to be starvation and other grizzlies.

Because of their highly flexible diet, however, starvation is relatively rare. Grizzly bears have the longest gut of any carnivore, and hence a highly developed ability to digest even low-quality foods.

Despite their size, grizzlies are adept at disappearing from sight. In Yellowstone, about eighty percent of their time during daylight hours is spent in timber, where sight lines are short. An adult grizzly's knowledge of nearly every nook, cranny, cave, gully, canyon, brushpatch, and defile in his home range enables him to slip quickly into hiding somewhere very near almost every place he goes. Some recent data also seem to suggest that when human presence in his habitat increases, the grizzly tends more toward nocturnality. Bedded down for the day, almost always in thick brush or jumbled downfall, he is practically invisible.

By far the grizzly's greatest defense against trouble is his extraordinary sensory apparatus. It has been popularly believed that bears' eyesight is poor, perhaps because rather than stare hard and steadily at you they tend to look sort of blinky and dim-witted. But the very arrangement of the eyes in the grizzly's face should tell us there is something wrong with that impression. Most of the ungulates and smaller animals that serve as prey to others have their eyes mounted well out on the sides of their heads, so they can see all around, and their vision is set up primarily to detect movement. Most such animals are color blind. Carnivores, on the other hand, including the grizzly bear, have their eyes set relatively close together and facing forward, for more effective prey location and depth perception. A predator obviously has to have good eyes, and while it is true that in some habitats grizzlies are rarely predatory, their evolutionary history puts them squarely in that category. They are by no means color blind, and although the technical acuity of their vision may not be the equal of the human ideal twenty-twenty, an experiment by E. Kackuk in 1937 showed unequivocally that young European brown bears could recognize their keeper visually at a distance of three hundred sixty feet. Obviously, it should not be assumed that a squinting, blinking, head-bobbing, dopey-looking grizzly bear is having trouble picking you out of some kind of blur.

The grizzly's sense of hearing is far more sensitive than man's, and it is undoubtedly an important aid in the pursuit of such subterranean prey as pocket gophers, ground squirrels, mice, and voles, which grizzlies locate blindly and pounce on with noteworthy accuracy. The sweet, high tinkle of even a minuscule bell on your backpack will serve nicely to warn a grizzly of your approach around a blind turning in the trail or over a rise, and most bears who hear such a sound, once they have learned to associate it with people, promptly make for elsewhere. A study by Katherine McArthur Jope in Glacier National Park has shown that bear bells are a significant deterrent of grizzly attacks, since violence tends to come only from bears surprised at close range.

An old Indian proverb goes, "A pine needle fell in the forest. The eagle saw it fall. The deer heard it. The bear smelled it." The acuity of the grizzly's olfactory sense is almost inconceivable to us. Andy Russell says the grizzly bear's nose is "as much better than a bloodhound's as a bloodhound's is better than a man's." At a single whiff, a grizzly may veer abruptly from the path he was on and thence follow the scent on a beeline for mile after mile, up hill and down dale, until at last he homes straight in on a carcass not even rotting yet. The biologist Charles Jonkel says that a human can detect as little as a single molecule of skunk-stink, but to a grizzly bear the whole world smells that eloquently.

At home in Houston, the young man and woman had picked their destination from a topographic map spread out on their living room floor. The topo map took in over two hundred square miles, but a tiny slice of road down in one corner ("Cody 51 mi.") and four abandoned prospectors' cabins were the only human artifacts shown on it. They had never been in the Yellowstone country before—indeed the closest thing they had ever had to a wilderness experience was a two-day commercial whitewater rafting trip in Georgia, where the boatmen put up your tent for you and cooked your T-bone to taste—but they wanted to get really *away* from it all, and they liked the sound of the name of Hoodoo Basin.

The map showed you could see forever from up there, maybe all the way to Yellowstone Lake, and they had heard that such areas above timberline could be spectacular with wildflowers. The young man figured he might also follow the ridgeline cross-country down to a couple of alpine lakes beneath Sunlight Peak, and get in a little trout fishing.

He had argued angrily that one of the reasons you went into the wilderness in the first place was to get away from crap like rules and regulations, but his girlfriend had finally worn him down, and yesterday morning he had consented wearily to driving all the way back to the park visitor center and applying for a backcountry camping permit. The ranger at the backcountry desk, with an altogether too smug look at their unscuffed hiking boots, politely urged them to consider another destination. That was mighty rough country, he said, still mighty cold, and while nobody had been in there yet this year to make any confirmed sightings, there were usually a lot of grizzly bears around.

As far as the young man was concerned, that settled it. He was *damned* if he would let some wimpy ranger or a rumor of bears stop *him*. Just to be on the safe side, however, and since there didn't seem to be anybody around, at the trailhead he had strapped to his backpack's hip belt his tooled-leather holster with the big blue three-fifty-seven magnum inside.

He felt better right away. This was against the law, and his girlfriend, although she didn't say anything, was obviously annoyed.

The trail didn't go a hundred yards before they had to ford a brutally cold creek, where they both lost their footing and ended up on their hands and knees, soaked. Their sleeping bags were wet, too. After they crossed the grassy valley floor—fording another freezing, roaring, malevolent creek on the way, this time rather more cautiously—they entered the forest, and here in shade the snow was still on the ground, in places having drifted to crusted-over man-trapping depths. The going was very slow. Occasionally the tree canopy would open, disclosing a brief wet meadow where the snow had melted and the trail had turned to soupy, boot-snatching mud. By nightfall they had covered about five miles. The freeze-dried beef stew was disgusting, and the young man spilled his ration of Rémy Martin.

The night was full of noises—rustlings, snufflings, creaks, and moans—all sounding like a grizzly bear on the prowl for human meat. The young man and woman both woke early, with headaches, despising each other and all the wretched world. A light, fine, all-insinuating rain began to fall.

Twenty years ago, five miles farther in toward Hoodoo Basin, a lightning-kindled fire had raced up a little spur ridge, raced down to the creek, and gone out. Now the stark black-and-silver trunks of the few firs left standing are all that remain of the forest. Here, open to the sun, the snow melts in most years by mid-May. At the edge of the burn, where half-shadowed islands of white still linger, the glacier lilies, *Erythronium grandiflorum*, enriched by charcoal and ash, are already in bloom, their delicate yellow bells quivering and nodding in the storm wind whipping up the canyon. The grizzly bear mother and her cubs are placidly mowing them down. From time to time the big bear stops grazing and, as the cubs watch closely, digs up the starchy roots as well.

The sky is ugly and low. The slow, steady rain is now punctuated with stinging gusts of sleet. The peaks of the magnificent Absaroka are invisible, buried in cloud. The trail winds on, and up, through endless dark dripping forest, as the snow grows deeper, softer, more wintry. The young woman is crying. She drags her feet through the clotting snow like a hopeless lifer from the Gulag. They are near eight thousand feet now, and the slightly lowered concentration of the atmosphere adds to her discomfort; she cannot seem to catch her breath, and the blood pounds loud in her neck. "I told you you had to get in shape for this trip," the young man whines. "I told you it wasn't going to be easy. I mean, listen. I really want to make that meadow before dark, okay? So let's try to keep moving, okay?"

"*Meadow!*" the girl fires back. "*Meadow!* You told me we were going to see *wildflowers*, and it's still the middle of *winter* here."

The young man still believes that if only they can make it out of the shade and to timberline—about ten thousand feet—the snow there will have melted, and the alpine meadows will be ablaze with flora. In fact, the only flowers between here and Hoodoo Basin are the glacier lilies in the old burn half a mile ahead. Hoodoo Basin itself is still under ten feet of fine-powder snow which even with snowshoes—which of course they do not have—the young couple could not possibly walk on. The alpine lake where the guy was planning to go fishing is frozen hard, and will be until late July.

This snow! He can't believe his girlfriend is so slow, and he wishes she would stop her sniveling. Isn't *he* just as miserable, just as cold, just as apprehensive, just as disappointed?

The wind is savage and ragged, and it blows the people's scent up the slope opposite the burn, away from the grizzly family. Then the mother bear and her cubs hear an ambiguous scrap of the young man's muttered cursing. The trail is hidden in the unburned forest across the creek and downcanyon, and the cubs bound forward to investigate the novel funny noises. They have never seen a person before.

With a single peremptory huff and a furious slap to each cub's head, the mother grizzly puts an immediate stop to their curiosity. One cub bawls, and she bashes him again, and he falls obediently silent. She rises on her back legs and takes a few heavy steps forward, tilting her head to one side and sniffing, not quite sure yet what could have made the noise. Then, on a sudden shred of wind, she

smells man. With a quiet grunt to the cubs to go ahead of her, the mother grizzly races up the slope and over the ridge, and the three bears vanish into the shadows of the spruces.

A few seconds later, where the trail emerges from the forest and crosses the little creek to enter the old burn, the young man recoils in disgust at the thought of the forest fire rampaging through the wilderness uncontrolled. The scene fills both the young people with desolation, and draws them briefly together. "God, this is awful," the young man says, taking the young woman's hand. "No wonder there's not any wildlife around here."

JUNE

A̲t the Cooke City Corral, you hear the same thing over and over. Three hairy, lethal-looking Hell's Angels types and their three pin-eyed speed-burnt molls uncoil out of three Harley-Davidson chopper trikes and demand besides burgers that the waitress enlighten them as to where all the bears is at. A pair of representatives of Yellowstone's most prominent constituency, American Retired Persons, bilious and cramped from hours of cheese doodle consumption at the helm of gargantuan Winnebagos, grumble that so many years ago you could walk right up to the bears out here and they'd practically eat right out of your hand. One little boy, who proclaims his future occupation to be explorer, has been driven all the way from Iowa to explore for bears and clearly holds it against his parents that he has seen not one. His father beards a Western-looking sort whom he takes to be a local—actually an insurance adjuster from San Bernardino who spends two weeks with his wife every June at the campground up the road and who therefore considers himself kind of an honorary semilocal—and this established authority on the state of the ecosystem solemnly informs his interlocutor that if the fedderl gummint had only kept their cottonpicking noses out of the problem and left it to the citizens there'd be plenty of bears, but as it is the Park Service has near-about killed them all, and those they haven't killed they're studying to death, and as a matter of fact there was a big old grizzly with one of their durn radio collars choking him, must have been half starved, going through his garbage just the other night, and like to scared the missus out of her wits.

One real live local—runs a restaurant and motel—finally got weary of the summer-long litany of disappointment and decided to take the matter in hand, private-enterprisewise. He figured that if the only bears turning up around Cooke City were doing so for garbage's sake, he might as well make a regular thing of it and see what happened.

Now, Cooke City, Montana, is not really a city. It consists of a single commercial strip about a quarter of a mile long, gas/motel/café/bar/souvenirs, and a few houses and trailers scattered here and there up the hill behind the strip. It was named City in expectation

82

of a great mining boom that never quite materialized, and except for the eroding mining access roads and a few flecks of private land it is pretty much surrounded by howling wilderness, the Absaroka-Beartooth on three sides, with Yellowstone Park just to the west, beyond the still less prepossessing motel strip called Silver Gate. Cooke City comes alive only in the few months, roughly June to September in a favorable year, when the road from Billings and Red Lodge to the park's northeast entrance is open over Beartooth Pass—ten thousand nine hundred thirty-three feet above sea level—and even then this is by far the least-used approach to Yellowstone Park. A number of businesses are boarded up, abandoned. Looking both ways before crossing the main drag may feel like something of an urban affectation. During the eight months or so when the pass is snowed under, the nearest civilization is Gardiner, Montana, fifty-six winding, slippery, blizzard-prone miles away through the park, and Gardiner's not much of a town either.

Since 1979, when the Park Service succeeded in getting the town dump closed by agreeing to haul the residents' trash the hundred and nine miles to Livingston—all on behalf of the bears who were feeding at the dump and so becoming a problem—Cooke City has had very little impact on the superlative grizzly habitat in which it is a tiny island. That is, it *had* little impact until that insightful entrepreneur started parking a dump truck under the stairs on the downhill side of his restaurant and shoveling his surplus french fries, T-bones, strawberry-rhubarb pie, and garlic bread into it every evening. The Hell's Angels and the Retired Persons and the little explorer are all delighted, of course, to find the truck full of scavenging bears, and the restaurant man congratulates himself for performing a valuable public service which also happens incidentally to facilitate the movement of visitors into his commercial premises. Everybody seems happy—excepting of course the fedderl gummint, which has been through all this before and seen how poorly it tends to turn out. The feds' problem is lack of legal ammunition. The Park Service, the Forest Service, and the Fish and Wildlife Service have all sat down and tried to hash it out, but there seems to be nothing in the Endangered Species Act or anywhere else about please do not feed the endangered species, and anyway the restaurant is private property and as such sacrosanct. The state of Montana has always considered Cooke City rather too remote to fool with much, but under pressure from the federals they reluctantly wrack their lawbooks for . . . anything. They find a sanitation statute that may apply, but it's going to take time.

Meanwhile, the bears are getting bolder every night, less and less fretful of the gabbling, flashbulb-popping tourist hordes. The guy's motel and restaurant business is booming. Down the road a few dozen yards, Bill and Betty Sommers are out on the porch of Sommers Motel with highly dubious looks on their faces, watching little girls of six and their chirping mamas troop down the hill to see the bears. Besides their motel, the Sommerses run a backcountry guide service, and they have been in these parts a good long time, gaining ample knowledge of wildlife behavior along the way—to which the snowy-bearded mountain goat heads on their living room walls and the stupendous grizzly rug attest. Like most of their Cooke City neighbors, they know that their fellow citizen up the road is asking for big trouble. "Somebody," Bill Sommers muses quietly, "is going to get killed."

"Most likely a bear," adds Betty Sommers. Both the Sommerses were here in the days when the mountains harbored many grizzlies and there was a limited legal hunt, and they'd like nothing better than a truly recovered population.

Because a huntable population would be good for business?

"No, no," says Sommers. "We just like having them around."

"Just not in town, please," cracks his wife.

It has become a regular annual custom for the mother grizzly that as June comes on and carrion and prey grow scarcer, she moves north and east toward Cooke City. In her youth there had been the town dump to forage in, and in mating season, as we have seen, the neighborhood remains an important social center. With cubs now, of course, she will avoid as much as possible any contact with other grizzlies—a stipulation against which she must weigh the temptation to use concentrated food sources. We may assume that as the bear and her cubs move into this area where grizzlies in fair numbers are already living in close proximity, she will be carefully investigating the traces of urine and other scents by which she can identify her fellow bears. It is likely that by scent alone she can tell the sex and the sexual status of the bears whose sign she is reading. She may also know how long ago the scent was left. With such information she can devise a route for herself and the cubs which will minimize the likelihood of conflict. As they approach Cooke City, however, the smell of garbage from somewhere nearby is deliriously intoxicating, and in its spell she lets her caution flag.

The scent leads right to the edge of town, to Soda Butte Creek, just across which, up the hill, there is the dump truck full of garbage and bears. She waits till midnight to approach, when the black bears have gone home to bed and the human gawkers are likely to be all asleep. Eventually the truck is free of grizzlies too, and the coast is clear. Still hanging back indecisively at the edge of the forest, she recognizes trotting out of the woods upcreek in the moonlight her own flesh and blood—none other than the calf-killing demon whose littermate was shot two springs ago. His easy stride and his blithe disregard for a sudden flash of truck lights from the road above suggest that he must be a regular at the chuckwagon jubilee. With a quiet woof of hard-earned restraint, the mother urges her cubs back into the gloom of the forest, and takes up another scent.

This one leads her east and south, across the state line into a valley of virgin timber interspersed with meadows where small herds of cows, grazing by Forest Service lease, have provided occasional prey and carrion for grizzly bears for half a century. The smell, unmistakably, is of beef, and plenty of it. Oddly, when she follows it to its source, the meat is up in a tree. You may have heard, and prefer to believe, that grizzly bears never climb trees, in which case you may wish to avert your eyes as this one proceeds unhesitatingly to do so. The meat, however, is hanging by a rope from a high limb, and try as she might she cannot reach it.

Returning disgruntled to earth, the mother bear discovers what her cubs have long since discerned: this place is a wonderland of good things to eat. There's a pile of cantaloupe peels over here, and over here a smelly dead ground squirrel, and over here some apples. Bacon is scattered everywhere. There is a length of steel culvert up on wheels, and at the far end of it, inside, there lies a huge and gorgeous chunk of beef, already swarming with delicious maggots.

She licks up a few, then sinks her teeth into the meat, and barely has she given it one good tug when CLANG! behind her, unimaginably, a steel-barred door has slammed shut.

She whirls. She pounds and pulls and butts and gnashes her teeth, and, *waaaw*, bawl the cubs, and, *aaargh*, she bellows, but the door holds tight. She crouches panting in the pipe and pushes her

nose softly against the bars. The cubs come and stand on their hind legs and sniff back. As she claws in fury at the steel, the cubs begin excavating around the trap, trying to dig her out, or dig their own way in. All night, in panic and terror, the futile struggle continues.

At dawn, the mother bear lies exhausted in the culvert, smeared with her own excrement. The cubs pace hopelessly around the trap, wailing, hungry, scared.

A pickup jounces down the rutted track, and two men emerge. "Look, Larry!" one whispers. "We got another one!" This is Bart Schleyer, graduate student in wildlife biology.

"Bart, those bears are just waiting in line to get in your trap.

They're getting to be worse than the girls up in Cooke." This is Larry Roop, research biologist for the Wyoming Department of Game and Fish.

As the men approach the culvert trap, the mother grizzly barks an impassioned dismissal at her little ones, and they hightail it dutifully for cover. "Cubs!" whispers Schleyer, smiling hard.

"All *right!*"

A female with cubs is an important capture. The trapping has been yielding many more males than females. That may be due to the fact of females' smaller home ranges, or because females are less bold and therefore less likely to approach the roads and developed areas where most of the traps are set, or simply because females are more cautious about getting into traps—but the sex ratio of trapped grizzlies has recently been so uneven that even allowing for trapping bias, the researchers have concluded that females are in severely short supply.

This bear shows very little gratitude for the biologists' concern. When they come near the trap, she lunges at them with all her might, smashing headlong into the bars. "Shhh," Schleyer tries to soothe her, "easy, easy, old mama. What do you say, Larry? Three twenty-five?"

"That sounds about right. I'm going to dose her on the light side anyway, so we can get her back to her cubs quick."

"Come on, come on, turn around," Schleyer says softly to the bear as Roop draws three and a quarter cubic centimeters of Sernylan into the syringe. Sernylan is the trade name for phencyclidine hydrochloride, or PCP, a veterinary anesthetic—and, in smaller doses, a rather violent hallucinogen, also known as Angel Dust. A dose equivalent on the basis of body weight would kill a human being several times over, but all it's going to do to the bear is put her swiftly to sleep. On top of the Sernylan, Roop draws in an equal amount of acepromazine, a tranquilizer, which will insure that she comes out of this strange experience in a relatively placid frame of mind. The syringe is fitted into a stainless-steel dart, and that in turn is loaded into an air pistol called a Cap-chur Gun. Schleyer prods the bear with a stick, and as she whirls in rage Roop aims at her haunch through the bars at the other end of the trap and fires. A little fluff of pink yarn in her fur marks the spot where the dart has sunk home. Again she whirls, but now rather than charge she sits down and curls around to see what this thing is pricking her derrière. She licks at it a couple of times, and seems not much concerned. Soon her head begins to droop, and then her legs give way. Her tongue begins to move slowly in and out as though she were lapping up water. Her eyes glaze over, and finally she lays down her head and sleeps.

Roop and Schleyer lift the heavy trap door open, grab the bear's back feet, and slide her gently to earth. Stretched out limp on the ground, she looks like nothing so much as a scruffy fur bag of assorted bear parts, but poke beneath that almost comically floppy caparison and you can feel an awesome musculature. Schleyer dabs at her lifelessly staring eyes with a tube of antibiotic ointment, and shields them from the sun with a scrap of towel. Roop pulls a pre-molar, a count of whose annual rings in the lab will tell her age, just like a tree's. A funny-looking pair of pliers, faced with reversed numbers made of little needles, is briefly clamped to the inside of her lip, and an indelible ink is painted over the tiny holes it has made—a tattoo. A bright yellow plastic tag bearing the same number is clipped through a hole Schleyer has punched in her ear. They take a blood sample with a syringe, and they pluck out a sample of her fur. (There has been some speculation that lighter-colored fur may be correlated with certain blood chemicals that are indicators of aggres-siveness; they will send the fur sample to the scientist who is trying to find out.) The bear gets an injection of a diuretic, and after a few minutes—"Thar she blows!" cries Roop—a urine specimen is taken. They measure her from stem to stern, recording all on a schematic bear diagram:

Total length	150.2 cm. [58 in.]
Contour length	189.4 cm. [74 in.]
Girth	118.5 cm. [46 in.]
Height	102.9 cm. [40 in.]
Neck circumference	76 cm. [30 in.]
Head length	41 cm. [16 in.]
Head width	32 cm. [12 in.]
Fore foot pad width	140 mm. [5½ in.]
Fore foot pad length	65 mm. [2½ in.]
Length from heel to middle toe	125 mm. [5 in.]
Length from heel to middle claw tip	162 mm. [6 in.]
Hind foot pad width	130 mm. [5 in.]
Hind foot pad length	192 mm. [7½ in.]
Length from heel to middle toe	204 mm. [8 in.]

Length from heel to middle claw tip . . . . 205.7 mm. [8 in.]
Furred arch of hind foot . . . . 9 mm. [½ in.]

Roop and Schleyer lash a block and tackle to a stout pine limb, gather up the bear in a surplus cargo parachute, and hoist her aloft to be weighed. She is down to three hundred thirty-two pounds. This is probably her low point for the year, since as summer comes on, berries will be ripening and other bear foods more abundant in the subalpine and alpine zones. Finally they fit the bear with a radio collar—a tiny transmitter and battery imbedded in waterproof plastic molded in turn to a heavy leather belt. The ends of the belt are joined together by a several-layered strip of cotton canvas, which is calculated to rot through so the collar will fall off at about the time the battery runs down. Schleyer records her description: "Dark underparts. Light grizzling on back. Light-colored stripe behind forelegs. Head quite light colored. Pelage thick and unrubbed." The sun is growing hot, and they drag the bear to a nice cool spot in the shade, and wait. (The researchers must stay with her till she comes out from under, because some other bear might happen along and try to take advantage of the situation—that is, eat her.)

While Roop and Schleyer wait for the mother grizzly to come around, the cubs reappear, timid but not especially afraid, and apparently not much bothered by their mother's condition. They both go to work kneading her teats to start the milk flowing, and soon they are nursing contentedly, producing a low, soft humming that sounds like a hive of bees.

Sernylan wears off from the top down, so the mother bear's first sign of life is a woozy shake of the head. "Describe recovery reactions," commands the study work sheet, so Schleyer is writing, "0905, tightening of muscles. 0910, some head movement." A few minutes later, she can rise on her front legs and turn to gaze in groggy mystification at her still useless hindparts and her humming progeny. "0920, head up, sprawled on stomach unable to get up. 0925, crawling. 0930, on feet but collapsed. 0938, staggered out of trap site into timber, followed by cubs."

Our heroine is no longer her wild and private self alone. She is now also a source of data for the Yellowstone Interagency Grizzly Bear Study, one of the most comprehensive wildlife research projects ever undertaken, and as such she has gained a degree of power beyond even that mythic primacy with which grizzlies were invested in the days before the birth of modern firearms. She has the power now, as long as we continue to grant it to her, to reshape human values in the preeminent, most influential human culture in the world—the power to deflect American history from its collision course with her survival, and from the moral tragedy which that course represents. If we can come to know her and to love what we know and so to wish it to endure, we cannot but be the better for it, for her kind's survival will be an objective correlative of our kind's having come at last to the conviction that there is a higher good than the subjection of all nature to human will. For the grizzly bear will never yield to our will. This grizzly, like every other, will be herself, or perish.

Partly for such deep reasons, perhaps, the people involved in formal efforts to save the bear tend toward ferocity themselves; perhaps there is as well a measure of identification with the bear's own unforgiving character. Whatever the reasons, to both their friends and their enemies grizzly bears *matter*. Jobs are lost, careers are ruined, and sometimes, it seems, even sanity is imperiled.

For the bear to be saved, the bear must be understood, so scientific inquiry is at the heart of almost all the myriad disputes over the grizzly, and it is often the wildlife biologists who find themselves caught in the middle and nearly torn to bits. Edward Hoagland has written that "Wildlife biology . . . is a stepchild among the sciences . . . badly paid, not quite respected, still rather scattered in its thrust and mediocre in its standards, and still accessible to the layman, as the most fundamental, fascinating breakthroughs alternate with confirmations of what has always been common knowledge." Because of wildlife biology's seeming accessibility, virtually every nonscientist involved with grizzly bears considers himself an expert, and that makes practicing good science rather hard for the real experts. Furthermore, the study of grizzlies as it is currently practiced is something of a hybrid, or perhaps more accurately hodgepodge, of three distinct traditions, each with its own extrascientific assumptions, values, and biases.

The first antecedent of modern bear study is wildlife management, in the old-fashioned style of state departments of fish and game. Wildlife management has its historical roots in the response of government to the needs of hunters whose quarry was becoming scarce because of unrestricted hunting; thus it began as a set of rules regulating and enabling the "sustained harvest" of particular favored animals. It is for the most part from among hunters themselves that wildlife management's practitioners have been drawn. Their backgrounds are often rural, often agricultural, and they are comfortable with the idea of manipulating nature in such a way as both to make it still "feel" wild and to insure that it produces the desired sustainable yield. From their point of view, human influence is an integral part of every ecosystem. Their approach to science seems to overlap a bit with game-wardenry, and so does their personal style. They are more likely to ride a horse into the wilderness than to shoulder a backpack. For office wear they prefer cowboy boots to running shoes. They shave every morning, the whole face.

The second source of bear inquiry is pure science, as practiced in the universities. From this subculture come long fuzzy beards, heavy hiking boots, a preference for camping stoves over campfires, and a sense that wilderness ecosystems should be as free as possible from human interference. These biologists' backgrounds are often urban, and their bias is toward the theoretical, as wildlife managers' is toward the practical. The pure scientists are more likely to be concerned about the functioning of whole ecosystems than the wildlife managers, who tend to see the wilderness's health in terms of the success of their chosen favorite animals. The pure scientist cares about pine beetles as much as pine trees, fungi as much as the elk harvest. The wildlife management people, on the other hand, seem a great deal more effective at getting things actually *done*.

(All this, of course, is much more black-and-white in the telling than in real life. Both traditions are active influences, but no pure example of either type actually exists among the scientists engaged in the contemporary study of the grizzly bear. There are cowboys in the colleges, and intellectuals in the Forest Service.)

The third inheritance of the current effort to understand the grizzly is the one that ties it most directly to the values of the people at large—the history of the national parks. In not much more than a century, the values reflected in that history have undergone a great deal of change, and although many grizzlies live outside the national parks, the park idea—of preserving natural beauty in its primeval state—continues to inform grizzly bear research everywhere. Nowhere have the changes been more characteristic of the evolving national personality, or more intertwined with ideology and philosophy, or more fiercely struggled over, than in the United States', and the world's, first national park.

Yellowstone Park was born in the mature years of the Romantic movement, the embodiment of the ideals of Emerson and Thoreau. Nature had been so quickly and thoroughly subdued in nineteenth-century America that wildness, so recently a dark and fearsome enemy, was beginning to be seen in the soft light of nostalgia. People of the cities already ached for what their pioneer fathers had abhorred.

In 1869, three men from Montana, Charles Cook, David Folsom, and William Peterson, penetrated the previously all but unexplored interior of Yellowstone to confirm the rumors of glory beyond description that had been spread by what establishmentarian America regarded as not quite trustworthy frontier illiterates. While camped amidst the steam-shrouded splendor of the Firehole River's geyser basin, so the (probably apocryphal) story goes, the expeditionary party first talked about what a shame it would be if such a beautiful place were to be settled and subdued in the usual fashion.

The idea of preserving unmanicured natural beauty as such was already in the air, especially since Thoreau's advocacy of establishing wilderness sanctuaries. Yosemite had been granted to the state of California by Abraham Lincoln in 1864 to be set aside in its wild condition. And now, as authoritative word spread to the Montana Territory's capital of Helena, a banker there became one of the first to be thoroughly possessed with the idea of protecting and preserving Yellowstone. Nathaniel P. Langford brought to his romantic motivations a classically American admixture of practicality, for besides a democratic opportunity for citizens to return to nobly savage nature he saw tourist dollars on the Yellowstone horizon, and he had a strong interest in the Northern Pacific Railway.

Langford and his friend and lawyer, the Surveyor-General of Montana, Henry Washburn, mounted a major expedition in 1870, with an eye specifically to national influence and publicity. Langford wrote an article describing their journey for *Scribner's Monthly*, and went east to give a series of lectures to carefully selected well-heeled audiences. Other members of the expedition published their accounts, and soon the romance of an already vanishing Western wilderness began to fire the national imagination.

The head of the U.S. Geological Survey, Ferdinand V. Hayden, heard one of Langford's lectures, and was inspired to send a still grander, government-sponsored expedition to Yellowstone in 1871, with a kitty of forty thousand dollars. The railroads, with characteristic perspicacity and characteristic wide publicity, transported the men and matériel for free. Among the party were the photographer William H. Jackson and the painter Thomas Moran, whose pictures went up on exhibit that fall in the rotunda of the Capitol. The lobbying to protect Yellowstone was intense.

On March 1, 1872, President Ulysses S. Grant signed into law the bill establishing Yellowstone National Park, to be protected "from settlement, occupancy, or sale under the laws of the United States, and dedicated and set apart as a public park or pleasuring-ground for the benefit and enjoyment of the people." The law decreed that rules and regulations should be promulgated "for the preservation, from injury or spoliation, of all timber, mineral deposits, natural curiosities, or wonders within said park, and their retention in their natural condition." Until that day, the whole history of civilization had been a story of the conquering of wilderness. Now, for the first time, a society had chosen officially to ordain the preservation of wilderness in its untamed state as an object of reverence. The creation of Yellowstone National Park marked an epoch in man's relation to nature.

Grizzly bears were not counted high among the new park's natural curiosities or wonders. There were, after all, still grizzlies throughout the mountain West, and those in Yellowstone were sparsely distributed and seldom seen. It was just as well that they did receive so little attention, for the preservation from injury or spoliation not only of bears but of all of Yellowstone's resources was very slow in coming. Typically, Congress, so proud of having established the park, had not bothered to provide any money to take care of it. They had, however, given it plenty of notoriety. Soon hunters came in droves to slay the bison, now extirpated from most of its ancestral range. Elk hunting rapidly became big business. Cowboys drove their cattle into the luxuriant meadows to graze. Timber was cut, hay harvested. Squatters built cabins. Indians attacked. Robbers waylaid stagecoaches. Somebody opened a saloon. With the active participation of the park superintendent, a lucre-minded cabal called the Yellowstone Park Improvement Company was formed for the purpose of turning over all the major sites to private enterprise. Meanwhile, the grizzly bear mostly lay low. When he did appear, he was usually shot without a second thought.

Nevertheless, the original national park *idea* was still alive, and soon enough there was public protest against the ruin of the Yellowstone wilderness. In 1883, all killing of animals except fish was prohibited, and the Yellowstone Park Improvement Company was legislated out of existence. The next year, the park superintendent behind the Y.P.I.C. scheme resigned in disgrace. In 1886, the U.S. Army took over administration of the park. They threw out the squatters and burned down their cabins. They hounded the poachers out of the park, and beat up the bandits. As well as they knew how, they tried to return the land to its natural condition.

Natural condition, however, was still a pretty loose notion in those days. Public enjoyment of the park as a pleasuring-ground took easy precedence over the preservation of its natural wonders in their natural condition. Roads were built. Hotels and other buildings were erected without regard for their effect on wildlife. The magnificent Old Faithful Inn, for example, still stands in the midst of some of the park's best grizzly habitat and ungulate winter range—and practically on top of the park's finest geyser. The romantic heritage of the park idea included an assumption of a hierarchy of animals ranging from the lordly elk at the top down to the hated wolf at the bottom. Accordingly, first the army and later the newly formed National Park Service went after the "bad" animals with a vengeance, thinking it would aid the recovery of the "good" ones.

In the latter part of the nineteenth century, the "good" animals had indeed been disappearing at a frightful rate. The bison had been exterminated from most of the United States, and even within Yellowstone Park poaching had decimated an already small population. Bighorn sheep and antelope were becoming rarer throughout the West; even the beaver was endangered in much of its range. Elk and deer numbers had been severely reduced. Under army protection in Yellowstone, however, they were increasing rapidly by the turn of the century, but the belief persisted that they were in bad trouble, and the army felt it needed to take action. It was not understood at the time that predators are virtually never capable of wiping out prey populations and in fact usually contribute to their viability, and that protection from poaching would alone have been sufficient for the "good" animals to recover.

Beginning in the 1890s and continuing into the teens of this century, therefore, the government mounted a number of large-scale antipredator campaigns in Yellowstone. Coyotes were slaughtered by the thousands, but their reproductive capacity is such that they always bounce back fast, and there was little impact on their numbers. The mountain lion, however, was reduced nearly to zero, and has only recently begun to recover. The Yellowstone wolf was officially hunted and poisoned into extinction. (Or almost: there are still occasional reports of wolf sightings in the backcountry, but there is no breeding population. For wolves to return to Yellowstone, they will almost certainly have to be reintroduced.) There was even a massive egg-stomping campaign on the islands in Yellowstone Lake where the trout-eating white pelican nested, and dozens of those magnificent birds were killed.

People did not quite know whether to classify the bears as good or bad. It was true that grizzlies did kill the "good" animals, but luckily their predation was confined mostly to early spring and late fall, when the chances of observation were slimmest. Grizzly numbers in any case were always so low that they would never have been considered wholesale killers like the wolves. And, especially after Theodore Roosevelt and the national craze for the teddy bear, bears began to be regarded as sort of cute. People liked them so much that for their amusement at the new hotels that had gone up in the park, grizzly bear cubs were kept chained to posts.

Even before the turn of the century, with the advent of comfortable lodgings and decent roads, visitation had been rising fast, and with it rose the production of garbage. It was dumped in open pits near the hotels and the popular campsites, and, now that the protected animals were becoming habituated to man as part of their world, the familiar scenario rapidly became a major park attraction: bears came to feed at the dumps, and people came to watch the bears.

Undoubtedly this rich new source of food boosted the reproductive rates of both black and grizzly bears, but it also introduced new dangers. For years, the bears remained harmless, and they seemed so plentiful now that every year a number were shipped out to zoos. Harmless though the bears may have been, the park administration recognized that trouble might be in the offing, and they tried to regulate the feeding of bears. All feeding was restricted to the supervised dump sites, and park visitors were forbidden to feed the bears themselves—a rule that was widely, repeatedly, and openly broken, with the inevitable dénouement.

The first injury to a bear-feeding tourist was recorded in 1902. The first fatality—former park historian Paul Schullery cautions that this story may be apocryphal—came five years later, when a rather less than smart aleck who had been watching a grizzly family feed at one of the dumps decided to chase the cubs up a tree and poke them with his umbrella, and their mother did her motherly duty. In 1916, another man was fatally mauled by a camp-raiding bear. With the coming of the automobile, visitation, bear feeding, and human injuries all increased sharply, and a new kind of bear entered the scene —the roadside panhandler. People came to Yellowstone from all over the world for the express purpose of feeding bears.

What could be more adorable? The bears quickly learned what was expected of them: they stood up on their hind legs, they waved their paws about, they leaned into cars and let folks breathe their peanut-butter breath. There is a story, perhaps also apocryphal but entirely plausible, about a father who wanted to take his kid's picture with a bear licking the kid's face and so painted same with honey. Most of the beggar bears were blacks, but eventually the dignity of even some grizzlies capitulated to temptation. The rangers, although most of them didn't like it, were under orders not to interfere. Wasn't a national park's purpose, after all, the enjoyment of the people?

In 1916, the National Park Service was created, and in 1918 that agency took over from the army. The law that established the Park Service set forth the park idea in somewhat clearer terms: the aim of a national park would now be "to conserve the scenery and the natural and historic objects and the wildlife therein and to provide for the enjoyment of same in such a manner and by such means as will leave them unimpaired for the enjoyment of future generations." At last the principle of nonconsumptive use had been formally propounded. But between it and the still unfulfilled original idea of retaining the park's natural condition, there remained a long way to go. Predators continued to be killed. Elk and bison were fed hay to help them through the winter. Under the misguided aegis of good old Smokey the Bear, wildfires were suppressed, radically changing the natural vegetative makeup of the ecosystem.

Beginning in 1919 and continuing until 1941, the bear-feeding spectacle at the dumps had reached such a pitch that grandstands were erected and the garbage spread out buffet-style on raised platforms. There were regular feeding schedules just as in a zoo, and the parking lots nearby overflowed with five to six hundred cars nightly. On a good night, you might see seventy grizzly bears.

In *The Bears of Yellowstone*, Paul Schullery quotes a park report

that in 1931 eighty-seven bear bites and three hundred eighty-seven cases of property damage were recorded, along with "numerous other complaints." By the mid-thirties, the authorities had begun to realize that things were getting out of hand. After 1935, the bear-feeding shows took place only at one central location, and in 1938 the amount of food made available there was reduced. In 1942, when visitation had plummeted because of the war, the shows were finally stopped altogether, and there was a brutal crackdown on the newly cold-turkeyed garbage addicts: fifty-five black bears and twenty-eight grizzlies were officially dispatched that year. Late that summer, one of the bears they hadn't yet killed, probably a grizzly, killed a woman.

There was widespread criticism of the Park Service afterwards, but the financial strictures of the war effort made effective action impossible: garbage continued to be dumped inside the park, and bears continued to feed on it. The only difference was that it all took place now out of public view.

For those educated only in the humanities and denied a background in the sciences, the very recentness of most of science's understanding of the world's workings is almost incredible; even for scientists, the sheer bulk and complexity of scientific knowledge tend sometimes to obscure the suddenness of its provenance. Yet the fact remains that two generations ago the simple idea of studying wildlife was almost unheard of. In 1944, when Olaus Murie began the formal study of bears in Yellowstone National Park, nothing like it had ever been undertaken. Even then, however, not very much was possible. You could watch some of them feed at the dumps, but as for identifying individual bears, or determining movements or home range or natural feeding habits, or coming up with any kind of information on mating or reproduction or social organization, or assessing the state of the population—forget it. Except for their appearances at the dumps, the grizzlies naturally kept to cover or the cover of night, and they were most adept at evading observation. Murie nevertheless came up with some useful conclusions about the behavior of bears in dumps and campgrounds, and he recognized that the only way to end this unnatural behavior was to remove the source of attraction.

"And here," Paul Schullery writes, "a great opportunity passed. With substantial scientific evidence to support them, the Park Service might have capitalized on the reprieve of the war years with a massive sanitation campaign, so that when visitors returned bear feeding would be much less common." But no dice. For one thing, there wasn't enough money to take care of the garbage any other way. For another, people liked watching bears, and the Park Service liked pleasing people—sometimes to the detriment of the health of the park. After Murie's brief report, bear research and indeed any evidence of special concern for Yellowstone's bears came to an end.

Serious inquiry would have to wait for two crucial technological innovations. The first was the gradual—and accident-fraught—development of safe and reliable immobilization techniques. If you want to study bears, you will not get far unless you can tell one individual from another with perfect assurance even at a distance or in bad light. That means they must be tagged. But freshly captured wild bears are impressively uncooperative about having holes punched in their ears and colored plastic streamers attached. They also lack enthusiasm for having the insides of their lips tattooed, giving urine specimens, and undergoing dentistry. When Albert W. Erickson, then a graduate student at Michigan State University, began the first serious modern bear study in 1952, he and his crew trapped their black bears in foot snares and had to wrestle them to the ground to clap an ether-soaked mask over their muzzles. Too little ether, and the bear could wake up suddenly, with imaginable results. Too much, and the bear departed with equal celerity for paradise. In a 1978 article for *National Wildlife* magazine, Peter Steinhart reported that of the first hundred bears Erickson handled, "ten suffered broken bones, including two whose shattered jaws had to be bolted back together. Two bears died of heat prostration, one of strangling by handlers, and two were shot by hunters who didn't know they were in foot traps." Artificial respiration brought several more of Erickson's bears back from the far side of never.

When new veterinary anesthetics like phencyclidine hydrochloride (Sernylan) came along a few years later, life became much less stressful for both bear researchers and their subjects. With the new drugs you could knock a bear conclusively out of service, you could even overdose him quite a bit without killing him, and you could mark, weigh, examine, sample, measure, probe, and in general get intimately to know the savage beast while he lay as passive as a babe through it all.

But to maintain meaningful contact with a marked bear you still had to keep him in sight—which meant that extensive study of bears in the wild remained impossible. The second technological revolution changed all that. Almost as soon as they had begun their study of the Yellowstone grizzly in 1959, the twin brothers Frank and John Craighead had recognized the problem, and had gone into consultation with electronics engineers from the rapidly advancing aerospace industry to investigate the possibility of using miniature radio transmitters to locate bears in cover and darkness. After two years of design and testing, on the night of September 21, 1961, the Craigheads stayed up late putting together a two-ounce transmitter, a fourteen-ounce battery pack, and a short loop antenna, all sealed in a fiberglass-reinforced acrylic resin collar. The next morning, it was fitted around the neck of their Bear Number Forty—later to know fame as Marian, the doomed heroine of Frank Craighead's book *Track of the Grizzly*—and, after recovering from the anesthetic, the world's first radio-collared grizzly bear wobbled off into the wilderness. For the next eight years, Marian and twenty-three other Yellowstone grizzlies were to transmit their whereabouts to the Craigheads' hand-held antennas, and to make possible the first penetration of human light through the ancient opacity of bearhood.

The quiet beep-beep of each radio-collared grizzly's assigned frequency now allowed the researchers to begin to compile an extended history of his movements, his range, his contact with other bears, his habitat use, and his times and places of denning. When a bear came close enough that there was an opportunity for direct observation, the researchers might now pinpoint his location and move quietly in from downwind to watch. When transmission suddenly ended or the bear ceased to move, mortalities of the sort that had never before been remotely traceable could now sometimes be quickly discovered. And by a comparison of the numbers of marked and unmarked bears observed, some inference about the size and trend of the population was feasible.

The Craighead study still stands as the longest-running, most thorough, most fertile, and most definitive of them all, the standard by which all subsequent study of bears has been measured. Some of their conclusions are still debated, but they are never ignored. Almost none of their findings has been conclusively disproved. Those which are still disputed are at most a very small part of their work, for their hypotheses were aimed precisely at those questions which it was most important to answer definitively, and their study methods and perceptions were so accurate that almost all the answers could be known beyond cavil.

The Craighead study touched on virtually every aspect of grizzly bear life. They learned the sizes and shapes and seasonal patterns and year-to-year variations and interrelationships of grizzly home ranges, and how those factors are affected by the distribution, availability, amount, and quality of food, by mate availability, by the proximity of denning sites, by the relative locations of seasonally critical habitat types, and by the age, sex, physical condition, and individual experience of each grizzly. They found that Yellowstone's grizzlies occasionally make long excursions out of their customary home ranges, and they discovered that the grizzlies being seen at the dumps represented a large proportion of the population of the entire ten-thousand-square-mile Yellowstone ecosystem, many of them having traveled far from home to visit the dumps to feed or to find a mate. They described a grizzly's life range—that is, the life-long home range of an individual—and showed how and why the area used by a bear varies from season to season and year to year.

The Craigheads also pioneered the study of grizzly habitat use. Over the years of the study, a picture of food habits began to emerge. Combining direct observation with scatology—the analysis of droppings—they learned how variable grizzlies' feeding regimes can be, according to time of year, habitat conditions, weather patterns, and even the quirks of individual bears, presumably learned from the idiosyncratic food habits of their mothers. The Craigheads defined the habitat types which are crucial to the grizzly diet, and identified the elements within them which grizzlies depend on, as well as how those elements or habitat types are used seasonally by grizzlies. They learned that Yellowstone grizzlies are scavengers, and on occasion cannibals, and that some are quite effective predators, and that in Yellowstone the availability of carrion or prey just after emergence from the den can be critical to grizzly survival.

Aided by the concentrations of grizzlies at the Trout Creek garbage dump in Hayden Valley, the Craigheads were able to observe grizzly mating habits at length. From their marked bears they learned the usual age of first reproduction, and how widely it can vary. They studied grizzly bear estrus, determining its typical length and discovering the hiatus that sometimes divides the period of fertility in two. They recorded the courtship and copulation of grizzlies for the first time, and they observed the roaring, battering, vicious fights of competing males—an opportunity which, again, was conveniently amplified by the high concentration of bears at the dump. They observed how concentrated populations of grizzlies, unlike the less sociable bears of more dispersed populations, work out an elaborate hierarchy, and how social order is maintained. They watched mothers defend their young against aggressive adult males, and they learned how devotedly female grizzlies play with their cubs, nurse them, discipline them, and teach them. They learned when and how the young are weaned. They contributed to an analysis of the nutritive values of grizzly bear milk. They studied the manifold differences between males and females.

Grizzly behavior, hour on hour, was constantly before them, and they made the most of it. They observed and recorded the use of aggression in the social hierarchy and how it is expressed in threat behaviors, postures, and actual physical violence. They observed the formation of alliances among family groups and individuals; the role of individual spacing and the importance of "critical distance" (fight-or-flight zones) between members of the hierarchy; vocalizations and body language; flight from danger; use of the senses; play; feeding techniques; curiosity; homing and navigation; swimming; climbing; speed; patterns of sleep and rest; day-bed construction and location; cub adoption; cannibalism; and so on, and on.

They followed grizzlies to their dens, and learned at what elevations, toward which point of the compass, in what soils, in what ecotypes, with what relation to prevailing winds and snow deposition, how, and when grizzly bears construct their winter quarters. They learned when the bears enter and leave their dens, and how those dates are related to weather, to the insulative properties of individual dens, to sex, to age, and to reproductive status. They observed the gradual onset of predenning lethargy and the reestablishment of normal metabolism after emergence in spring. They found that grizzly dens sometimes occur in groups within relatively limited areas, and that dens are usually dug each fall and are only occasionally reused, and that denning areas seem to be maintained by tradition through the generations. They went into grizzly dens themselves, measured them, identified the plants used for bedding material, monitored the temperature, and, finally, developed hypotheses about the effects of den location and construction on the microclimate within the den. They implanted radiotelemetric sensors in the bodies of both wild and captive hibernating bears to record their body temperature, responses to disturbances, and movements within the den.

Once a few life histories of their marked grizzlies began to emerge, the Craigheads were able to consider the variability of reproductive cycles and rates, and how such variations can be affected by food quality, food availability, habitat use, and the individuality of particular females. They calculated the age and sex composition of the Yellowstone population, and eventually they were able to carry out a detailed mathematical analysis of the dynamics of the population. They monitored mortality, and recorded the particulars of over half of all known grizzly deaths in the ecosystem for twelve consecutive years. They identified many of the sources of this mortality—most of it man-caused—and learned which classes of grizzly were most vulnerable.

They studied the movements of grizzlies with relation to human presence, the presence of other bears, and other kinds of disturbance. They found, as old Grizzly Adams himself had speculated in the nineteenth century, that by extracting a premolar, sawing a slice out of it, and counting the annually deposited rings of cementum, one could precisely determine the age of a grizzly. By pioneering the techniques of trapping, immobilizing, marking, and radio-tracking grizzlies, they helped to develop and perfect methods which have since become indispensable to the study of wild animals from caribou to whooping cranes. In cooperation with the National Aeronautics and Space Administration, they began to experiment with the possibility of tracking wild animals by satellite telemetry, a project on which they are still at work.

The Craigheads benefited Yellowstone and its bears also in ways quite beyond the realm of research. Despite the fact that only a small part of their funding came from the National Park Service, and although they had no official responsibility for actual bear management, they instructed and assisted park rangers in the handling of bears, and they often took on the riskiest and most delicate tasks themselves, such as capturing marauding grizzlies in the middle of the night in the middle of heavily populated campgrounds, where a wounded or infuriated bear could have wrought fearful carnage. Although some rangers had some bear-handling experience, there was no regular training in this skill which left so little room for error, and the Craigheads were old hands at trapping, tranquilizing, and releasing bears, so it was natural that the park staff should turn to them for aid and advice, and the generous extent of their response eventually made them indispensable participants in Yellowstone Park bear management: often the Craighead brothers would roll out of bed in the wee hours of the night to lend a hand, driving as far sometimes as a hundred miles to the scene of the problem. A few employees of the Park Service, which like many another institutional subculture had a history of xenophobia, resented what they saw as intrusion by outsiders. But many more were grateful for the Craigheads' contributions, and for their incontestably selfless concern for Yellowstone's grizzly bears.

Wildlife research and wildlife management have always been inextricably—if also uneasily—intertwined. As a rule, because research funding tends to come either directly from management agencies or from independent organizations whose goal is to recommend management measures, the very questions posed in wildlife research derive from wildlife management problems. Funding bodies are rarely if ever motivated by simple scientific curiosity; they want answers they can act on—applied research, not basic. Such answers, therefore, can rarely be strictly descriptive. Managers nevertheless often rankle at researchers' *pre*scriptive findings. The distinctions can be rather absurdly semantic: "The killing must end" will prove unacceptable where "The present pattern of man-caused mortality is likely to lead to extinction of the population" is okay. A researcher may point out that grizzlies raiding unsanitary hunting camps are frequently shot, but let him also recommend that grizzlies' lives can be saved if hunters are required to keep their camps clean and to hang their game meat out of reach, and suddenly he's treading managerial turf. Some managers welcome such recommendations; some act as if their toes had been stepped on.

The uneasy relationship between research and management engenders other kinds of trouble too. University-bred researchers may already be writing with the turgid banality so typical of scientific prose, but when they find themselves in government-funded projects, what had been at least clear is then corrupted and clouded by the requisite—or at least highly infectious—jargon of bureaucracy. Managers reluctant to involve researchers in planning find themselves around the conference table arguing scientific points in which they have zero expertise. Researchers may have furnished knowledge, but it is the managers who own it, and, as Sun Tzu said twenty-four hundred years ago, knowledge is power.

On the other hand, many researchers' prescriptive conclusions concern only the narrow field of their particular expertise, without consideration of management's other obligations. Sometimes a researcher's philosophy is hopelessly incompatible with the mandate or the philosophy of the agency he is serving. Researchers could not *be* researchers if they had to deal with the complexities, contradictions, and inevitable compromises that consume so much of managers' time. Unavoidably, the very psychologies of researchers and managers profoundly differ.

Yet divorce is not an available alternative for this insalubrious marriage; both parties are doomed to cooperation. It seems as if it ought to be simple enough for each faction to exhibit a modicum of respect for the other's allegiances and obligations, and once in a while it does happen, but more often the vagueness of who really ought to be doing what renders true cooperation impossible in the atmosphere of blind self-interest that customarily prevails. For the cultivation of suspicion and mistrust, the common ground of wildlife management and wildlife research is exceptionally fertile soil. Just ask anybody who ever had anything to do with what has come to be known as The Craighead Controversy.

When the Craighead study began, Yellowstone Park had little in the way of a bear management policy beyond ad hoc problem solving, but park management recognized the need for much greater knowledge of grizzly bears and for a system of procedures derived from that knowledge. In the 1962 memorandum of understanding that was to govern the study, therefore, the park formally requested that one result of the Craigheads' work be a set of management recommendations.

Then, in 1963, a committee appointed by Secretary of the Interior Stewart Udall and headed by the ecologist A. Starker Leopold produced a paper entitled "Wildlife Management in the National Parks," which recommended as a primary goal of national park policy "that the biotic associations within each park be maintained, or where necessary recreated, as nearly as possible in the condition that prevailed when the area was first visited by the white man." The Leopold Report, as it has come to be known, has taken on something of a biblical aura over the years, and it has had great influence on the management not only of the national parks but of other wildlands as well. The report did not fully recognize the role of ecological change in wild environments, for it seemed to suggest that the primeval condition of the parks could be stabilized indefinitely, and it urged that where necessary considerable manipulation of nature's handiwork should be practiced in the name of that stability; but a more important, indeed rather a revolutionary idea grew out of the Leopold Report, based on a perhaps creative and undoubtedly beneficial misunderstanding of the committee's intentions. There developed from the report a profoundly philosophical ideal: that nature, at least in the largest and wildest national parks, might simply be allowed to take its course—wildfires allowed to burn uncontrolled, bighorn sheep allowed to undergo epidemics of eye disease and fall off cliffs, the mountain pine beetle allowed to devastate whole forests, grizzly bears allowed to starve to death when their numbers exceeded their habitat's carrying capacity. Twenty years ago, that was a shocking idea, but it has since proved its worth over and over. It has meant that our biggest and most natural national parks have become vast ecological laboratories, where the processes of life and death may be seen and studied in all their richly baffling complexity.

An ecosystem manipulated by man, after all, can never tell us the clear truth about how nature works, for modern technological man's influence is so powerful that it inevitably obscures the subtleties of natural processes. (In this sense, man can no longer be seen as merely a part of nature, just as the hydrogen bomb cannot be called just another engine of war: each is capable of obliterating the reality from which its definition derives.) Human impact is so pervasive in the twentieth century that observation of how nature works when spared it is an ever rarer and more precious opportunity. Of course, compromises with the recreational and other obligations of the national parks have always been and will always have to be made, and human influence, though it may be minimized, will never be eliminated, but especially in the largest wilderness parks, like Yellowstone, where whole complex biotic communities may be wholly or mainly contained within park boundaries, the idea of "natural management" which had its genesis in the Leopold Report has begun to yield profuse rewards to human understanding.

Although this ideal has had revolutionary effects on park management, its foundation was laid long ago, in the original national parks credo of the preservation of wild nature. The Leopold Report was the closest the National Park Service had yet come to a formal statement of philosophy, and as such it was of great value, for a national park is at bottom an expression of belief, and that belief had not yet been fully articulated. Indeed there is still a long way to go toward a consensus of belief; the Leopold Report must not be thought of as an eternal code of principle, but rather as a step, albeit a big one, toward a difficult and still distant conclusion.

Some of the report's ideas may already be seen as having been a bit misguided, such as the proposed stabilization of ecosystems' natural flux. As earlier advisors also had done, the Leopold committee recommended as well that scientific research in the parks be expanded —a worthy goal, in consonance with the role of the parks as natural laboratories—but when it urged that the Park Service conduct that research itself, it may have cleared the way for unintended consequences. When it is suggested that any institution's domain be quickly expanded, the prospect of abuse of power always looms. If the Park Service was going to do its own research from then on, what was to become of the ongoing independent research in the parks, especially that which was not prealigned with government policy and answering government-propounded questions?

In some national parks, independent research is still thriving, and working in harmony with the Park Service's own personnel. Indeed, that was the case for the Craigheads in Yellowstone, for the first eight years of their study. But if decision making was to be concentrated entirely within the Park Service as the Leopold Report recommended, obviously the Craigheads could no longer be participants in the formulation of Yellowstone's bear policy. And, indeed, in 1964, one year after the report's appearance, the requirement that the Craigheads and their associates contribute management ideas was rescinded. Their job from then on was to be strictly research. John Craighead insists that he and his brother never received official notice of any such change in their responsibilities. Park Service officials note that the new memorandum of understanding no longer mentioned management responsibilities for the Craigheads.

Written understandings aside, however, the Craigheads continued to help out when bear problems arose and were, as ever, de facto part of Yellowstone Park's bear management, and park superintendent Lemuel Garrison and his successor John McLaughlin were content with the situation—that is, one thing in writing and quite another in fact. Then, in 1967, a new superintendent, Jack Anderson, took over, and brought with him the park's first biologist to serve in an influential executive capacity, Glen Cole.

Yellowstone Park's centennial celebration was due in 1972, five years away, and an international conference of park managers was to be held there in honor of the occasion. If the world's flagship national park was to be shipshape in terms of the Leopold Report by then— restored as nearly as possible to its pristine primeval condition—work would have to begin at once, and one of the new leadership's primary goals was to close the open-pit garbage dumps. For one thing, the dumps were in violation of federal water quality standards, and, for another, they had created a concentration of bears, both black and grizzly, which had certainly never been a feature of prehistoric Yellowstone. There was also the crucial question of whether bears who fed on human foods in the dumps were therefore more likely also to seek the same foods elsewhere—in the campgrounds, for example, where bear raids were a continuing problem.

The park staff believed that garbage bears were garbage bears, and not picky about where they found their garbage. On the basis of that reasoning, the campground problems—and the attendant danger to park visitors—could be traced directly to the dumps, where many of Yellowstone's bears had clearly become addicted to garbage. The sooner these addicts began their withdrawal, the park staff held, the better. The dumps were therefore to be closed at once, cold turkey, and those bears who could not readjust to a regimen of natural foods would be eliminated—shipped to zoos, or killed. The park staff believed that the number of grizzly bears who would have to be eliminated would be small enough that the population could easily sustain the loss. That belief was based in part on the hope that most of the park's dump-feeding grizzlies would be able to adjust rapidly to the loss of garbage, and in larger part on Glen Cole's conviction that the population was much larger than the Craigheads thought. Cole believed that there were in effect two populations of Yellowstone grizzly bears: those who fed regularly at the dumps, and who formed the bulk of the Craigheads' study sample; and another, backcountry population who rarely or never visited the dumps, and who had mainly gone unrecorded by the Craigheads. Cole felt that even if the number of incorrigible garbage bears who had to be eliminated should prove to be substantially larger than the park staff was hoping, there would still be plenty of backcountry bears. These uncorrupted bears, Cole maintained, would then come to dominate the population, and the passing-on of garbage-feeding habits to the young of garbage-feeding mothers would be minimized. Yellowstone's grizzlies would thus, he reasoned, soon be on the road back to a more natural way of life, and Yellowstone's visitors would soon be much safer.

The Craigheads, on the other hand, held that there were not two separate dump-feeding and backcountry populations; their data, they said, showed that nearly all of Yellowstone's grizzlies used the dumps at one time or another, and they felt that the number of non-garbage-feeders was therefore much too small to sustain the elimination of many of the dump bears. They believed, moreover, that because the dumps were closed to human visitors, the bears who fed there were *not* habituated to humans, and that garbage was just as natural a food for grizzly bears as biscuitroot. Indeed they felt that the dumps helped *prevent* campground problems, by drawing grizzlies to a high-quality food source isolated from the park's developed areas. Recalling that there had been a camp-raiding rampage following the garbage reductions of 1941, and knowing how important a food source the dumps had been for a number of bear generations, the Craigheads reasoned that a cold-turkey dump closure would bring about a sudden, confused dispersal of suddenly very hungry grizzly bears, who would then inevitably be drawn to the campgrounds, and big trouble. An abrupt dump closure, they argued, would be bad for both bears and people.

This, then, was the core of an essentially scientific disagreement which was soon to be shrouded in layer after layer of extrascientific dispute. The Park Service held that garbage bears were ipso facto habituated to humans and therefore dangerous; that most of the garbage bears would be able to adapt relatively easily to natural food habits; and that the population was large enough in any case to sustain the loss of even a goodly number of bears who might not be able to adapt. The Craigheads held that feeding on garbage at the isolated open-pit dumps and habituation to humans were not necessarily related; that an abrupt dump closure would cause severe difficulties for the bears who had fed on garbage every summer of their lives, and would lead inevitably to widespread bear-human confrontations which would in turn necessitate the elimination of many grizzlies; and that the population was too small to sustain such a loss.

The next, extrascientific layer of the conflict concerned the intractable philosophical question of just what is *natural*, and whether that represented a legitimate ideal for national parks management. The Park Service was acting on the ideas expressed in the Leopold Report, which advocated a return of park ecosystems to a condition as nearly as possible replicating the primeval; that, of course, meant minimizing the influence of modern man. The Craigheads, believing that modern man must be included in any idea of nature, advocated a much more active and ongoing human manipulation of the park's ecology. They believed, indeed, that without man's intervention the park's grizzly bear population might not survive.

The park staff, still in keeping with the Leopold Report, held that philosophical questions and the management issues they raised were properly a Park Service matter, entirely beyond the researchers' mandate. The Craigheads, who had been used to participating in the resolution of management questions under previous administrations, felt that the danger of the park's proposed actions was so dire that they had to take action despite the limitations of their official mandate, and this added a third layer to the conflict—the question of whose views should take precedence in management.

It was time, in 1967, for the Craigheads' first major report on their study, and with it they staged what may be thought of as a preemptive strike in the obviously imminent battle over the grizzly bear. The paper they submitted to the Park Service was boldly titled, "Management of Bears in Yellowstone National Park"—openly flouting the stipulation that management was not to be their bailiwick—and it made many specific recommendations (such as killing bison and elk to feed bears deprived of garbage) which were in direct conflict with the tenets of the Leopold Report. The Craigheads contested the Leopold committee's (and now also the Park Service's) most fundamental assumptions: "Within Yellowstone," they wrote, "some of the natural population-regulating processes have been so altered since the establishment of the park that these are not now effective. Since there is no possibility of these being wholly restored, and since management must do the job, artificiality becomes inevitable." The Craigheads now accepted that closure of the dumps was going to happen whether they liked it or not, but they insisted that the transition from dependence on to freedom from artificial supplementation of the bears' diet had to be gradual. Implicit in their assertions, of course, was the confidence that they knew a lot more about bears than the park staff did. Which was true. But the Craigheads' apparent belief that greater knowledge should result naturally in greater influence indicated a certain naïveté about the nature of institutional authority, which tends not to like having such gauntlets slapped down before it.

Indeed, it was immediately clear that the park staff regarded the Craigheads' report as an attempt at gross usurpation of Park Service authority. And the park staff's aggressive taking-up of the gauntlet indicated in turn a certain naïveté about the nature of the Craigheads, who were not only strong-willed but also famous—able, if the need should arise, to mobilize public opinion, which tends not to like seeing valiant animal-lovers kicked around by the government.

And somewhere in here begins the accretion of the final layer, which was eventually to envelop and almost to smother the central biological questions: personal animosity. It started small—a few individuals on the Yellowstone Park staff dead set against John and Frank Craighead, and vice versa—but it was going to grow.

An unrelated incident in the summer of 1967 contributed to the already overheated atmosphere. On a single night that August, two young women were killed by grizzly bears in Glacier National Park—a stunning coincidence, since these were only the fourth and fifth fatal grizzly maulings in the whole history of the national parks, yet no more than a coincidence. The killers were two of the many Glacier grizzlies who had been hand-fed summer after summer right under the indulgent eyes of the National Park Service and who had therefore lost their fear of man. The Park Service's official report on those incidents stressed that both young women had been menstruating and were wearing perfume, and it absolved park bear policy of any blame.

After the storm of indignation that followed what came to be called (after the book of the same name by Jack Olsen) the "Night of the Grizzlies," Yellowstone Park's management saw trouble on their own horizon: they, too, had many grizzlies feeding on garbage who were, they felt, also habituated to humans and therefore dangerous. The Craigheads, on the other hand, contended that there was a big difference between the garbage-bear problems of Glacier and of Yellowstone: the Glacier bears, the Craigheads said, were strongly man-conditioned because much of the garbage they were getting came in the form of direct handouts from people, whereas Yellowstone's dump-feeding grizzlies did not associate garbage with people; only the relatively few regular campground-raiders were truly conditioned to people and therefore dangerous. But the Park Service smelled lawsuits in the garbage-scented air, and the Park Service encouraged Yellowstone Park to move ahead with the dump closures forthwith, the Craigheads' warnings be damned. Furthermore, the Craighead's unsolicited management recommendations, with all their overt and veiled criticism not only of Park Service management but even of Park Service philosophy, had now been circulated at high levels in Washington, where they had been received with little gratitude. It was not long, therefore, before wider battle lines were drawn—the National Park Service arrayed in a united front against two stubbornly quixotic biologists.

In 1968, at the Trout Creek dump, the park's largest, edible garbage began to be separated from nonedible, and the supply was also reduced in volume. And, just as the Craigheads had predicted, there was a sudden increase in bear problems in the campgrounds. During the previous two years, according to Frank Craighead's citation of official park bear logs in his book *Track of the Grizzly*, the number of control actions (bears relocated or killed) at the Yellowstone Lake campground, about eight miles from the Trout Creek dump, had been thirty-three and nine, respectively; in 1968, according to Craighead, it was eighty-four.

The Park Service's own official records show only twenty-four control actions. But the Craigheads maintain that those records are grossly incomplete. Frank Craighead writes that "according to rangers sympathetic to the bears' plight, the unofficial policy of the park superintendent was: get rid of the bears, just don't let anybody know."

John Craighead adds: "This was actually incorporated in an official inter-district memo which I saw. It has been authenticated by park personnel who also received the memo."

Former park archivist Paul Schullery comments: "I looked, but I could never find such a memo in the park files."

Park Service spokesmen admit that record-keeping may have been poor, but they insist that the very idea of some sort of systematic campaign against grizzlies would be sheer anathema, both personally and institutionally, to the kind of people who work in a national park.

And so it goes, round and round, impossible to get to the bottom of. What is clear, though, is that by now what had at first been a scientific disagreement and then a philosophical dispute and then a conflict over management prerogatives was now open personal warfare.

In the early fall of 1968, a wooden mess hall which had served as the Craighead team's research headquarters was bulldozed and burned by the National Park Service—in preparation, they said, for the centennial celebration coming up four years later. The Craigheads were denied use of any other vacant park buildings, and had to operate from a house trailer belonging to the U. S. Fish and Wildlife Service. They were also forbidden any longer to handle or relocate bears. The Craigheads suspected that more bears were being killed than anybody was saying, and when they later (in 1971) requested access to park records of captures and control actions, writes Frank Craighead, access was denied. The Craigheads believe to this day that there was a coverup and that the records now available do not reflect the true numbers of bears killed, although there is no conclusive evidence that this is so. Some rather suggestive circumstantial evidence, John Craighead writes, is the skewed age structure shown in later studies, and the small number of Craighead-marked bears recaptured after 1974 by the interagency team. These facts, Craighead believes, imply mortality well beyond the numbers officially admitted.

The Park Service categorically denies any sub-rosa killing of grizzly bears.

Officials of the Atomic Energy Commission, which had been providing funding for the Craigheads' radio-tracking work, were denied permission to visit the Trout Creek dump site with the researchers. In early 1969, acting on his belief that the colored ear streamers and radio collars placed on grizzlies by the Craighead team were esthetically unacceptable to park visitors—ninety-nine percent of whom never saw a grizzly at all, marked or otherwise—superintendent Anderson ordered all such eyesores removed whenever possible, and forbade all further marking or collaring. Even the removal of a premolar to determine a bear's age was forbidden.

The Park Service maintained that the Craigheads were refusing to furnish data to support their recommendation not to close the dumps cold-turkey. In fact, they had no data that would predict the future. What they did have was an intimate knowledge of grizzly bear behavior; their predictions had been intuitive. What was going to happen, neither the Craigheads nor the Park Service could say with utter certainty. It was simply that the Craigheads felt that theirs, on the basis of their years of experience, was the better-qualified speculation.

The Park Service by now was claiming that the Craigheads were not furnishing them with any data at all. Frank Craighead, however, says that he and his brother "actually supplied a wealth of reports and papers." When he tried to hand two of their finished reports to Jack Anderson, Craighead writes, Anderson shoved them back at him and said he didn't want to see them.

On the other hand, the incivility to which the conflict had sunk was not all on one side. When the Park Service's Natural Sciences Advisory Board—chaired by Starker Leopold, author of the national parks policy in whose face the Craigheads' recommendations so defiantly flew—met at Yellowstone in September of 1969, the Craigheads would present their testimony against the dump closures only on the condition that all National Park Service employees leave the room first. The board concluded that there was no hard proof that the Craigheads' predictions would prove right. Neither, of course, could they say that the Park Service's own predictions would be borne out.

The Park Service nevertheless took the board's report as a green light. In October of 1969, the Rabbit Creek dump was closed, and in the fall of 1970, Trout Creek followed.

Before the dump controversy had come to a head, the Craigheads had thought that their study might soon be ended; in a January 1969 report, John Craighead had stated that the project was ninety-five percent complete and would require only two more years to complete. By 1970, however, when the memorandum of understanding under which their research had been conducted was due to expire, the grizzly bear scene was changing radically, and the Craigheads wanted to monitor the dispersal and behavior of the grizzlies who were now being deprived of garbage. It would take several more years to know if their predictions had been right.

The new memorandum of understanding the Park Service then offered contained the astonishing stipulation that all publications or even oral comments made by the Craigheads pertaining to Yellowstone grizzly bears be approved in advance by the director of the U.S. Bureau of Sport Fisheries and Wildlife (now the Fish and Wildlife Service) and that *he* in turn get the approval of the director of the National Park Service before a mouth could be opened or a word printed.

The absolute and utter kibosh, in short, had been put on the Craigheads' academic freedom, not to mention their personal rights under the First Amendment to the Constitution of the United States. The Craigheads refused to sign the agreement. Most of their work had already been made impossible, anyway, by all the earlier restrictions. The study was over.

The trouble, however, was distinctly not. Stories about the Craighead controversy continued to appear in the press. Bloody murder was being screamed by the likes of the animal-rights advocate Lewis Regenstein and the columnist Jack Anderson. *The New York Times* and the *Washington Post* did stories. Members of Congress were getting involved, and pressure on the Department of the Interior (the Park Service's parent agency) was mounting. The Craigheads were widely seen as persecuted underdogs.

Meanwhile, all hell was breaking loose in Yellowstone. According to Frank Craighead in *Track of the Grizzly*, "In the years 1969 through 1972 there were a total of one hundred sixty known deaths [of grizzly bears], an average of thirty-two bears per year, with highs of forty-six and forty-five in 1970 and 1971, respectively"—not counting, of course, the undiscovered illegal kills, of which there is always a substantial complement. In 1971, Craighead writes, when the garbage dump at West Yellowstone, Montana, was bearproofed, nineteen grizzly bears were captured near that site and relocated, and by spring of the following year all but one of them were dead.

In and around the town of West Yellowstone itself, Craighead writes, there were an additional twelve known and four probable grizzly bear mortalities in 1971 alone. In that single year, a total of either (according to which source you decide on) forty-three, forty-four, forty-five, or forty-eight grizzlies were killed (both legally and illegally), including Marian, the study's first radio-collared grizzly, and seventeen other of the Craighead team's marked bears.

By 1973, conservationists were sufficiently inflamed, and government was feeling enough of the heat, that the Secretary of the Interior formally requested the National Academy of Sciences to convene an authoritative committee to evaluate the mess. Under the chairmanship of the ecologist Ian McTaggart Cowan—who was considered to be a genuinely disinterested observer, as none of the previous arbiters had been—the committee sought out everybody who had anything to say, boned up on the literature, pondered awhile, and issued a report.

The report, though its language was conservative, came down hard on the Park Service, especially on the assumptions about grizzly bears under which they were being managed by Yellowstone Park— assumptions which pointedly ignored the previous decade's wealth of data and the conclusions the Craigheads had drawn from them. The population figures supplied to Yellowstone Park management by Glen Cole, for example, were based entirely on reports of bear sightings, and without visible markers it had obviously been impossible for observers to differentiate individuals. "Estimates of bear numbers for 1971 to 1973," the report stated, "are based on hypothetical numbers and there are no data to verify them."

The committee's dismissal of the park's own research effort was stern: "The research program carried out by the National Park Service administration since 1970 has been inadequate to provide the data essential for devising sound management policies for the grizzly bears of the Yellowstone ecosystem."

The report supported the Craigheads' conclusion that there were not separate dump-feeding and backcountry populations, and it endorsed the Craigheads' estimate of the small number of grizzlies not using the dumps. The committee accepted the Craigheads' belief that their censuses had counted seventy-seven percent of the population, that the population size was approximately two hundred twenty-nine bears, and that a sharp decline had occurred after the closing of the dumps. The committee recommended, as the Craigheads had, an extremely conservative policy on the removal of grizzlies. They also insisted that proper research was impossible without the marking of bears. All in all, while the committee did criticize some of the Craigheads' conclusions (mainly on the grounds that they needed more data, which of course they would eventually have amassed if the study had been allowed to continue), and although its treatment of the Park Service's conduct was so circumspect as to be almost opaque, the National Academy of Sciences report amounted to a nearly complete vindication of the Craigheads.

In 1975, however, in a stunning reversal, committee chairman Cowan recalculated the Craigheads' numbers, and now concluded that not seventy-seven percent of the entire population but only about fifty-nine percent were represented in the dump censuses—yielding a population estimate of not two hundred twenty-nine but three hundred one! In other words, Cowan now figured that the Park Service's figures, despite the inadequacy of their techniques, were closer to the case than the Craigheads', and that there had been a substantial number of backcountry bears all along.

The original report's major criticism of the Craighead study was an important one, concerning the critical issue of population projection. In 1974 the Craigheads and their associate Joel Varney had published "A Population Analysis of the Yellowstone Grizzly Bears," documenting the severe effects on grizzly population parameters brought about by the dump closures and control actions, and projecting a further steep decline if current management practices were to continue. The committee held, however, that the population should soon begin to recover its losses, largely because they believed that the Craigheads' new computer model failed to take into account a potential compensatory increase in reproduction and cub survival that could be expected as population density fell and competition for food therefore decreased. The Craigheads argued that because the population decrease had been accompanied by a sharp decline in food supply, and also because falling density for such an already sparsely distributed animal would make it harder for potential mates to find each other, no compensatory increase could be anticipated.

This dispute continues even now between adherents of both positions. Dale McCullough, of the University of California at Berkeley, who sat on the National Academy of Sciences committee, has recently published a paper demonstrating density-dependent behavior in the Yellowstone grizzly population, and John Craighead and a group of associates have published an updated version of their population analysis showing exactly the opposite.

The Cowan report concluded by recommending that further research be undertaken immediately, and that it be carried out by *independent* scientists—with none of this stuff about advance approval from directors of government agencies for the researchers' comments and reports.

Meanwhile, a proposal to establish a new Yellowstone grizzly study was already aborning in Washington. Since a conspicuous lack of interagency cooperation was one underlying factor in the Craighead hassles (John Craighead was an employee of the Fish and Wildlife Service as well as a member of the University of Montana faculty), the idea was now to forge a real team effort, with representatives from the National Park Service, the Fish and Wildlife Service, the Forest Service, and the states of Idaho, Montana, and Wyoming. No nonagency participation. Team leader to be appointed by—tadah!—the National Park Service. Specifically none other than Glen Cole. So much for independent research.

Yet the person Cole picked to head the study team, a wildlife biologist from the University of Idaho named Richard Knight, was about as far from a Park Service mouthpiece as it was possible to get. For Knight turned out to be one of the least bossable, most independent characters in the West. Park Service man or not, he and his study met with a rather chilly welcome at Yellowstone National Park, where Jack Anderson still reigned as superintendent and, no matter what the National Academy of Sciences committee said, still didn't want anybody telling him how to deal with his grizzly bears. Anderson still wanted those colored ear streamers *off*. He forbade the new researchers to carry firearms to protect themselves in case of bear attack: in a letter to Robert Finley of the Fish and Wildlife Service, who had been trying to work out a memorandum of understanding that would enable the study to conduct research in the park, Anderson wrote, "I have been traveling in the Rockies, the Sierras, and other remote areas for some thirty-five years and never felt the need of a firearm"—conveniently ignoring the presumable fact that during all those years he had not been handling anesthetized grizzly bears who might just wake up a little early and in a bad mood.

The Yellowstone Interagency Grizzly Bear Study was to have begun work in the spring of 1973, but by midsummer not only had no field work been conducted, the whole project was already in disarray. Finley wrote in July to Assistant Secretary of the Interior Nathaniel Reed, "The present situation makes sound and unbiased research in Yellowstone National Park impossible." He also wrote to the study team that they would have to proceed without access to the park— the heart of the grizzly's range.

Furthermore, almost from the beginning, there was personal conflict among some members of the study team. One can look for explanations in the traditional interagency rivalries and in the states' longtime mistrust of the feds and in the wide philosophical gulf between the likes of the mainly conservationist Park Service and the mainly utilitarian Forest Service, but in this case the story is probably simpler and more individual: some of these people just couldn't get along, or weren't trying. Accusations flew wildly back and forth— lack of communication . . . nonutilization of talent and experience . . . failure to live up to official responsibility . . . secrecy . . . conspiracy . . . empire building.

Dick Knight's solution was not the kind of soothing reconciliation so popular in management schools these days. Basically what he seems to have done is just start bashing the pieces into place. Those that didn't fit, he tossed aside. Knight was going to be boss, and *he* would decide what research was to be done, when, how, and by whom —like it or lump it. Thus, from the early days, the Forest Service representative on the team had little contact with anybody else and performed little of the field research he had been assigned. Idaho's man took care of administrative tasks, and stayed in Idaho, well away from the study area. Montana's biologist did at least work at the team's headquarters on the Montana State University campus in Bozeman, but he occupied himself mainly with autopsies on dead bears and rarely communicated with Knight—a situation that still prevails today, although, perhaps thanks merely to the healing passage of time, more amicably now. After the first few years of the study, the Fish and Wildlife Service biologist left, and that agency dropped out altogether. Only Wyoming's Larry Roop, the Park Service's Dick Knight, and Knight's associate Bonnie Blanchard remain today as active and truly cooperating members of the team. Funding comes only from the National Park Service and the state of Wyoming. "Interagency" "team"—ha.

In the agencies' defense, however, it must be said that when the personality problems of the team were threatening to sink it, the government executives got together and established a steering committee so that at least at the planning level there would be some interagency cross-fertilization. The main idea seems to have been to try to exert some kind of control over the headstrong and irascible Knight—an effort which is still touch and go. Knight has mellowed, in a certain clever way: he may often be seen smiling now at meetings where once he would have brooded and snarled, and he diplomatically accepts the criticism, advice, warnings, injunctions, plans, philosophy, and crackpot schemes that are heaped on him—then goes ahead and does what he thinks was right in the first place. If the Park Service wanted a researcher temperamentally opposite to John and Frank Craighead—an organization man, who would think long and hard about what was best for the government's public image—they definitely picked the wrong guy.

"Of *course* the agencies *all* say they want to save the grizzly bear," Knight croons in a voice saccharine with sarcasm. "Every winter I sit through meetings with the Fish and Wildlife Service, the Forest Service, the Park Service, the states—I sit there till I'm sick of them, listening to everybody tell each other how great they're doing, saying, 'By God, I'm for the bear!' And they are, as long as it's easy. But let them come up against something that's difficult from a public-pressure standpoint—well, then, the bear takes it. They doze him away."

Many of the people living around the periphery of Yellowstone Park feel nothing but malice for the grizzly bear, and it is from them that a significant part of the illegal killing comes. Many of these people know nothing but folklore about grizzlies, and nothing at all about the study. Wouldn't a little public relations benefit the bears?

"Look. We're not in business to educate the public. Our job is to provide information to the managers, so they can make the wisest possible decisions about grizzly bears. They're the ones with the money to hire the public relations people. I'm a scientist, not a public relations man."

In the early days of the study, Knight felt that Cole's estimates of the grizzly population were much too high, but he had great difficulty in coming up with a figure of his own that he could be really confident of. After the dump closures, the population dispersed to the remote corners of the wilderness, so even if there had remained a number of conspicuously color-marked bears—which, thanks to the Park Service, there didn't—it would have been extremely hard to perform any realistic sort of census. Furthermore, given the technical difficulties and the wide range of statistical probability, Knight was really not comfortable with the idea of stating any number at all. He preferred to address the *trend*, rather than the (unknowable) *size*, of the population. But officialdom wanted a number. So he gave them a number. For a long time, the number he gave was three hundred and fifty.

Eventually, however, as radio-collaring was reinstituted and the data base grew, and man-caused mortality continued at a rate higher than known reproduction could possibly compensate for, the study team began to revise its population estimates downward. Their confidence in the accuracy of the numbers they were stating remained low, but as long as numbers were demanded of them, it was clearly necessary to be as conservative as possible—for a high overestimate might mask doom. By the summer of 1982, Knight and the team were saying that it was possible that fewer than two hundred Yellowstone grizzlies remained. As the years of the study had passed and the data accumulated, in other words, the new study had come closer and closer to the Craigheads' original prognostications. This, even more than the National Academy of Sciences report, was the kind of exoneration the Craigheads needed. Yet it had been so long in coming that during the intervening years both the Craighead brothers had developed something of an idée fixe about the villainy of the Park Service. Despite the fact that after the departures of Anderson and Cole the management of Yellowstone Park began to deal reasonably with their grizzly bears, cutting back sharply on the number of control actions and in general bending over backwards to save every possible grizzly, and despite the fact that it was land use policies and failure of law enforcement *outside* the park that were now the principal cause of grizzly mortality, the Craigheads continued to focus their ire on the Park Service as though it were the source of all the trouble, relentlessly and in detail and, some said, intemperately criticizing every official proclamation they considered wrong, of which there were many. By now the Park Service had learned to reply coolly and smoothly, and a few observers of the scene began, behind their backs of course, to call the Craigheads crackpots—which was utterly wrong, but unsurprising.

The Craigheads had predicted that an abrupt dump closure would lead to a sharp decline in the grizzly population, and, though there are other factors involved as well, the population seems indeed to have declined sharply. Although not quite to the extent the Craigheads had predicted, the Yellowstone grizzly has been shown, by Knight and his study team, to be in real trouble. "Last year," Knight said in 1981, "I was giving twenty or thirty years until the Yellowstone grizzly would be extinct, or a remnant. This year I'm more pessimistic. But nobody ever said saving the grizzly was going to be easy. Just look at the habitat encroachment around here. Three hundred and fifty thousand acres under lease application for oil and gas exploration in the Washakie Wilderness. Thousands of acres in the heart of the Teton Wilderness, clear into the Thoroughfare. Applications all over the North Absarokas. Mining and logging in the Gallatin. Geothermal on the west. Residential development all over the place. We're surrounded! Not to mention the poaching rings working out of Cooke City and West Yellowstone. You can walk into some of those souvenir shops over in West and pick up a nice grizzly claw for two hundred and fifty bucks. A big hide might bring ten thousand. Meanwhile, where's law enforcement? We do have a couple of good law enforcement officers, and I hate to downgrade them. The problem is that there are too few of any kind of officers operating in grizzly bear habitat, and fewer good ones.

"And the habitat encroachment is always considered by the Fish and Wildlife Service item by item. They're always saying, 'No, *this* or *that* won't jeopardize the bear by itself.' But what about the cumulative effect of five or six developments? They won't address that. Yellowstone Village is a big real estate development right in the middle of where there used to be lots of bears. Then you've got Ski Yellowstone, and that by itself wouldn't wipe out the bears—just take a few more. And right here in the park, forty million dollars' worth of development at Grant Village is coming, sitting on top of five Yellowstone Lake trout spawning streams—some of the most heavily used grizzly habitat we've got.

"I'd say that the way things are going, the future of the grizzly bear as we know it is bleak."

Nevertheless, there are now in and around Yellowstone almost as many human beings professionally involved in trying to avert that bleak future as there are Yellowstone grizzlies themselves, and, despite the personality conflicts, bureaucratic lethargy, interagency infighting, and philosophical confusion that seem to dog the grizzly bear through the years, the human effort on the bear's behalf is slowly coalescing. And the main reason for that progress is that through the work of the Craigheads and their scientific heirs, what is good and what is bad for grizzlies and how they live their lives and die their deaths and what changes they can and cannot stand are finally coming to be understood. If a viable population of grizzly bears remains in Yellowstone at the end of this century, it will have been a success against the odds for government, but for science a triumph.

The mother grizzly and her cubs are moving back into the central peaks of the Absaroka now, as the snowcrest creeps upward and the succulent vegetation follows. Days of harsh cold wind-driven rain and of hot sun hasten toward the brief high-mountain summer. Nutrients and energy surge through the system, from the minerals of the soil into the microorganisms into the vascular plants into the herbivores and through both the latter into the grizzly bears, who are gaining weight fast now. The mother bear is full-grown, and any energy she may accumulate beyond what is required to establish adequate fat reserves for next winter will go toward milk production and thus her offspring's growth; she may grow fatter at times, but in skeleton and muscles she will never grow larger. High nutrition in females without cubs also does not contribute toward their further growth; it will be reflected, rather, in increased reproductive fitness, in the form of enhanced fertility, larger litters, larger and therefore more viable cubs, and shorter reproductive intervals. Male grizzlies, on the other hand, continue to grow all their lives long, as long as there is enough to eat, since greater size enables them to dominate their peers and therefore to have more success in winning the favor of mates.

At no time are the differences among the different classes of Yellowstone's grizzlies more pronounced than now, in June. Mothers and cubs like our protagonists are placidly eating like pigs and keeping out of excitement's way in small subunits of their home ranges, usually in the remotest and least accessible food-producing terrain they know. Females with older young may be ready to breed again, and they will have been weaning their yearlings or two-year-olds, or even, in some cases, three-year-olds. These newly liberated mothers, as well as females without young, are now moving toward traditional areas of amatory rendezvous, their appetite for food low and their hormonal states in an uproar. Newly weaned female subadults are moving modestly around the edges of their mother's home ranges looking to carve out a little place for themselves not too far from home, while their brothers are roaming far afield, crisscrossing sometimes the whole ecosystem and even pushing out past the edges of occupied bear country in their quest for a place not already being hogged by some belligerent older and bigger subadult male or, worse, by a testosterone-maddened and inhospitable old male grizzly. It is because such older males never want them around that dispersing subadult males are by far the most vulnerable segment of any grizzly population. Their dispersal usually coincides with spring hunting seasons for black bear, and the young grizzlies' small size, their wide-ranging movement into accessible fringe areas, their youthful inexperience, and the inability or unwillingness of some black bear hunters to make the correct identification frequently prove a fatal combination.

According to the sort of country they inhabit, Yellowstone grizzlies in June have extremely various feeding regimes. Those who live in the drainage of the upper Yellowstone River above Yellowstone Lake are being treated to a tremendous spawning run of four-year-old cutthroat trout into the tributary streams. On some nights, especially in the remote wilderness of the lake's southern and eastern hinterlands, it can look almost like salmon-time in farthest Alaska, with grizzlies plunging up and down the riffles in pursuit of whole glittering shoals of foot-long fish. Even in little trickles no more than a foot wide, big trout may lurk under the undercut banks of meanders, and bears will work their way splashily upstream reaching beneath those overhangs. In the broad, shallow riffles of larger creeks, where cutthroats gather in dozens to fight over mates and spawning nest sites, grizzlies pin the trout under their paws, sweep them shoreward till they flop onto sandbars, or sometimes just bite them straight out of the water.

The grizzlies of the moist and mainly forested southwestern region of the ecosystem, with its fertile, flat river bottoms, have access to large meadows at moderate elevations where plant phenology progresses rapidly in spring, and here the bears are already digging for

carbohydrate-rich roots and the year's firstborn abundance of rodents and insects. Wet-meadow forbs are also plentiful and at their peak of protein content.

Back home with our grizzly and her cubs in the high mountains of the national park's northeastern corner, we find spring beauty and glacier lily still following the snow's recession, and horsetail abundant in the swales and at waterside; soft young grasses and the juicy tops and starchy roots of yampah move through grizzly guts by the ton.

Above it all, a small airplane with a branched antenna slung under its wing skims low over the landscape. Within, with his ear pressed to a Telonics receiver encased in leather elegantly tooled with the image of a great bull elk, Larry Roop is listening hard for the static-smirched and mountain-bounced *tock-tock* of a radio-collared grizzly bear. When he locates one, the spot is recorded on a map on his lap. When a bear is in or near one of the Interagency Grizzly Bear Study's habitat-analysis transects, word will go to an assistant somewhere on the ground, and scats may then be collected, sorted, air-dried, soaked in water, pulled apart, and painstakingly examined; the researcher will record species present, frequency of occurrence, percent composition per item, percent of total diet volume, importance value, sometimes nutritive composition. Certain highly digestible items, like mushrooms, hardly appear in the scats, and their significance must be guessed at; others also leave little behind, but you can tell them by the smell. Meat scats, for example, really stink, while spring beauty scats smell sweet as new-mown hay. After a number of continuous years of scat analysis—in order to account for the great seasonal and year-to-year variations in food supply and feeding habits—food preferences and importance can be assessed. After enough locations for an individual grizzly have been amassed on the map, the study team can draw a minimum-home-range polygon and delineate the bear's biocenters within it. That diagram may be over-laid with those of other grizzlies to enable consideration of avoidance patterns and other social behavior. Preferred plant communities can be defined, and use of those communities investigated on the ground. Responses to disturbance can be recorded. The success of transplants of problem bears can be assessed. And bit by minuscule bit, the grizzly bear is revealed.

Roop tunes in to the broadcast frequency of the mother grizzly's radio collar. For several days, she and the cubs have been moving up and down a remote subalpine ridgetop, miles from the nearest trail, turning over rotting logs at the edge of timber and slurping up the ants and grubs beneath, digging for glacier lily bulbs among silver patches of snow tinted strawberry-ice-cream-pink with the spring growth of algae, stalking and chasing but never catching an occasional elk calf, and, once, unearthing a marmot dead in its burrow. There will be no trouble with backpackers or anybody else around here, for even now, as June shades toward July and the campgrounds and motels and dude ranches and cafés are aswarm with vacationers asking one another if they've seen any bears, the mountain passes that separate this wilderness from the nearest outposts of civilization are still under deep snow and impacted ice, and there is no human at all in these parts except one single-minded young man with a hundred-pound pack on his back, containing food, tent, sleeping bag, all the usual camping stuff, plus snowshoes, ice axe, zip-lock plastic bags (stuffed with grizzly bear scats), camera, notebooks, plaster of Paris for track-casting, extra batteries, tape measure, thermometer, hygrometer, and radio receiver, tuned just now to the frequency of the mother bear's radio collar.

The young man lifts and rotates the antenna and frowns, listening hard to the empty static. In this region of grotesque rock towers and jumbled talus-footed cliffs, the signal ricochets and splays apart and is often, as now, lost. To keep in radio contact he must stay within a mile of the bears, yet so skillful a tracker is he that the grizzly and her cubs, although he has been on their trail for almost a week, have yet to discover his presence. He stays downwind, and to keep up must run headlong through seemingly impassable windfall timber. When the bears move, he moves. When they sleep, he sleeps. When they rise at midnight in a thunderstorm to forage through the mud and streamside willow beaver-stobs, he must rise and follow in the dark and rain. When, as now, the signal is lost, he must climb to a high precipice, and perhaps to another and another, until the quiet *tock-tock* of the bear's radio is heard again.

JULY

T HERE seems something heroic about grizzly bear research. Some of that something is intrinsic, and felt fully perhaps only by the practitioners—the struggle to break through the adamantine otherness of the beast; the challenge of finding the clear facts amidst a foggy welter of supposition and hope and the ever few rarely unambiguous data; the persistence in the face of what must seem, on many a dark day, one's subject's inexorable doom; the loneliness at the heart of knowing how little what matters so much to oneself may matter to the world beyond.

There can be heroism also in making it matter at large. That is something the Craigheads have always known, and never flinched from. Other researchers, their very livelihoods contingent on their ability to work smoothly within the cantankerous machinery of government agencies and funding bodies and overstrictly limited job descriptions, are content to find the facts, present them, and let others who may be better suited to combat do the fighting. Yet even these partisans of the quiet and unmettlesome approach know that their findings can be dynamite, and will, if so, most likely be used as such.

Although the forces ranged against the grizzly bear may lack coherent intention, their power is so great that they may be seen as constituting a single juggernaut of destruction. The grizzly bear's defense, such as it is, consists entirely in the weapons of biological truth and of the ethic it generates. Considered singly, the weapons— the biologists' findings—can seem puny. But as this chapter and the next one will attempt to show, there is an edifice abuilding around the bear which may yet repel the assault of his enemies.

It is ten o'clock at night, two days past the full moon. Light rain is falling; two tenths of an inch have fallen in the last twenty-four hours. There is no wind. Fog billows up from the river below. The humidity is eighty-nine percent, the temperature forty degrees Fahrenheit. It is grizzly bear time, and grizzly bear weather, par excellence.

Where a steep sidehill park bottoms out in a level strip of wet meadow above another, timbered slope, the mother bear is noisily cropping the tender new tops of emerging cow-parsnip (*Heracleum lanatum*). The cubs are racing in circles, working up an appetite. Crouched in the woods half a mile below, with cold rain trickling down the back of his neck, Bart Schleyer is scribbling in the dark. The subject of Schleyer's master's thesis will be the daily routine of Yellowstone grizzly bears—twenty-four hours a day, spring, summer, and fall. Most of what has been learned about grizzlies has come in discrete bits and pieces, a grizzly here, a grizzly there, most of the data gathered in daylight and good weather, when field work is comfortable for biologists. Schleyer's study, on the other hand, yields to neither storm nor night. Conducted under the aegis of the Yellowstone interagency team, Schleyer's work focuses on the behavior of individual grizzly bears hour after hour, day after day, from emergence until denning, and so is intended to discern the elements common to most grizzlies' behavior and to distinguish from them those which vary among individuals.

He has found the idiosyncrasy category to be large indeed. One of his study bears, for example, is a highly successful predator even in summer, when large prey animals are supposed to be too healthy and fleet-footed for a grizzly to catch. Others are almost exclusively vegetarian, ignoring even weakened prey that could be dispatched with a lazy swat. (The usual scat-analysis techniques would not have turned up this variability. The data would simply show a certain amount of meat, and intuition might well lead the researcher to conclude, wrongly, that all the bears were doing some killing or carrion feeding.) Schleyer knows a male and female who struck up acquaintance, quite normally, in mating season, but then stayed together until fall—a gross violation of grizzly bear standards. Two of a trio of yearlings who had seemed to be conclusively weaned in May showed up back with their mother in midsummer; the third stayed independent; sometimes one or the other would stay with the mother, sometimes both would, sometimes they ventured out on their own, sometimes together, sometimes apart—playing havoc with the general assumptions about grizzly family dynamics.

In addition to the wide range of individual variability, Schleyer has also found a number of common patterns, mostly related to activity budgets and therefore, presumably, to bioenergetics. Grizzly bears are catnappers, up and down both day and night, but each season's pattern of activity has its own distinctive conventions.

In spring, Yellowstone's grizzlies are most active during the day and around dawn and dusk. There are clear peaks of activity at 6:30 a.m. and 10:00 p.m., and less definite peaks at 12:30 a.m. and 12:30 p.m. At 3:30 a.m. and 2:00 p.m., most grizzlies are almost certain to be bedded down.

In summer, things change dramatically. The grizzlies continue to be active at dawn and dusk, but now most of their feeding and travel is nocturnal. There are peaks around 6:00 a.m. and 10:00 p.m., and the bears maintain a moderate level of activity almost continuously from 10:30 at night until 6:30 in the morning—fattening up while potentially irksome humans sleep and the air is cool.

In fall, activity becomes erratic, varying more widely from bear to bear—probably a reflection of increased dependence on carrion and prey, a single item of which may provide steady food for several days and so can allow a very low level of activity. There does seem to be one common peak of activity, around 2:30 in the afternoon. In good grasshopper years, these insects crawl around sluggishly in the chill of dawn and dusk, and then the crepuscule becomes grizzly prime time: grasshoppers are excellent high-calorie food.

It still must be remembered that all these numbers represent only statistical probability. One of Schleyer's grizzlies seems reliably to be up and around when all the others are asleep, and vice versa, all season long.

Weather, Schleyer has found, is probably the most important single determinant of grizzly activity on any given day. When the thermometer rises past seventy-two degrees Fahrenheit or falls below twelve above, you will almost never see a Yellowstone grizzly. Most of the highest level of activity takes place in the narrow range between forty-two and fifty-two—just right for light fur attire. Grizzlies seem to like fog and rain, as long as there's not too much of the latter: activity increases up to about a quarter-inch of rainfall, and then falls sharply off. There is often intense activity in the first couple of hours after a rainstorm. Perhaps because moist air conducts odors and sound better than dry, grizzlies are more and more active as relative humidity increases, up to ninety-five percent—at which point it usually starts raining. They tend to hunker down uneasily if the wind is high. It will come as small surprise that they don't much like to go out in hailstorms, either.

Grizzlies are least active on nights when the moon is full or almost, and most active in the week centering on the new moon, except—too dark?—on the night of the new moon itself. Like your basic human homebody padding groggily up and down the hall in his slippers, a grizzly bear wakes up slowly, usually shuffling around his bed site for a good half hour before setting out on business; he winds down equally slowly.

Like her peers, the mother bear in July is settling in to a regular summer circuit of biocenters. Schleyer keeps track, and he finds that many of these heavily used areas are smaller than a square mile each, and that grizzlies will move from one to the other even when the ecotypes and food availability seem to be identical—probably in order to maintain maximally intimate acquaintance with their whole home ranges and to keep on the lookout for more and better sources of food, especially carrion, whose location is unpredictable. Constant movement also means higher security, and, in the case of mothers with cubs, it can be a source of continuing education as well, in botany, geography, navigation, escape, and general behavioral flexibility.

The grizzly's travel circuit, regular though it may be, can easily be interrupted. The appearance of a large male on a family group's domain will put them over the mountain in a hurry. Wherever the grizzly population is near the carrying capacity of a given habitat, there is a good deal of such dominance-governed intraspecific social displacement. And there is no surer disrupter of grizzly itineraries than people. Because human trails usually offer the easiest way through the woods, grizzlies often use them at relatively secure times of day, but even then they are exceedingly skittish. During Schleyer's study, every grizzly who has become aware of the presence of people has been off like a shot, and not one has stopped running until he is at least *two miles* away. Now, it is true that as grizzlies become more used to people in their midst, as some bears in Glacier have apparently done, they may eventually learn not to spook so easily, but for most grizzly bears today, having too many people around can definitely be a problem. The fact that human trails often follow creek and river bottoms, lakeshores, ridgetops, and scenic meadows means that people are frequently routed straight through the best, most heavily used grizzly habitat. Some new trail plans have begun to take grizzly travel patterns into account, but most trails are already in place, and building new ones and returning the old to nature cost a lot of money. It is seductive to think that with increasing backcountry use, a few more people will get chewed on by grizzlies and then the money for new trails will magically be found, but a far more likely effect of increasing wilderness recreation is increasing displacement of grizzlies, therefore stress on grizzlies, lowered nutrition, and higher energy expenditure, and therefore, ultimately, diminished grizzly reproduction.

Research like Schleyer's on grizzlies' responses to disturbance is essential to land use planning both in the national parks, where the possible human uses are relatively few, and in the national forests and on other government lands where the multiple-use mandate may allow hunting, fishing, trapping, livestock grazing, logging, mining, oil and gas exploration and extraction, roads, airstrips, off-road vehicles, ski resorts, second-home developments, dogs, and all manner of other potential shatterers of grizzly bear felicity. Many people erroneously assume that the wilderness status that has been granted to much grizzly habitat in the national forests is sufficient to protect the bear, but in fact the wilderness law is as full of loopholes as Great-aunt Alice's lace antimacassar. Sport hunting is hardly a loophole, but it needs to be mentioned here because men *legally*

carrying guns in the wilderness are unquestionably the leading source
of illegal grizzly bear killing. Mining and oil and gas extraction in
classified wilderness areas are technically permitted by the law, although those activities are supposedly subject to the stipulations of
the Endangered Species Act. In reality, however, whether profit or the
biosphere shall prevail in a given situation is sometimes determined
by land managers' whims, according to how much pressure they're
under and from whom. Even new roads are occasionally allowed to
penetrate the wilderness—for access to mines and oil wells and to the
sometimes numerous private inholdings. Moreover, as a look at the
Yellowstone ecosystem map will show you, wilderness areas are often
sliced up into smaller chunks by road corridors, through which rivers
of traffic may flow in summer and along which any number of potential hazards to grizzlies—restaurants, houses, garbage dumps—may
act first as attractants and ultimately as killers. How such activities
are governed and when they should be restricted or altogether forbidden can be intelligently decided only on the basis of good research
—which developers and their allies in government tend to be reluctant to underwrite, on the sound principle that when there are no
data you can't have data jammed down your throat. When fed good
data, however, they may gag, but they've got to swallow.

Research on grizzly behavior is essential also to keeping people
safe in grizzly country. Only about one in every thirty million visitors
to grizzly bear habitat is ever going to be killed by a bear. Your
chances of meeting a violent death in your car on the way to the
trailhead are far greater than those of being eaten up by a bear in
the wilderness. Rare as they are, however, there have been some
seemingly unprovoked fatal grizzly attacks, and, while there are
always a few people who get a thrill out of daring fate, most of us are
happier if we know how to minimize our odds of gory dismember-
ment in the jaws of a grizzly bear.

There's actually not that much to it. The Forest Service and the
Park Service hand out a little brochure that covers the subject pretty
well, and their ideas and others' are included in the following recommendations.

❨ Avoid surprising grizzlies. Let them know you're around, and
they'll clear out long before you ever have a chance to know
they're there. A little dinging bell on your pack is usually sufficient. In a study in Glacier National Park, Katherine McArthur

Jope found that about twenty-five percent of hikers there used bear bells, but of all hikers charged by grizzlies not one was carrying a bell.

(If you do see a grizzly, give him a wide berth. No quick moves. No hollering for your mom. Circle slowly upwind if you can, so the bear can get your scent. If no detour is possible, move slowly back the way you came, or just wait quietly till the bear leaves. Whatever you do, *don't run*. Running is a personal invitation for any bear to give chase, and even if you're an Olympic gold medalist you won't outrun him.

(Minimize food odors. This one cannot be overemphasized. Keep your sleeping bag and whatever else you're going to have near you at night free of food smells. Don't sleep in the clothes you've cooked in. Freeze-dried food is less attractive to bears than fresh. Store all your food, empty food containers, garbage, and cooking and eating utensils unequivocally out of reach of bears. Since black bears readily climb trees, just hanging your stuff from a tree limb isn't good enough. The best method is to string a line between two trees with your food and gear in the middle at least ten feet off the ground. Sleep somewhere well away from your cooking and food-storage area. Burn cans and containers to suppress their odor, and then pack them and *all* your garbage out.

(Leave your dog at home. (Dogs are illegal on national park trails anyway.) The classic scenario: dog scents bear spoor; dog tracks and finds bear; bear displeased; dog turns tail, runs whimpering back to master with bear in hot pursuit.

(If you are charged by a grizzly, try to get up a tree—but only if you're sure you can get *at least* a good ten feet up it before the bear reaches you. Many charges are actually bluffs, and will stop short of actual contact, but if you're fleeing, or tangled up in pine boughs three feet off the ground, a charge may quickly turn into serious pursuit. The government brochure recommends that you toss something out to divert a charging bear's attention—your pack, say—but charges have been so few that this theory has not been well tested. (If the bear follows you up the tree, he's either a black, and probably just curious, or an idiosyncratic grizzly, in which case you can kiss your ass goodbye.) If there's no tree handy, try standing your ground with as much false air of courage as you can muster. Some people recommend playing dead and rolling up in a ball on the ground, but that would seem to invite some kind of investigation, probably painful in nature. In the highly improbable but nonetheless dreadful event that a charging grizzly turns out not to be bluffing, *then* rolling up into a ball, with your legs drawn up to your chest and your hands clasped over the back of your neck, is probably the best way to minimize injury.

The government brochure makes several other recommendations based on slightly less indubitable evidence:

- It suggests that traveling in larger groups is safer. Jope's study, however, showed that grizzlies in Glacier were slightly more likely to approach larger groups than singles or couples. Of course, approaching is not the same thing as attacking. Larger groups also tend to make more noise, which helps, and if you should get chewed on it's nice to have somebody to go for help or carry you out to the hospital.

- The brochure recommends not using perfumes, deodorants, or other sweet-smelling substances, and it states that women should stay out of grizzly country during their menstrual period. It may be that bears are attracted by perfumes or by the smell of blood or some pheromone in menstrual discharge; some recent research with polar bears indicates that menstrual blood is an exceptionally powerful attractant. Both the girls killed in Glacier Park in 1967 were menstruating. On the other hand, there is no evidence that menstruation actually incites attack.

- The brochure also asserts, "Human sexual activity attracts bears." If you cannot bring yourself to remain celibate, the next best thing is probably to have your fun somewhere out in the open in broad daylight, where the bear can at least see what's going on. Also preferably not too far from a good climbing tree, or two.

If you are hunting, fishing, and/or on horseback in grizzly country, a number of other precautions should come into play:

❰ Bears are crazy about horse feed, so it must be kept unavailable. It may be heavy, but you've got to hang it high.

❰ The same goes, but even more so, for game meat and fish. There is no surer bear attractant than fresh meat, and it must be kept out of reach. That means ten feet off the ground and well away from the nearest vertical object. It should also be kept at least a hundred yards outside of your camp, since even though it may be unreachable it is almost certainly going to attract the attention of bears. Gut piles and other refuse should be as far away from camp as humanly possible. Throw fish remains back in the water.

❰ Get your game meat out of the backcountry fast. The quicker you do, the fewer bear problems you'll have.

❰ Many of the foods that are too heavy for hikers are often brought along on horseback trips or kept in semipermanent hunting camps—bacon, fresh fruit, beer—and even a small spill of such items can bring bears scrounging into camp in the dead of night. Keep it clean.

❰ If you're hunting black bear, be sure you can tell blacks and grizzlies apart. This is not nearly as easy as it has sometimes been cracked up to be. Even the biologists themselves see bears sometimes they can't identify. Black bears can be just as blond as some grizzlies, and they can get pretty big too. The old saw about grizzlies always having dish-shaped or concave profiles is also not a reliable guide: grizzlies' faces vary widely, and a few have distinctly Roman, black-bear-like noses. Most grizzlies have long front claws, although those of active diggers may be worn short; all black bears have short front claws. Some people say that a black bear's nose is more like a dog's, and a grizzly's more like a pig's; but making the distinction would put you rather uncomfortably close to the object of your scrutiny. The most certain distinguishing characteristic is the grizzly's shoulder hump. If the light is too low or the bear is moving too fast for you to make indisputable identification, hold your fire.

Better still, don't go hunting for black bear in grizzly country in the first place. There are hundreds of places all over the continent where blacks are the only bears present.

Some of the precautions listed above may seem aimed more at protecting grizzlies from you than you from grizzlies. But don't forget that jail can be a kind of grizzly trouble too.

Protecting people from bears turns out to be pretty simple. The converse gets much more complicated, and here researchers sometimes find themselves the sole obstacles in the path of the juggernauts of commerce and industry. It is in that confrontation that the full magnitude of the cost of saving the grizzly bear can be seen.

At the national level, the complete removal of every acre of occupied grizzly bear habitat in the Lower Forty-eight from any form of exploitation would have insignificant impact. But at the edge where civilization is constantly probing, trying to ooze into grizzly country, the effects can be locally very significant. Laws, regulations, guidelines, and procedures seem to be sprouting up everywhere between the bear and disaster, but threats are blooming at an even faster rate. No sooner are strict timber harvest rules propounded in some national forest than there is suddenly a proposal for a ski resort. The local economy, typically, has been highly dependent on the timber industry, which has lately been in bad straits due to high interest rates and the resulting depression of the building industry. So: ski resort? Construction! Jobs! Terrific! And the pressure mounts fast. Management calls on biologists to do a quick-and-dirty analysis of the ecological impacts of the proposed development, and although what the biologists want to do is throw up their hands and insist that a really realistic assessment is simply not possible given the time and money available, the biological analyses are often indeed quick and dirty. Yet like the effects of some carcinogens, land development's impacts on the grizzly bear often take a long time to show up. Small changes in population dynamics or distribution patterns may seem insignificant in the short term but nevertheless spell doom over the long. As we have seen, sometimes a very slight change in population parameters results in an inevitably declining population. Likewise, disruption of a movement corridor which is significant only in time of drought may not become important until perhaps twenty years into the future—and then, in one critical year, the population may be decimated because grizzlies can no longer reach indispensable feeding sites. Arguments like that, however, find scant welcome from development-oriented, multiple-use management. The biologist is seen as squawking over "esthetic" "preservationist" trivia. Since biological assessments are almost always performed by people whose bread is buttered, whether proximally or distally, by development-minded government executives, those assessments tend to reflect the short-term thinking that characterizes the people in charge. There are occasional dramatic exceptions to that pattern—national forest supervisors who really take the long view and care deeply about the bear, biologists who stand up at the risk of their livelihoods, even timber executives who are dedicated to preserving viable grizzly populations on their private lands—but the overall movement is still toward development of grizzly habitat. Even in the case of major developments, when the participation of the Fish and Wildlife Service is called for and therefore some judgment is exercised outside the usual chain of command, every new proposal is treated as a whole new situation, and cognizance of development's cumulative effects on whole ecosystems can be hard to come by.

Obviously what is missing is a guiding philosophy, straightforward and concise: nature first in grizzly country. Which is, after all, exactly what is mandated by the Endangered Species Act. In the real world, however, it is seldom what results. For one thing, endangered species laws are often in direct conflict with other laws, like the Surface Mining Act of 1892, and the decision of which view to favor in case of conflict is often a judgment call. For another, the likes of the Forest Service and the Bureau of Land Management have a long tradition of *using* the land, and it is hard to get it through some of their managers' heads that maintenance of grizzly bears can count as a valid use.

Who profits? how much? Such questions are a good deal easier to answer than, How much is a grizzly population worth? and to whom is it worth that? When the alternatives to grizzly preservation are considered—the ski resort, the timber sale, the subdivision, the oil field—the profits are clear, and among the principal beneficiaries, usually, are the longtime familiars and even friends of the land managers: the industry people with whom they've worked closely for years; the stockmen who have grazed livestock under federal permits and who may have coffee every morning at the same café as the feds; the mining company that has a few congressmen in its pocket. The extent of local influence on the management of national lands is a disgrace, but it is also perfectly expectable in terms of human nature. Of course one cares more about what one's friends and neighbors want than about the distant noise from Washington or New York. Which is not to say that the situation could not be changed.

Sufficient pressure from the national level could change it—and it is at that level that there is a constituency for the grizzly bear.

There is also a sizable local partisanry for the bear. Many people who have grown up in or moved to Montana, Wyoming, or Idaho are where they are precisely because of their love of wild country, of which there is no more potent symbol than the grizzly. Sportsmen, backpackers, professional outfitters, and just plain nature-lovers all over the West see the grizzly as the foremost emblem of what they love in their homeland, despite the fact that few of them have ever seen a grizzly bear in the flesh. In 1983, despite heavy opposition including that of the governor, the schoolchildren of Montana mounted a huge petition campaign that resulted in the grizzly's being declared the official state animal. But far too often, when it comes to dollars-and-cents issues, local support for the bear is drowned out by the typically more skilled and more tenacious proponents of development. The people whom land managers *hear from*—day after day, vociferously, and often in person—tend to be those who would profit at the grizzly bear's expense.

The complexity of the task of assessing and then mitigating the effects of development in grizzly country is best seen in northwestern Montana, where the bear's habitat is a hodgepodge of jurisdictions—national parks, national forest wilderness areas, multiple-use national forest lands, Bureau of Land Management rangeland, state parks and refuges and forests, corporation-owned timberlands, Indian reservations, ranches, even towns—almost all of them under one sort of assault or another, or several at once. Let us leave Yellowstone awhile and look there.

The wretched gravel road that ascends the North Fork of the Flathead River fosters an inescapable sense that one is very near the tip-tail-end of nowhere. The generous and orderly ranchlands and cherry orchards of the plains surrounding Flathead Lake fall away behind, and ahead the savage shadow-forests of the north close in. Only twice, as the road crests a rise above broad riparian meadows, can one see, across an unbroken sea of valley-bottom timber to the east, the awesome jumble of snowpeaks that is Glacier National Park and the continent's spine. From the west, dirt spur-roads debouch logging trucks rampaging out of the highlands of the Whitefish Range. Some-

where far to the north, the river spills from the glacial crest of the British Columbian Rockies, and even down here, many granite miles into Montana, the water retains a frigid, sterile clarity. Because of its low concentration of dissolved minerals, the river supports relatively little aquatic life besides the massive yearly spawning runs of Flathead Lake's cutthroat trout, bull trout, and landlocked salmon, on which the eagles and the ospreys then feast.

There is one "town," of a sort, called Polebridge: a store, a bar (lit by Coleman lamplight), a few cabins, and one public phone, whose number, in its entirety, is 13.

Ten miles farther north, there is another log cabin, a community center serving the scattered old-timers and young exiles whose dwellings are strung sparsely up and down the sixty miles of valley. Today, however, it is other local residents who are represented here—the grizzly bear and the timber wolf. The annual meeting of the Grizzly-Wolf Technical Workshop has filled the center to overflowing with some hundred and fifty people from all over North America. The size of the crowd is due in no small part to one man, a biology professor at the University of Montana named Charles Jonkel.

Besides having founded the Border Grizzly Project and presiding over the many ongoing grizzly research endeavors in the region of the Northern Continental Divide, Jonkel is chairman of the Bear Specialist Group of the International Union for the Conservation of Nature and Natural Resources, the Geneva-based organization whose offshoot the World Wildlife Fund is perhaps better known. In this capacity Jonkel monitors the status of six bear species (and now, since the possible discovery of a whole new species in Nepal in 1983, perhaps seven) scattered throughout seventy countries, with thirty or more languages involved. Getting jealous, mutually resentful, and often fiercely opposed jurisdictions to cooperate on behalf of bears, therefore, is a frustration Chuck Jonkel knows well—although he has had remarkable success getting such cooperation here along the North Fork of the Flathead.

"Now, be sure to watch old Chuck," another biologist has warned. "First of all, every time I see the guy he's a little bit hairier. Notice how when his back itches he'll just back up to a tree and slide up and down. And you've got to see him do his grizzly body language routine to believe it. Sometimes I think Chuck speaks better bear than most of the bears I know."

Jonkel also, in a voice strangely high and soft for so bearish a mien, speaks very persuasive English: "Our task as researchers," he tells the assembled group, "is a lot more than just basic science. Wildlife biologists have often found themselves in the position of the poet whose wife divorced him because he never seemed to do much of anything but look out the window. Development in the border grizzly area is coming so fast that every day we researchers fall a little farther behind, so it's more and more true that if our research can't be put directly to work by managers, they're just going to do what they always used to do—ignore it. Our findings aren't worth a damn unless we *coordinate* them—with previous data, and with one another—and then *communicate* them to the land managers. It's our responsibility to make them realize, for example, that even in the relatively small border grizzly area, research and management problems are different in the Selkirks, in the Cabinets, on the Black-feet Reservation, in Glacier National Park, or in any ecologically distinct area. Take the Rocky Mountain Front, east of the Bob Marshall Wilderness. That's probably the hottest area in the U.S. for oil and gas exploration, and there are grizzly bears living eighteen or twenty miles east of the mountains, out on the prairie. The oil companies and the agencies want to extrapolate a standard approach from existing data, which makes me ask them, 'Are you planning to use seismic data from Texas to look for oil in Montana?'

"Or right here, in the Glacier View Ranger District of the Flat-head National Forest. They've done a cumulative impact statement that's really a magnificent achievement. They've projected the effects of all development on grizzly bears for five years, and they've tried throughout to mitigate the negative effects. When they cut timber, for example, it will be done in such a way that it may even improve grizzly habitat. They'll be closing roads, and keeping out of essential spring and fall habitat components, leaving travel corridors for bears. The cutting will be timed so as not to interfere with known patterns of grizzly use, and the ground will be treated in such a way that desirable vegetation will spring up fast—similar to the effect of a natural fire. All this is great. But the fact is that what they're doing is only *reducing* an impact that is fundamentally negative. I'm alarmed as hell to see this seismic exploration proceeding at such an extremely rapid rate. Just here in the North Fork valley alone, Amoco has got three helicopters and fifty-two men on seismic crews. They're spending sixteen thousand dollars a day just on helicopters. Of course"—here Jonkel pauses for a wry chuckle—"somebody did blow up a quarter million dollars' worth of helicopter for them last year. Of course, it was insured. Anyway, nobody has any idea what effect this seismic stuff is having on grizzlies—and the companies are unwilling to pay to find out. Have we got anybody here from Amoco? No? Well, they said they were going to send a representative."

Over breakfast, over lunch, over dinner, through meetings all day long and bull sessions long into the nights, the bear talk goes on. There are plaid-shirted biologists in from Alaska and Canada, deep-tanned sheep ranchers convinced that radio collars make bears kill sheep, professional conservationists with earnest looks and bulging files, forest rangers in Smokey the Bear hats and no-nonsense bare-necked haircuts, cheery student volunteers (Jonkel's acolytes) eagerly laboring at the endless chores, dogs racing gaily underfoot, and even, briefly, until his arrest by the local constabulary on suspicion of suspicion, a wild-eyed and impressively begrimed wanderer passing through on his rather indirect way overland from Oregon to Arizona in the company of a white mule, a brown horse, and two large rifles—which, he asseverates, serve only to keep him in roasted ground squirrels.

There are as many opinions here as experts. University of Washington professor Albert Erickson, whose pioneering study of black bears was cited in an earlier chapter, is now under contract to the American Smelting and Refining Company (Asarco) to survey the area in and around the Cabinet Mountains Wilderness where the company has proposed an enormous silver and copper mining operation at Chicago Peak. Erickson has estimated that there are no more than eight or ten grizzlies living in the Cabinets.

"On the basis of a few days flying around in helicopters! It's ridiculous!" is Jonkel's response. Three of Jonkel's students—unpaid but for their groceries, which he buys out of his own pocket—are conducting their own grizzly search in the Cabinets, and theirs will be the only data available to pose against or corroborate Erickson's. "Chicago Peak is the worst possible place for a mine in that area, and you know it. It chops the corridor between the east and west Cabinets right in two."

"The attitude in industry today," Erickson replies, "is that researchers are always crying wolf. Resistance to development in many cases is over marginal habitat, where one or two grizzly bears stand in the way of critical resources."

"But industry has been sandbagging legitimate concerns," Jonkel counters. "We've gathered a lot of data that's been disregarded because they didn't like the findings."

"Researchers are such copout artists!" Erickson shoots back. "The manager asks a question, and the researcher says, 'Give me forty thousand dollars and five years and I'll try to find out.' But industry has to move forward."

There will be plenty more discussion of Asarco's Chicago Peak mining complex and its metastasizing ilk in the next couple of days, so Jonkel is content to deflect this blow. "Like the man who asked an engineer what two and two was," he smiles. "The engineer said, 'Exactly two plus exactly two is exactly four.' Next, the man asks a lawyer how much two and two is. The lawyer answers, 'Well, how much do you want it to be?' Finally the man comes to a wildlife biologist and asks him how much two and two is. After a long, thoughtful pause, the wildlife biologist says, 'Um, I think we need more data.' "

The joke comes to unfunny life on the East Front of the Rockies, where the two-plus-two is the effect of oil and gas exploration and extraction on the grizzlies who live there. The biologist who must continue to postpone giving a definitive answer to the question— because it is just too complicated—is Keith Aune (pronounced *awny*). He has been doing grizzly research on the Rocky Mountain Front for three years now, and a picture of the unique life of bears there is only beginning to emerge. In high summer, most East Front grizzlies live like most other Rocky Mountain grizzlies—foraging in the remote sanctuary of the peaks and alpine plateaus of the central wilderness (in this case, the Bob Marshall). But in spring and fall, and for some of these bears in summer too, the most productive habitat is to be found well out on the plains to the east of the mountains, in a region of cattle ranches, roads, towns, Minuteman missile silos, and, increasingly, oil wells.

The East Front is a topographic dazzler. The Great Plains roll treeless for miles in a gently rising westward wave toward the jagged wreckage of tectonic collision that forms a spectacular mountain wall. There are virtually no foothills. There is very little sense of transition at all except, in the last few miles of the plain, the limber pine savanna, where the dwarfed wind-bowed conifers produce an occasional bear bounty of nuts. Out of the canyons, many of them mere cracks in the mountain wall, pour streams whose waters sweep preternaturally fast through the mild slopes of the savanna, and along these streams grows luxuriant early succulent vegetation that draws many grizzlies down from the snowbound heights in spring. Where the pine-flecked savannas give way to open prairie, there are extensive, virtually impenetrable wetlands, nourished from underground strata of mountain aquifers leaching sidewise into the edge of the flats, and here the abundance and diversity of bear foods are spectacular. For the bears to reach these feeding paradises, however, they must cross a great deal of distinctly nonwilderness land. Although the dense streamside vegetation affords adequate cover through which to travel from the mountains to the prairie swamps, movement from one feeding site to another frequently involves trips overland across open, treeless range. Until very recent years, the density of human use has been sufficiently low that, despite a hundred years of active ranching and agriculture on these high plains, the bears have learned to steer clear of conflict. These grizzlies are only very rarely cow killers (although they do sometimes feed on cattle carrion). The occasional pickup truck raising a plume of dust down a nearby road, a pair of cowboys on horseback pushing their stock through the limber pines to the next creek north, a platoon of yelping children playing tag amidst the cottonwoods behind a remote ranch house— none of these has ever really disturbed the grizzlies living here. When the truck goes by, the bears lie low; when the cowboys and cows rumble through, they flee to the riverine thickets; ranch houses and children and all that smells of constant man-use they simply avoid. In turn, the local people have left them alone. The people here are proud and jealous of the old-fashionedness of their way of life—the open spaces, the neighborliness tempered with stern self-sufficiency, the wildness which they are always so near. Elk and deer and even bighorn sheep winter on these ranches and are welcome, despite the fact that they reduce cattle forage. A few bad-tempered old curmudgeons abominate grizzly bears on general principles and occasionally shoot them, but by far the majority of the citizens hereabouts see the grizzly as an exemplar of the differentness, the naturalness, the non-nostalgic anachronism of a life that is still, unaffectedly, the real Old West. There is little of this kind of living left anywhere in the world, and they know it. The ranchers and the townsmen of the East Front see the sun set, splendidly, over the mighty horizon of one of North America's wildest and richest wildernesses, and they like it like that.

It may be said, however, that the naturalness and old-fashionedness of this way of life have been a case of necessity made virtue. There has been no more profitable a use for the prairies of the Rocky Mountain Front than low-impact spread-out ranching and agriculture. Even the installation of the awesomely mute Minuteman complex has barely marred the land. All you can see of these monstrous engines of death are little squares of bare land ruled off by mild-mannered chain-link fences bearing small signs that read, "Restricted Area: Use of Deadly Force Authorized," plus a bunch of small-print military gobbledygook with the general import that if you were going to climb some fence or another, pick another. Within each square you see a gray steel gate flush with the earth, beneath which may or may not lurk a missile aimed at Leningrad, and a gray steel grate through which air softly rushes, whether in or out is hard to say, somewhere beneath which there may or may not be a crew of rocket-sitters at their computer displays, with red phones to their high command and forty-fives strapped to their sides for assassinating their colleagues should same go bananas. There is no parking lot for the crew, no evidence of human occupancy at all. Strange, is it not, that a technological development capable of ruining all civilization should have so little impact on the lives of grizzly bears; yet at night grizzlies graze unperturbed at the very edge of the missile silo quadrangles.

The real explosion on the East Front has been the coming of the oil industry. With the advent of new techniques for extracting the deep-lying hydrocarbons beneath the tectonic overthrust, ranchers have begun to set their sights on real money. *Big* money. And because so much of this land is privately owned and thus not subject to the conservation rules that apply on even the least restricted multiple-use government property, exploration and drilling have been able to move right in, without worrying much about environmental damage.

The visible effects of exploration or drilling for oil can seem quite minor. You look out across the plains west of U.S. 89 toward the Bob Marshall Wilderness, and the gentle rhythm of the little rocking-horses of the oil wells seems as placid and modest as the white spin of an old-time farm windmill. But linking those wells are pipelines, and maintaining pipelines and wells requires roads, and roads bring people, and people bring guns. Seismic testing brings lots of people, and the kind of folks who work on the crews are not, frankly, exactly the first ones you would pick for not taking potshots at grizzly bears. Even once the exploration is over and the well is in, and quiet has seemed to return, the roads remain open, and what has been remote rangeland with little enough human disturbance that grizzly bears used it freely is now the domain of jeepers and rough-necks and motorcyclists and come who may, and no longer the grizzly's own. The oil fields here are proving to be rather rich ones, and exploration and extraction are moving rapidly closer to the mountain front, where the government lands begin. Here environmental information becomes crucial, and here, to their credit, several private companies have kicked in a bit of funding for the interagency research effort which Keith Aune leads—Williams Exploration Company, Sun Exploration Company, Superior Oil, and American Petrofina. It need hardly be added that there are a good many other companies making millions on East Front oil without spending a nickel on grizzly bears. In that light, the initiative of the contributing companies warrants strong praise, for in most cases private developers have shown that they would much rather not know the impacts of the activities they profit from.

Aune has gathered data that seem not just to look his gift horse in the mouth but to kick it in the teeth. Seismic exploration for oil and natural gas is a noisy and dramatic affair. Long lines of high explosive charges are set off at or near ground level, and a battery of electronic monitors can then analyze the shock waves reflected from deep underground for the possible presence of oil or gas. The explosives must be powerful and spaced fairly close together for an accurate picture to emerge, and that, in this deeply quiet country so blessedly unriddled with roads, means helicopters, off-road vehicles, lots of workers, and lots of noise. Aune has tracked a number of radio-collared East Front grizzlies before, during, and after such disturbances, and in every case the effect, not surprisingly, has been for grizzlies in the area either to expand their home ranges substantially or to move out altogether. "And you need to realize," Aune points out, "that if the directly affected grizzly is a really dominant adult, he may just be able to move and will make out fine. He may displace another bear, who may also do fine. But somewhere down the line, maybe far away from the original disturbance, some bear is going to lose crucial habitat. Sure, we can look at the local bears and show how well they get along with the seismic work, and that's just what everybody wants to hear. But it's not the whole story. The real story may be miles away."

The Northern Continental Divide's grizzly country is a land where, despite the superficial appearance of pristinity, the ripples of development are already overlapping. Although the central grizzly population is still believed to be healthy enough to support a limited hunting season, almost all of northwestern Montana is under assault from resourse development. Among the most dramatic incursions into grizzly country here is the proposed Asarco operation in the Cabinet Mountains, which may well do irreparable damage to a small and increasingly isolated population of grizzlies.

As a biologist for the Kootenai National Forest, Alan Christensen has had to figure out ways to mitigate the Asarco project's many negative effects. His position is inherently an uncomfortable one—

tugged forever back and forth, on one side by the Forest Service's multiple-use mandate and its longstanding utilitarian psychology and, on the other, by a scientist's naturally longer-term concerns and the love of nature that draws people to such jobs in the first place. Unlike some others caught in the same sort of bind, Christensen does not try to have it both ways. "We're caught in the middle of a conflict in the laws," he explains. "The Endangered Species Act says we have to protect the grizzly bear, but the Surface Mining Act and the Wilderness Act tell us we have to provide reasonable access for mineral claims. So what we've tried to do is minimize Asarco's impact on the bear. We've got very strict guidelines on on-site disturbance. The drill rigs are set on pads so the soil won't be compacted. We require complete restoration of the site, and the company has been very cooperative about it. There was a small spill this past year that stained some rock, and Asarco sent in a cleanup team to scrub it off with biodegradable detergent. We also require them to fly out all their slurry. I'll tell you, those drill sites are hard to find after they've finished.

"The real stress to the bear is not habitat loss, but displacement because of human access, and the biological evaluation that we did recommends very significant restraints on access. The helicopters they use to reach the rigs have to fly in very narrow flight corridors, and they're limited to certain times of day and certain times of the year. There's a total prohibition of exploration during the grizzlies' emergence and denning periods. And, according to patterns of habitat use, some segments are closed entirely until the first of August, and others are closed after that.

"Still, we did get a jeopardy opinion from the Fish and Wildlife Service." (All large-scale federal activities that may affect a threatened or endangered species must be reviewed by the Fish and Wildlife Service, and if the species is found to be jeopardized, either the project must be modified or the affected habitat must be replaced by other land of equal suitability.) "There's no question that the exploration will affect the bears' travel patterns. So we've agreed to compensate for the lost habitat. We're delaying a number of timber sales, and we're going to be closing quite a few roads—which has been a big hassle with the local people. And then we were sued because we did just an environmental assessment, which doesn't require public participation, instead of an environmental impact statement, which does. We won the suit, but it's still under appeal. A lot of people don't understand that the big problem is not the mining but the increased settlement and increased human activities that come in with it."

Hank Fischer, of Defenders of Wildlife—which is one of the plaintiffs—responds: "First of all, the Surface Mining Act of 1872 is not inviolate. The Forest Service is supposed to decide if mining is in conflict with *surface* resources. They usually duck the issue, but they *can* decide in favor of protecting the resource. Next, you have to realize that all of this concerns only the exploration phase. Extraction is a whole new ball game. You don't notice Asarco or the Forest Service talking about that."

The Forest Service is often cast as the villain in these dramas, and there is no doubt that in some cases they have richly deserved the opprobrium. Bill Schneider, author of *Where the Grizzly Walks*, says, "If the grizzly bear goes extinct, it will have been the Forest Service that did it." But here and there, by fits and starts, even the Forest Service is changing. The men and women who came aboard in the late sixties and the seventies are now moving into positions of influence, and bringing with them the sensibilities of a new generation. Management direction is frequently still purely development-oriented, but voices of ecological reason are now heard even in the small, private meetings where, for all the big talk about public input, the really important planning—the formulation of options—is carried out. The result so far is a great discordant hash of Forest Service policies, often widely at variance even between national forests sharing long common boundaries. For those who are trying to coordinate the grizzly bear's recovery, this is a nightmare. But perhaps from a more distant perspective it can be seen as an encouraging sign of change under way.

Probably partly in response to the lawsuit against Asarco's Chicago Peak development, for example, Christensen and the Kootenai National Forest have carried out an ambitiously detailed analysis of all their grizzly habitat, using the habitat component and cumulative effects mapping techniques developed by the Border Grizzly Project. They have stratified with admirable precision those areas which provide for year-round habitat needs, including denning; those which provide certain critical elements, although they may lack others; those which are seasonally critical, such as low-elevation spring and fall range; those which are essential primarily as movement corridors, with cover needs rather than food values predominant; and, finally, those areas considered unsuitable for grizzlies. Thus, as the Kootenai National Forest's integrated forest plan is developed, and the computers rattle out the options, a highly specific understanding of the grizzly's needs will be taken into account.

The Kootenai's management planning, as in many other Western national forests, is complicated by checkerboard ownership, where every other square-mile section of some parts of the forest is in private hands. In much of the Kootenai's grizzly habitat, those hands are Burlington Northern's. It is much to BN's credit—and a sad index of other companies' indifference—that Lorin Hicks and his staff at Burlington Northern are the only corporation-employed wildlife biologists in the Rockies. "What's been of greatest importance to us," he says, "is learning that every grizzly population is different in its habitat use and its movements. If there's no literature existing for a given area, we go in and do the research ourselves. Of course, we've done a lot of cooperative work with the Forest Service—most recently, mapping habitat in the Cabinets and the Swan Valley, and working to establish a protected movement corridor between the Missions and the Bob Marshall. I don't like to brag, but BN is the first private company to win the Group Achievement Award of the Wildlife Society—that's our professional biologists' association—and I'm very proud of that. Because of work like ours, polarization between industry and the agencies is on the decrease. We've started to try to look at our use of the land through grizzly-colored glasses."

Scratching his back grizzly-fashion against a tree, exactly as his colleague had predicted, Chuck Jonkel pauses for breath on a mountain crest in the Whitefish Range, where he has led a field trip from the Border Grizzly meeting. At his feet is a shallow excavation where a root-grubbing grizzly has been churning up the ridgetop, and far below there stretches a ravaged clear-cut at the head of the drainage. "All these conflicts, the way they end up in the press, it's always the grizzly standing in the way of development. But just look down there. That whole bottom was wet woods, full of grizzly foods, superb spring and fall range—and it was all but worthless as timber. And this cut didn't ruin it just for bears. They've got downstream erosion now, and the way they scarified the soil"—plowing up the root systems of understory perennial vegetation so that trees can be replanted immediately—"has meant that none of the usual successional plant species are coming back—the berry bushes, and the succulent forbs. So it's just about useless for any wildlife. It'll probably take this land two hundred years to recover. I always stress that although the grizzly's needs are prominent because their scale is so big, when you save the grizzly you save the whole ecosystem. Luckily, I don't think we're going to be seeing much more of this kind of thing. Forest Service timber-cutting practices are supposed to take grizzlies into account now. But we've still got plenty of problems."

Plenty is something of an understatement. Besides the onward rush of oil and gas exploration on the Rocky Mountain Front, there is extensive hard rock and uranium exploration under way in the Kootenais, and oil and gas exploration on the Blackfeet Indian Reservation. A ski resort has been proposed adjacent to the Cabinet Mountains Wilderness in some of the best grizzly habitat in the entire Kootenai National Forest. There are conflicts between grizzlies and residential subdivisions in the Flathead Lake basin, and between grizzlies and a bitterly hostile local populace in the Selkirks. Because many timber sales were held back due to the depression in the construction industry, timing constraints meant to diffuse pressure on grizzly habitat are flying out the window. In Glacier Park itself there is continuing fear of strife between visitors and those grizzly bears there who seem to be habituated to human food sources: at the Many Glacier campground, backpackers now sleep inside a chain-link fence, and park management is considering closing off whole areas to human use, despite burgeoning backcountry visitorship. Glacier's grizzly population will inevitably be affected by the explosion of development outside park boundaries. A proposed widening and paving of the gravel road up the North Fork of the Flathead has been stopped by a Fish and Wildlife Service opinion stating that the massive expected increase in traffic along the new road would jeopardize the grizzly, but pressure for development along the North Fork—mining, logging, and residential construction—is likely to keep the issue alive for years to come. U.S. Highway 2, the principal access route to Glacier Park, is slated for widening and straightening, which will radically increase traffic and its speed through the heart of grizzly country, and that is bound to disrupt grizzly travel patterns. Virtually all the proposed logging, mining, oil and gas drilling, and residential developments will require new roads, some of them extensive networks, and studies on the North Fork of the Flathead have already suggested that grizzlies in this ecosystem consistently avoid areas within one-half mile of roads.

Direst of all, one of the world's largest coal-mining complexes is planned on the North Fork in British Columbia, just northwest of Glacier Park, and the pollution and disruption it will cause are likely to be devastating. One open-pit mine alone will be a thousand feet deep and one mile across. It will employ six hundred people, fifty miles from the nearest town, in the very middle of what until now has been inaccessible wilderness supporting one of the densest grizzly populations in North America. Mines already in operation there are producing twelve million tons of coal annually, and their yearly output will soon exceed thirty million tons. Planning is under way for several more huge mines to go into production within the next few years, bringing in thousands more workers. Moira Farrow has written in the *Vancouver Sun*: "Coal mining in the East Kootenay is not news. But its immensity, viewed from the air, is astonishing. Lakes are being drained. Overburden is piled hundreds of metres high. Mining camps are being cut out of the bush. And the smell of coal dust fills the air. Raw coal production in this area increased thirteen times from 1968 to 1975, and since then it has quadrupled again."

The cumulative effect of these activities can barely be even guessed at. Research has yet to show definitely how grizzlies will react to certain kinds of disturbance, but what little is known is mightily unpromising. Still, Chuck Jonkel clings to hope. "Sure, the projections are gloomy. But they often don't figure on the bear's intelligence and adaptability and individuality. Don't underestimate these damn grizzlies. They do things they're not supposed to be able to do. There are isolated small populations in northern Italy and along the Spanish-French border, just ten to twenty bears in each, and they've been self-sustaining for sixty years. There's a population in northern Norway of fewer than a hundred bears, and they've been surviving for more than a hundred years."

It must be reemphasized, however, that the encroachment on those European brown bears' habitats has come far more slowly than what is being experienced in American grizzly country, and European bears have had thousands of years to get used to living close to civilization. Moreover, as Jonkel himself makes clear, the long-term prognosis for the European population he cites is decidedly poor; the populations in the Italian Alps and in the Pyrenees are probably already doomed remnants, merely taking a long time to die out.

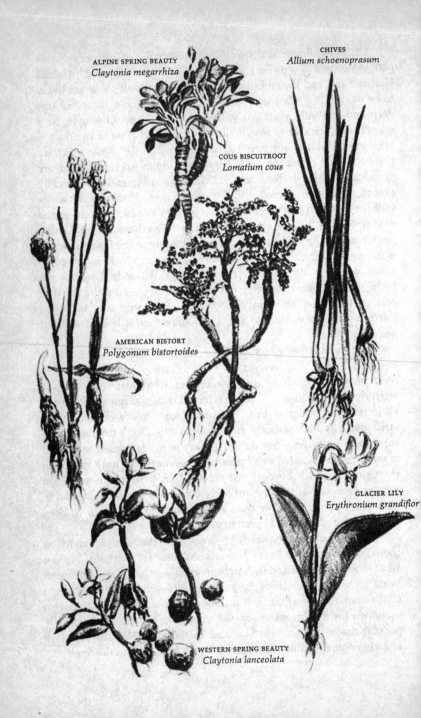

ALPINE SPRING BEAUTY
Claytonia megarrhiza

CHIVES
Allium schoenoprasum

COUS BISCUITROOT
Lomatium cous

AMERICAN BISTORT
Polygonum bistortoides

GLACIER LILY
Erythronium grandiflor

WESTERN SPRING BEAUTY
Claytonia lanceolata

Nevertheless, Jonkel's optimism may yet be justified if not through the grizzly's own unpredictable adaptability then perhaps by the rapidly increasing accuracy and utility of scientific research aimed at determining just how far the grizzly can be pushed and what measures will be most effective in insuring the bear's continued existence. There is a prodigious amount of bear research under way— the major part of it on the more widespread and more easily observed black bear, but much of that applicable to the grizzly as well.

Some of the research seems almost fantastic. John Craighead, for example, is now leading an interdisciplinary team in trying to establish a technique for analyzing grizzly habitat with satellite imagery. The researchers began by performing probably the broadest analysis of grizzly habitat ever carried out, in a primary study area in Montana's Lincoln-Scapegoat Wilderness and two secondary areas with contrasting ecological characteristics—identifying which plants within the study areas were significant as grizzly foods, determining their distribution and abundance, classifying the ecotypes and climatic zones that produced them, and finally relating all those data to actual grizzly use as indicated by scats and other sign.

With the next stage in research, the real magic began. NASA's Earth Resources Technology Satellites LANDSAT-1, launched in 1972, and LANDSAT-2, in orbit since 1975, measure the intensity of light reflected from the earth's surface in four wavelength ranges— green, red, photographic infrared, and near-infrared—and then electrically transmit to earth a continuous record of those measurements. Information from each band is converted into a photographic image covering a rough square about one hundred fifteen miles on a side. Each image contains something over six million "pixels," or picture elements, and each pixel covers a bit over one acre of ground. By comparing the multispectral values of each pixel with the vegetative communities which they had already "ground-truthed," the researchers were able eventually, after a great deal of technical struggle with the difficulties of mountainous topography and the density of forest canopy cover, to arrive at a range of energy reflectance which expressed the unique light-bouncing properties of each of the grizzly bear habitat types. Write a computer program derived from those reflectance values, feed it the appropriate LANDSAT images, and abracadabra! you have a vegetation map.

Needless to say, it did not come about quite that easily. There were months of ground-truthing, technical hangups, revision, and refining. Habitat typing involves a certain amount of artificial pigeon-holing, since in fact plant communities intergrade continuously with one another, and the transitional zones are hard to figure out how to treat. Extrapolation from the fully ground-truthed study plots to biologically similar areas was eventually able to reach eighty-five to ninety percent accuracy. Craighead and his associates believe that their satellite analysis techniques will prove to be tremendous time- and money-savers in a wide variety of applications, from evaluating elk habitat to laying out timber sales in remote wild areas. Satellite imagery can also be used to monitor the impact of development activities ongoing in grizzly habitat. For each new major ecological community, however, quite a bit of ground-truthing is required, and the new data must then be incorporated into the computer program. If that work can be accomplished for a broad range of ecosystems, the resulting data base can be used over and over again, charting the progress of various ecotypes through their seral stages. With each new use and the resultant refinements, the accuracy of the data base will grow still greater.

There do remain substantial technical difficulties with the use of satellite imagery. "Until it is more tested," writes biologist Larry Roop, "there are some bad problems. Others have looked into using this method and have been very disappointed with what could be done—hence the lack of excitement thus far from anyone but NASA and the Craigheads. When Dick Knight tried to get habitat readouts from satellite imagery, it gave Yellowstone Lake as being lodgepole pine forest! Not that it doesn't have great potential, but at present its value is overstated."

For the quality of its habitat analysis alone, however, the project has been a conspicuously excellent piece of bear research. Whether satellite analysis will prove to have broad practical applications remains to be seen, but the idea of monitoring the inner life of whole ecosystems on the largest conceivable scale is clearly one whose time has come—and nowhere more so than in grizzly habitat which is subject to resource exploitation, where the effects of disruption may be far separated in both time and space from the cause—and the Craighead group's techniques for remote sensing may prove to have been a bold first step toward an unprecedented degree of intimacy with large frames of ecological reference.

. . .

Every three years, most of the bear researchers in the world get together under the auspices of the International Association for Bear Research and Management to present new research findings, exchange ideas, take potshots at one another's data, and hoist a few, and it is at these meetings that the amazing scope of contemporary bear research is best seen. In Alaska, a group is studying the population dynamics of grizzlies on the north slope of the Brooks Range, at the northernmost limit of grizzly country, where they grow so slowly that females may be ten years old before they first give birth to cubs. Along Hudson Bay, a Canadian team is investigating the remarkable ability of polar bears to navigate accurately across trackless sea ice. Another group is studying the effects of capturing, chemically immobilizing, and handling bears. There is a report on the expansion of a brown bear population from the Soviet Union into Finland. The latest scoop on cranial variation in polar bears is presented. The differences in regional food habits of grizzly bears in Montana are analyzed. Breeding behavior, feeding strategies, social relationships, energy budgets, movement patterns, maternal care, bear-human interactions, computer modeling of populations, and correlations between bear distribution and habitat types are treated in research papers. Are there still a few grizzlies living in the remote highlands of Mexico's Sierra del Nido? (Maybe.) What changes in bear management should be made in Canadian national parks? (Many.) What are the effects of hunting on a black bear population? (Reduction of population size, decline in mean age of males.) Has anybody figured out an effective bear repellent yet, other than a thirty-ought-six? (No.) How important is the role of curiosity in learning in cubs? (Very, even when unrelated to food.) How can orphaned young bears most successfully be reintroduced to the wild? (Probably by planting them in dens in fall.) How is the brown bear doing in Bulgaria? (Fine. Population stable at about five hundred, hunting forbidden.) How do naïve barren-ground grizzlies in the far North react to oil pipeline construction? (Abandon dens sometimes, raid camps, decline in numbers, perhaps ultimately adjust if certain procedures are followed.) Why do there seem to be separate coastal bear populations on Admiralty Island, one feeding on spawning salmon in summer while the other remains above timberline eating berries? (No idea yet.)

The relevance of much of the bear research discussed at these conferences to the larger spheres of human activity may seem tenuous. A great deal of it is directed ultimately toward protecting the bear from human pursuits that will go forward whether bears figure into the plans or not, and this proportion of the research, therefore, may be said to profit mankind only at the esthetic level; certainly the survival or extinction of the grizzly bear will have negligible impact on the health of the earth as a whole. The significance of that esthetic or cultural aspect is a central assumption of this book, but it's also nice to think that there may also be tangible benefits from bear research. It must be remembered that time and time again, seemingly irrelevant basic scientific research has stumbled over immeasurable boons to humanity. One thinks, for example, of how bread mold turned out to produce penicillin. Perhaps one day we may also think of what came of the study of bear hibernation.

Ralph Nelson, director of research at the Carle Foundation Hospital of the University of Illinois School of Medicine, has been looking at the physiology and biochemistry of hibernation for some years now, and has turned up some pretty astounding facts. Bears do hibernate (there was once some question as to whether you could really call it that, since they are so much more easily roused than classic hibernators like woodchucks), and while doing so they maintain themselves in a fashion entirely unique in the animal kingdom. We will learn all about the process when our grizzly bear prepares for denning this fall. Suffice it for the moment to say that hibernating bears' ability to break down and reuse the poisons produced by their own bodies may offer exciting new avenues for research on human renal disease. Nelson has also suggested that the principles of bear hibernation might somehow be applied in prolonged space travel by humans, where food storage capacity and the ability of astronauts to endure long confinement would both be in short supply. He proposes as well that hibernating bears themselves would be ideal experimental space pioneers. "If the Russians can tame bears so that they can play hockey," he has written, "perhaps NASA or other organizations can teach them to navigate a spacecraft."

Meanwhile, back on earth—and back in Yellowstone—Dick Knight and his colleagues on the Interagency Grizzly Bear Study Team are deep in less cosmic pursuits. This is the height of the study season, and the height of the bear-problem season too. Lodges along the

North Fork of the Shoshone near the park's east entrance are having their garbage cans rifled nightly, and the miscreants are regularly being trapped, radio-collared if need be, and transported to the back-woods. Grizzlies are smashing up apple orchards near Gardiner, and robbing picnic hampers in West Yellowstone. Grizzlies are being spotted well outside what have been considered the limits of occupied habitat, and ignorantly optimistic citizens are shooting off their mouths in the newspapers about a grizzly resurgence and by God let's reinstate the hunting season to protect our women and children —when what these far-flung sightings really reflect are social discord due to the disproportionate number of males in the population (lead-ing to wider movements by dispersing young males), and continuing adjustment to a long-term decline in food supply due to the dump closures and perhaps also in part to climatic change. All these prob-lems must be addressed, usually *right now*, by the study team. They are the ones who must trap the problem bears, and argue with certain obstinate managers for hours that repeat offenders should be trans-ported yet again rather than shot, and keep up with all their radio-collared grizzlies' movements, and, if they're lucky enough to be listened to, try to get the complex facts into the papers to refute the simplistic slogans. Somewhere in all this, in between chasing trouble bears and sitting in meetings and dealing with the endless im-portunate trivia, Knight and his team are also supposed to be getting some research done.

Somehow, through the years, they have managed to do so. Drawing on the work of earlier researchers, they have described the physiography, the vegetation, the history, the climate, and the fauna of Yellowstone. Year after year they have traced grizzly move-ments, and learned much about grizzly home ranges and overall distribution in the ecosystem. They have done extensive work on grizzly food habits: carcass surveys to establish an index of carrion availability and use; long hours of scat collection and analysis to determine food preferences; examinations of feeding sites; transects of whitebark pine stands to assess nut production, grizzly use, and the effect of the current pine bark beetle epidemic; and even a study of the use and importance of ants as grizzly food. The team has investigated overall habitat type preferences, and the use of areas affected by wildfire. They have studied the nature of grizzlies' con-flicts with man, and grizzly predation on livestock in the Yellowstone area. They have located, measured, and analyzed grizzlies' day beds.

They have experimented with time-lapse cameras, and invented an expandable radio collar to be used on young, growing bears. They have discovered that grizzlies' use of forested country in Yellowstone is much higher than had been believed. They have studied the locations, habitat types, elevations, aspects, shapes, sizes, and construction of grizzly winter dens. And, to an extent perhaps equaling all those subjects combined, they have wrestled with the intractable questions of population—productivity, sex and age structures, survivorship, mortality, and, that bugbear of bear bugs, population size.

Knight's population work has elicited howls of protest, shrugs of disdain, interminable technical commentary, bureaucratic plot and counterplot, hirings, firings, resignations, transfers, sensational journalism, nasty rumors, personal vengeance, and even, occasionally, a bit of quiet support. As we have already seen from the Craighead brouhaha, the size and trend of this grizzly population have long been a touchy subject. Add a personality like Knight's—he is less apt to respond to a challenge to his data with a soft-spoken review of his reasoning than with a terse "You got better?"—and you have biopolitical nitroglycerine. As it happens, of course, nobody does have better data, and, although everybody seems to have an opinion nevertheless, the explosive nature of the Knight persona has contributed significantly to the occasional triumphs of sound bear management over the half-baked fancies of the many folks in bear land who don't know recycled biscuitroot from shinola.

For behind the bluster, the strength of Dick Knight's position remains that it is based on what Chuck Jonkel calls *asking the bear*. When some gung-ho fish-and-game man starts talking about limiting protection of grizzlies to Yellowstone Park alone—this really happened, by the way, not too long ago—Knight can furnish data showing that of the eighty-four grizzlies he has instrumented, all but nine spent some of their time outside the park boundary. If a development is proposed for important grizzly habitat, Knight has the documentation: he can produce data on vegetative communities and the critical bear foods they contain, he can show how human activities may interfere with those foods' availability to bears, and he can specify the extent and intensity of previous use of the given habitat by grizzlies. In the past, speculation, prejudice, and fantasy have all too often guided policy making. But with the likes of Dick Knight and the Interagency Grizzly Bear Study Team around, nobody can get away with that any more—not, at least, without a fight.

The study team's information base gets harder to quibble with with every passing season. Besides their perpetual struggle with population data, the team's main work these days is documenting habitat use. This part of the study is not only the most interesting from a pure-science point of view—tracking energy flow through whole ecosystems, a task which is complicated by the grizzly's being both a secondary consumer (plant-eater) and a climax carnivore (eater of plant-eaters and others, and rarely himself eaten)—but also essential to understanding how grizzly bears are likely to be affected by changes in their environment.

One of the most important revelations of recent research has been the nature of grizzly bear nutrition. Because of their evolution as carnivores, bears' adaptation to using plant foods has been highly specific, and it has been shown that protein, the same thing their ancestors got from their all-meat diet, is the most important ingredient bears extract from plants. Carbohydrates in roots, tubers, and fruits are the next most important element in their diets. Owing to the limited digestive capacity of their carnivore gut, grizzlies must get their protein from plant cytoplasm when it is in liquid form—which means that most plants are usable only within a quite brief time span. An understanding of the ecosystem-wide availability of liquid protein (and, to a lesser extent, of high-quality carbohydrates) will tell you pretty accurately at any given moment where grizzly bears are likely to be.

In July, there is good food almost everywhere. For the grizzlies living near Yellowstone Lake and in the drainage of the upper river above the lake, the enormous spawning run of cutthroat trout continues to wriggle up the feeder streams. For the digging-minded bears of the grasslands, the meadow and ridgetop soils are full of roots, bulbs, corms, and rhizomes, all crisscrossed with tunnels in which juicy little rodents cower. For a fruit-loving grizzly, the streamsides and woods offer ripening huckleberries, buffaloberries, strawberries, gooseberries, thimbleberries, kinnikinnick, and mountain-ash. For salad aficionados there is a smorgasbord of spring beauty, elk thistle, white clover, oniongrass, American bistort, dogtooth violet, yampah, yarrow, horsetail, biscuitroot, sedges, grasses, and dozens of other good green things each to be harvested at its maximum of savor, later and later the higher they grow.

. . .

159

High in the alpine country of the Absaroka-Beartooth Wilderness, near the national park's northeastern corner, the grizzly and her cubs seem to float in a sea of wildflowers. The big bear's winter coat is falling off in slovenly patches, revealing a dark new coat shot through with the long silver-tipped guard hairs that give the grizzly the name. As summer progresses, the dark new fur will gradually bleach out in the sun, and by fall her back will be a sunny blond. The little ones are sleek and fat. This is a time of rapid growth, and placid ease. The bears may feed eighteen to twenty hours a day, the mother packing away up to eighty pounds of food, perhaps forty thousand calories' worth.

With food in such generous supply, bears should be in their most benign frame of mind, but the mother grizzly has been smelling people-scent all over the place, and she is in a nettled mood. With every passing summer, there seem to be more and more campers and hikers around, and fewer places where grizzlies can feed in peace, even here in the remote high country. The mother bear has not felt obliged to attack anybody yet, although a few years back she did charge one interloper up a tree when he made the mistake of walking between her day bed and a carcass she had buried nearby. Just for good measure she had also torn his pack to shreds, but she was too nervous to get into the food, what with the man hollering at her from the tree, and so she still has not developed a taste for freeze-dried tuna à la Neptune.

As we have seen, all grizzly bears are constantly aware of cover, and they usually feed near timber where they can quickly disappear. The absence of visible threat, especially where (as here in this alpine meadow) sight lines are long, is also a kind of cover. Late this afternoon, as dusk has come on, the grizzly and her cubs have risen from their sheltered sleeping-thicket and moved well out into the open, digging up bulbs and ants, in which they are so absorbed that none of them notices the human form creeping toward them from downwind.

At the sound of a faint metallic click, however, the big female whirls around, stands up—a tidy seven feet tall, thus—and takes a look. Who does this guy think he is? Another click from the camera. She drops to all fours and directs the cubs to flatten themselves against the ground, and proceeds to do her maternal duty. First she walks sideways with her back humped up to show the guy how big she is. Then she pops her jaws together loudly, meaning, "You are on my turf, and I am politely but firmly asking you to leave." But the guy doesn't move. He's scared stiff. He has read the brochure the rangers gave him, and he remembers that you should not try to run from a grizzly bear. With the hackles quivering on her hump, the bear lowers her head almost to the ground, a real warning of imminent attack, and stares straight into his eyes. The guy *still* doesn't get the message. He stands up slowly, knees knocking, ankles like jelly. He figures that because she is not snarling—which, despite the predilection of taxidermists from time immemorial, bears cannot do, since they lack the requisite lip-curling muscles—she must not really be mad. The guy is mistaken. She hurls herself at him like a lightning bolt.

Out in the middle of the big treeless alpine meadow, and clinging fast to the maxim about not running, he simply stands his ground and prepares to die. As his life unreels before his mind's eye and the bear reaches the last bound before she will be on him . . . she stops. Stops cold. And just stares at him, silent. He is shaking so hard he can barely stand, but he tries not to move. The bear snorts, spins around, and as fast as she had charged races away, woofing at the cubs to get the hell into those woods.

What happened? Hard to say. It may have been something she perceived as authoritative in the guy's body language, perhaps merely his declining to yield, or it may have been that at the last second the bear just chickened out. The whole thing may have been only a bluff in the first place. Another grizzly, in any case, might easily have killed the guy. On another day she might have done it herself. Grizzly bears are funny that way.

Elsewhere way out in the boonies, at Cooke Pass, Montana, in a little café on whose windows a grizzly on the prowl for garbage this morning has smeared his unmistakable signature, Larry Roop and Bart Schleyer are sipping coffee and awaiting the arrival of Steve Mealey and his grizzly ecology class from the Yellowstone Institute. Schleyer has already been down to the old Cooke City dump site to check the trap, and for the third morning in a row—thanks mainly to the earlier-mentioned entrepreneur whose garbage buffet has been drawing in bears from far and wide—they have caught another grizzly.

"Roop, you old hick," booms Mealey from the door, "you sure can catch bears!" Mealey wrote his master's thesis on the Yellowstone grizzly while working with the interagency study team, so he and Roop are old pals. He is here now to lead an exhaustive week-long seminar on every aspect of the grizzly's situation—biological, administrative, and political. The class has drawn a wildly diverse crowd of bear-lovers, ranging from professional wildlife biologists with Ph.D.s to a little besneakered antivivisectionist old lady who has hitchhiked in from Aspen. This morning's bear will be the first non-zoo grizzly they have ever seen.

"It wasn't me," Roop rejoins. "It was Bart who caught that bear. He just charms 'em in."

"I heard it's old Number One."

"Yep." This is a bear they both know well, the first ever captured in the interagency study, back in 1975. Old Number One has been a pretty good bear. Apart from killing a little livestock down in the Sunlight Basin, he has kept out of trouble with people, and, as Roop continues, "You just can't keep that bear out of the trap. I can't even remember how many times we've caught him."

Meanwhile, back at the dump, Number One slumbers tranquilly in the culvert trap he knows so well, his belly full of bait. The arrival of the human crowd seems to bother him not in the least. Roop recalls that this bear weighed about five hundred fifty pounds when they caught him last fall, and so Number One gets darted with an appropriate dose of anesthetic and tranquilizer. After fifteen minutes, the bear slumps to the floor of the trap, rolling his eyes and licking his lips. As they drag him from the culvert—to delighted oohs and ahs from the assembled seminar—identical expressions of pale horror come into Roop's and Schleyer's faces. In the dark shadow of the trap's interior they could not really make it out, but this seventeen-year-old grizzly bear is not, as he ought to be, in his prime. He is hide and bone—pelvis and ribs jutting starkly beneath thin, sagging skin. His fur is falling out in handfuls. And his weight is down to three hundred and fifty pounds.

This is bad. He has gotten much too much drug. A violent convulsion jolts through the bear, and his limbs flail spastically. Schleyer jams a stick in the mouth so the bear will not swallow his tongue—and, as suddenly as it came, the convulsion passes. Number One is breathing evenly now. "Poor old bear," Roop says quietly, lifting the head to fit him with his new radio collar.

"He's not going to make it, is he, Larry?" says Mealey, turning now to speak to the class. "By this point in the summer, this bear ought to have been gaining weight to carry him through the winter. He should be absolutely swaddled in fat. His coat ought to be thick and shiny. But as it is now, if he makes it through the fall he may well die in the den, or soon after he emerges next spring. Do you have any idea what might be the matter, Larry?"

"Not really. Grizzlies don't get sick very much. I think this bear just hasn't been getting enough to eat—I don't know why. Still, if he gets a few good meals, he might pull through. Bart, don't you think we can leave him this bait?'' They lower the quarter of a calf from the tree where it has hung, and lay it in the shade nearby. Number One begins to stir, and lifts his head weakly. Roop also has a reeking road-killed marmot in the back of his truck, and has scrounged a supply of spoiled sirloin steaks from a dude ranch whose freezer broke down, and he leaves a heap of those too.

AUGUST

THE sky is bluer than it has any right to be this side of heaven—
even at midafternoon only barely paling at the horizon toward the
white of transpiration—and the racing hard-edged clouds, though
big and near, yield only hard-edged racing shadows. An alcoholic
pine-exhalation comes on a breeze, and the dry tang of sage. No birds
call; only a chattering ground squirrel is up and about in the heat.
The far peaks' glare-glazed crescents of snowpack attenuate daily,
sweating into spongy rubble at their downhill margins. An eagle
hooks into a thermal and rises a slow regal mile into the blue and still
is as vividly sharp to the human eye as a human below is to his own.
The light is without character, partaking of nothing of the fierce glit-
ter of desert or the softening modulations of deciduous woodland:
an air altogether of absence: the absence of free water.

There is still, to be sure, much water here, but it is all tied up—
sluicing hurriedly by in the creeks and rivers now free of snowmelt
silt and clear, or falling in lavender curtains from bruise-colored afternoon thunderheads and evaporating before it ever touches earth, or,
most of all, in use in living tissues. Yellowstone is never more alive
than now, when its weather is driest: although the tawning range-
lands at the eastward foot of the Absaroka are grazed and trampled
and parched halfway to death already, and the temperature there is a
hundred degrees, here a mile above them on the upthrust plateau the
grass is green, the flowers are blooming, and the air is cool. This is
the timeless summer of dream, an abundance the more poignant because it is so brief. In its fullness the creatures of the wilderness seem
to move with an easy grace, the wealthy and secure in a time of
plenty, coats sleek, muscles strong, neither struggling for mates nor
aching for food.

Behind this appearance of ease there is a brutal race against
mortality—not, we must suppose, a conscious but certainly a purposeful struggle against the looming, all-engulfing, pitiless winter to
come. The grizzly and her cubs are round and soft with fat, and, if
they are to grow more so, and so to be fat enough to make it through
five months of sleep, their feeding strategy in this time of seeming
repletion must continually change. Although the meadows and
streamsides and woods are never so lush as now, the nutritional

value of many of the plants they produce is in steep decline: as they mature and flower and begin to produce seeds, the plants' structural elements, the cell walls of indigestible cellulose, are taking over from liquid protein cytoplasm. The grizzlies' diet now shifts toward fruits, whose abundance can be extremely variable, according to late frosts, dry or wet springs, or last winter's snowpack. In good years for, say, the huckleberry crop, in fruit-rich places like Glacier Park, grizzlies may feed happily together in the berry patches even in considerable aggregations, and all gain weight at an impressive rate. In bad years, there will be social strife, and movements by subordinate bears far from safe central home ranges. Nutritionally stressed grizzlies, of course, are those most likely to come into conflict with man. Some may starve outright—although usually not until the following spring, when nutritional stress is always greatest—and some females, though they may be pregnant now, will fail to bear young, and those young who are born are likely to be puny, and prone to early death. One of a litter of three cubs almost always has trouble from his two more dominant siblings, but in an infancy which has been preceded by the likes of a berry crop failure the unlucky runt may be abandoned by his mother, may starve because third dibs on mother's milk is not sufficient to keep him healthy enough to keep up with the family in their travels, or may be tormented into exile and eventual death by his less severely disadvantaged littermates.

Does the bear in summer actually think of the winter to come? We cannot know. All we can know is what we see—that her actions now, in this season of supreme nowness, in the halcyon timelessness of utter summer, are all in service of the future. Although she divulges no legible evidence of dread or hope or any awareness of the future, there is behavior that would fit it.

The cubs now weigh perhaps sixty pounds apiece, and have gained much in dexterity, strength, and endurance. They can travel tirelessly to the subalpine ridgetops where the whitebark pine trees grow. These trees produce substantial crops of nuts only irregularly, some stands bountiful while others are almost barren, but this year, perhaps because the rains of early summer were generous last year, there are ripening pine nuts galore. As the cones mature, red squirrels will migrate to the whitebark groves and chew the cones from their stems by the thousands, and then store them in buried caches for winter and spring. These caches can provide crucial emergency rations for grizzlies in times of stress, especially in early spring, for the bears can locate them by scent even beneath the snow; but it is now and into the fall, when the nuts are fresh and high in oils and the caches are easy to find, that pine nuts provide a significant proportion of Yellowstone grizzlies' nutrition. In some years, the nuts may comprise as many as half the total calories grizzlies consume in late summer and early fall. One study by members of the Yellowstone interagency team found a single cache that contained nearly three thousand whitebark cones.

The bear is superbly adept at gobbling them up: she smashes the cones with her teeth or paws, spreads the debris out on the ground, and delicately licks up only the nuts. The few cone scales that find their way in with the nuts, she spits out the side of her mouth. With singularly ursine fair-mindedness, she will often also smash and eat the squirrels themselves.

One component of loving grizzly bears is probably a certain envy of their freedom: their world seems so their *own*—steal the nuts, kill the squirrel, slide down a snowbank on your back, fear nothing. For a modern consciousness too sophisticated to subscribe to rhapsodic ideas of *human* noble savages, a wild, free-roaming grizzly bear makes a perfect heir to the wild, free South Sea islander of the Rousseauvian tradition—which, after all, embodies a longing that has never left us and probably never will. But we must not forget in our green rhapsody that although the grizzly bear's freedom is a fact of his history, the means of its continuance is now a human artifact. If we wanted to erase the grizzly bear from the face of the earth, we could do it in a couple of years. But, no, we choose to preserve his freedom, like a museum specimen in a glass case, to remind us of what once was, and except by our sufferance no longer can be: a relic, an icon, a precious anachronism—an image of our ancient subservience to the wild, our long-lost helplessness and innocence. And even with our protection, as we have seen, the grizzly bear's little glassed-in freedom is a fragile thing indeed. The mechanism that makes its preservation possible is extraordinarily multifarious, because the grizzly's needs intersect (or interfere) with so many of an expanding human population's needs or desires, and like all complex systems it is highly vulnerable to breakdown. Frequently, the failure of one part endangers the working of all the others.

Yet among the approaches to grizzly bear salvation jury-rigged

into being over the years by state fish and game departments, national parks, national forests, hunters, conservationists, scientists, and bureaucrats, there has been little consistency of design. Points of junction have usually been whittled and hammered to at best a very approximate fit, and they often seem to be held together by chewing gum, bobby pins, and blind faith. Finally, however, just in the last few years, there has been growing recognition that common goals and uniform procedures could make life a lot easier for everybody, and more possible for the grizzlies of the future.

The first big steps toward rationality came with the Endangered Species Preservation Act of 1966, the Endangered Species Conservation Act of 1969, and, most important, the National Environmental Policy Act of 1969, which required that federal agencies consider the environmental effects of all activities proposed for federal property. This sounds like nothing more than common sense now, but it was a big deal then.

The next step was the Endangered Species Act of 1973, under whose authority the grizzly bear in the lower forty-eight United States was declared a threatened species—defined as one whose existence is likely to become endangered unless current conditions are improved. The law calls for action to improve those conditions. First, habitat critical to the recovery of the species must be designated. Thereafter, any federal or federally sanctioned activities that might affect that habitat must neither degrade it nor diminish any other aspect of the species' prospects for recovery. Finally, a detailed plan for recovery must be written and abided by.

The furor that followed the proposed delineation of critical habitat for the Yellowstone grizzly in 1976 provides an excellently depressing illustration of the gulf between legislative idealism and social reality. The law calls for public hearings on critical habitat, and these were humdingers.

Ranchers ranted, hunters raved, developers howled. Most of the hearings stopped just short of outright riot. The local citizenry did not understand the law—did not understand that the designation of critical habitat was not an automatic closure of the land to other uses, did not understand how complex the grizzly's needs were—and did not give a damn whether they understood or not. These were the first public hearings for the critical habitat of any endangered species that really required a lot of land, and they were an unmitigated disaster. The Fish and Wildlife Service (the responsible agency) rolled up their maps, slunk back to their offices, and tried to forget about critical grizzly bear habitat. It has still not been officially designated—in direct albeit perhaps well-advised violation of the law—and it may never be. To this day, federal officials in grizzly country wince at the very word *critical*. They prefer, and always try to say, *occupied* habitat. Everybody knows it comes to the same thing. The only difference is that to work with occupied habitat you don't have to have any more public hearings, and your family can sleep safely at night.

Quietly picking its way around the minefield of critical habitat, the Fish and Wildlife Service proceeded with the recovery plan. There were four main objectives: to identify all surviving grizzly populations south of Canada and establish a population size for each that would represent a reasonable assurance of long-term viability; to identify the population-limiting and habitat-limiting factors that have contributed to the decline of each population; to propose measures for the recovery of each; and to achieve recovery in at least three of the six populations identified, at which point the species could be "delisted"—that is, declared no longer threatened.

It took years of work, and the document that resulted is one of the most ambitiously detailed wildlife management plans ever conceived. The six grizzly populations the recovery plan targets are those of

- the Yellowstone ecosystem;
- the Northern Continental Divide, which takes in Glacier National Park, the Bob Marshall Wilderness complex, and a number of other jurisdictions including national forests, Indian reservations, and Bureau of Land Management lands;
- the Cabinet-Yaak ecosystem of far northwestern Montana;
- the Selway-Bitterroot Wilderness of north-central Idaho;
- the Selkirk Mountains of northern Idaho; and
- the North Cascades of Washington.

The North Cascades hardly ever see a grizzly—once in a while, one wanders through out of the medium-sized population just over the border in Canada—and the national forest managers and fish and game people in Washington state, although they have sort of half-heartedly identified suitable habitat, do not seem wildly keen on repopulating their neck of the woods with grizzlies. The Cascades seem to be one of those places where grizzlies might someday reestablish themselves, but if they do they are going to have to do it pretty much on their own.

The Selkirks are a little less discouraging. In the summer of 1983, researchers finally succeeded in trapping and radio-collaring a grizzly there, and a little work is finally under way. Very little is known about this area's biological potential, but it is contiguous with substantial occupied grizzly habitat in Canada, and if grizzlies decide to colonize it—or if, as may be possible, there are already a decent number there—it is probably big enough and rich enough to sustain an independent population. But it won't be easy in the Selkirks. The U.S. Forest Service has been singularly unresponsive to wildlife concerns in this ecosystem—fighting tooth and nail, for example, against the listing of the Lower Forty-eight's last caribou population as endangered. Many of the local people are poor, the economy is deeply depressed, and poaching is commonplace.

The Selway-Bitterroot is a big, fascinating question mark. It is part of a huge ecosystem—a million and a quarter acres in itself and an additional two and a half million in the adjacent River of No Return Wilderness making up the largest single piece of roadless wilderness in the Lower Forty-eight—but, until the beginning of a small-scale survey in the summer of 1984, virtually no formal grizzly bear investigations have been carried out there. There have been a few possible sightings of grizzlies, but they have been of doubtful reliability. Frederica and Everett Peirce, who operate a small guest ranch on a private inholding on the Selway River, in the heart of the wilderness and right in the midst of the kind of low-elevation riparian zone that would be prime spring habitat for grizzlies, have lived here for years and not only have never seen a grizzly bear but don't know anybody who has. Commercial float trips raft the Selway almost daily in summer, and they too have yet to see a grizzly. Nevertheless, this could be superlative grizzly country. It is huge, rich in bear foods—including a large elk population—remote, little used, and not much threatened by any kind of development. If there were ever a good candidate for the reintroduction of grizzlies, the Selway-Bitterroot is it. But try talking to the feds or to state officials about reintroduction—especially any of those who were around during the Yellowstone critical habitat hearings. The very idea gives them the creeping willies.

In the Cabinet-Yaak, there may be a fairly sizeable population, and there may not; nobody knows. What is known is that this habitat is under terrible pressure—from mining, from oil and gas exploration, from logging, and most of all from road building to serve those activities. The Kootenai National Forest, which takes in most of this ecosystem, already has over five thousand miles of roads, and their management plan calls for an eventual total of *ten* thousand. Grizzly numbers there may be critically low; the bears have certainly proved hard to find. In the summer of 1983, a twenty-eight-year-old female was trapped, but that was too old for her to be of much use. Two young orphan grizzlies from Glacier Park were relocated to the Kootenai National Forest and released wearing radio collars, but one was found shot, with his collar still transmitting, and the other suddenly and mysteriously went off the air and was presumed also to be dead. Although its future is cloudy at best because so much development has been proposed, the grizzly habitat in the Cabinet-Yaak is excellent, and the area is considered large enough to support a minimum population of about seventy grizzly bears. There are certainly, however, nowhere near that many there now.

In the Northern Continental Divide ecosystem, the grizzly population might perhaps be considered stable if development were to stop in its tracks and remain active only at present levels—of which, fat chance. This is a huge and still relatively pristine chunk of extremely rugged country, and it harbors the largest grizzly population left in the Lower Forty-eight; estimates, admittedly not well informed, range from four hundred forty to six hundred eighty grizzlies here—enough, the state of Montana believes, to allow a limited hunting season. The state permits twenty-five grizzlies to be killed each year (including those killed accidentally, illegally, officially, or in self-defense), of whom no more than six on the east side of the continental divide and seven on the west may be females. As soon as the limit on females is reached on either side, that side is immediately closed to hunting. When total mortality of both sexes reaches twenty-five, the season is shut down. This has turned out so far to be an entirely theoretical arrangement; as it has happened, grizzly range here is so remote and the bears themselves so hard to find that the twenty-five-bear limit has never been reached since its inception in 1975. An average of six hundred hunters go out for grizzly every year, and kill an average of eleven. The average total of control killings, accidental deaths such as road kills, and known illegal killings is another ten. This could also mean that the population is not nearly as healthy as Montana officials like to think. It must be remembered that these figures represent only the *reported* kill. Most grizzly experts make it a rule of thumb that for every dead bear you hear about, there is another you don't. The Shoot, Shovel, and Shut Up Club (as the grizzly's most dedicated enemies are known to his most dedicated defenders) may be small, but its membership is highly active.

Meanwhile, the habitat encroachment expected in the Northern Continental Divide ecosystem is only beginning to pick up steam. Many more miles of road are planned, especially in and near low-elevation spring habitat. There is a heavily hunted black bear season in spring, and the expansion of the road system will mean easier access to the backcountry for poachers as well as legal hunters. In the spring black bear season in 1983 alone, five grizzlies were illegally killed here. Actual habitat loss to development is also expected to be substantial, and that will reduce grizzly numbers still further. Disturbance and dislocation will reduce the reproductive rates of those grizzlies who survive. For all these reasons, Montana's grizzly hunting season may not last much longer, and the future of the grizzly bear population of the Northern Continental Divide is far from secure.

The size of the Yellowstone ecosystem population continues to be heatedly debated. Dick Knight's study team has suggested that to be on the safe side everyone should consider that the minimum population is no greater than one hundred eighty-three to two hundred seven, and that the trend continues downward. Observations of females have been in steady decline since 1959. Lots of people, most of them with axes to grind, assault the study team's population work, and Knight concedes that the population *might* be larger than his estimated minimum, but he is quick to point out that nobody else has any current data at all, and that all the indicators of trend point toward continuing decline.

The state of the Yellowstone population is attributable at the moment mainly to excessive illegal killing of grizzlies, but there is quite a bit of habitat encroachment here as well, both under way and expected. Much of the national forest land in Yellowstone grizzly habitat is classified wilderness, so one might think that road building and timber cutting were not major threats, but the wilderness areas are fragmented by numerous roads and other nonwilderness corridors, often following stream bottoms that provide crucial riparian vegetation and travel routes, and there is highly destructive exploitation planned for some of these corridors; although in some cases the absolute size of the affected areas may be small, the biological effects of such disruptions as new roads can be devastating. Along existing roads, moreover, there is a great surge in second-home building, including a huge condo development called Yellowstone Village near the town of West Yellowstone. Oil and gas exploration is expected to accelerate sharply, especially in the Bridger-Teton National Forest south of the park. Hard-rock mining, logging, livestock grazing, and road building are having an explosive renascence on the Gallatin National Forest, and there is rapid development on many parcels of adjacent private land. Geothermal drilling and energy production have been proposed for areas near West Yellowstone, to tap the great hot-water reservoirs that underlie the whole volcanic plateau. Such development could have disastrous effects on the national park's famed geysers and hot springs as well as on grizzly habitat. The vast former Forbes Ranch, which lies along the northern border of the park in excellent grizzly spring range, has been sold to a religious cult called the Church Universal and Triumphant, which is planning real estate subdivisions, sheep ranching, and apple orchards—the first, if as is likely the garbage is poorly handled, and certainly the other two activities all being irresistible grizzly bear attractants. A huge ski-resort complex has been proposed for the Mount Hebgen area—in the midst of important grizzly habitat. Throughout the ecosystem, backcountry recreation continues to increase, displacing grizzlies, altering their movement patterns, and denying them access to feeding sites.

Rather shockingly, one major act of habitat degradation is being committed by the National Park Service itself, whose record on behalf of grizzlies in recent years has otherwise been exemplary. The huge complex called Grant Village, on the shore of Yellowstone Lake, is one of those bureaucratic schemes so dazzlingly awful that their sheer inertia seems to take on a life of its own, irrespective of whatever may be gained or lost. Initially conceived in the nineteen thirties, and with a detailed plan worked out in the mid-sixties, this monstrosity will eventually include seven hundred lodging units housing a possible two thousand eight hundred park visitors a night; three restaurants; housing and a recreation area for two hundred seventy-five employees of the private concessioner operating the facility, including a fifty-site trailer park; a concessioner maintenance area; housing for Park Service personnel; a forty-person dormitory for the

Young Adult Conservation Corps; a Park Service maintenance area; a general store; a souvenir shop; a post office; a ranger station; a marina; a sewage treatment plant; and, of course, lots of parking lot. Projected cost as of 1979 was forty million dollars.

Moreover, this heroic enterprise is being built smack-dab astride five Yellowstone Lake trout-spawning streams, in the midst of some of the entire ecosystem's best and most heavily used grizzly habitat.

As we saw at the old Cooke City dump, grizzly bears continue to frequent places where they have previously found food. Thus it may be safely assumed that every once in a while one of the two or three thousand citizens bivouacked at Grant Village on a summer's eve is going to pull a cute stunt like trying to photograph little Tracy with the big cuddly bear. This may or may not be the end of little Tracy, but if it is you can bet it'll be the bear's end too.

The Park Service's mellifluously titled "Preferred Alternative for the Development Concept Plan" recognizes such dangers: "If a serious increase in bear problems occurs, the National Park Service will consider blocking all but the easternmost and westernmost spawning streams to trout. . . . The spawning streams that would be blocked have less than a five percent influence on trout populations in the lake."

Now that's a trick Rube Goldberg would have been proud of. And only five percent of the trout population? Pshaw; it's nearly nothing. One wonders nonetheless what Trout Unlimited might have to say. Also what happens when little Tracies get eaten up on the westernmost or easternmost still unblocked streams.

The funniest part of this is that Grant Village's principal purpose, as set forth in the P.A.f.t.D.C.P., is "to remove overnight facilities from environmentally sensitive areas"—namely, Old Faithful and the area of Fishing Bridge, both of which have a lot of buildings around and both of which provide excellent habitat for wildlife including the grizzly. So closing that down is great. In fact, in recommending that accommodations be reduced there, the Fish and Wildlife Service has said that "grizzly densities [are] higher [in the Fishing Bridge/Pelican Valley complex] than at other locations in the park"— but now get this—"*with the exception of the Yellowstone Lake spawning streams.*"

Maybe in 1966, when the Grant Village plan was hatched, the Park Service didn't know that. But they know it now. Dick Knight, for one, has made sure of that.

And meanwhile the Small Business Administration is left holding a bagful of defaulted low-interest federal loans to motel owners in the Yellowstone gateway towns who are going broke.

The unfunniest part is that Yellowstone Park's management has agreed, in writing, to abide by guidelines stipulating that "land uses which can affect grizzlies and/or their habitat will be made compatible with grizzly needs or such uses will be disallowed or eliminated." And somehow, although Grant Village obviously and grossly degrades critical grizzly habitat, and therefore violates the most basic provision of the Endangered Species Act, the Park Service managed to get a no-jeopardy opinion from the Fish and Wildlife Service. The deal was that the park would make up for the lost habitat by clearing out of Fishing Bridge and Old Faithful. But then, lo, word came from Washington that most of the Fishing Bridge complex was to stay. (It may yet go. The final decision has still not been made.) That did not, however, seem to slow down work on Grant Village.

Why was another location never considered? The park has plenty of potential building sites in areas of low grizzly use and just as well suited to Grant Village's requirements. Nobody in the Park Service has yet been found to answer that question.

It is true that Grant Village is an anomaly: Yellowstone Park has been doing a good job with grizzly bears lately. They have gone to great lengths to manage their garbage, which has classically been at the root of most human-grizzly conflicts. They work hard at educating their visitors about bears, and they rigorously enforce the rules against feeding them. The park's let-burn fire policy is reaping substantial benefits in grizzly food production. With diligent trail and area closures, they have managed to avoid serious injuries to people for the last several years. Nearly one fifth of Yellowstone Park is subject to seasonal closure to all human entry, solely to protect grizzlies from disturbance and dislocation. Park managers agonize over nuisance bears, and they are removed from the ecosystem only when they seem to be truly incorrigible. The park recently accepted two troublesome grizzlies from Cooke City's garbage jubilee, and when two cubs were caught in a study team trap outside the park and their mother was threatening to eat up anybody who tried to come near to let them out, the park provided a helicopter and crew for a dramatic paramilitary operation to chase the mother off while Bart Schleyer and Larry Roop air-dropped in to free the squalling cubs.

So Grant Village is hard to figure. A lot of people in the Park Service don't like to talk about it. But construction is already well advanced. It is, apparently, too late. Like the Tennessee-Tombigbee Waterway or the war in Vietnam, Grant Village seems to be one of those lousy things so hugely lousy that nobody can stop them. And it stands as a cautionary example of what happens when the National Park Service's idea of what people want comes nose to nose with what grizzly bears need.

The recovery plan sets a goal of three hundred for a fully restored Yellowstone grizzly population. That number came out of a rough extrapolation from Frank and John Craighead's reproductive data, most of which, you will recall, were gathered in the days when Yellowstone's grizzlies were getting a lot of garbage to eat. Now that the park dumps are closed and other garbage is becoming steadily less available to bears, it is possible that the ecosystem's carrying capacity for grizzlies might not sustain three hundred. The ecologist Harold Picton has hypothesized that climatic fluctuation has accounted for much of the decline in reproductive rate that followed the dump closures in the early seventies; if that is so, a continuation of weather with occasional severely dry years could mean that the maximum sustainable population is little larger than today's estimated two hundred grizzlies. By the same token, better weather, specifically snowier winters, could bring about a strong increase in reproduction, since deep snows result both in heavy winter and spring die-offs of ungulates and also in lush spring and summer vegetation. Since the dump closures, the average age of first reproduction has risen by a full year, and litter size has declined; if those changes are due chiefly to the loss of garbage, then the population may go lower yet, since adjustment to the decrease in available calories may still be going on. In that case, the ecosystem's natural carrying capacity could prove to be so low, without the possibility of immigration from adjacent populations, that the Yellowstone grizzly population's resistance to stochastic catastrophe would be perilously weak. On the other hand, it may be that the gross amount of available calories is irrelevant, and that natural foods are more than sufficient; in that case, gradual adaptation to natural food sources, combined with minimized killing, could lead to an eventual increase, perhaps even to the hoped-for three hundred. The problem in setting a goal is that it has been so long since natural food conditions and natural mortality rates prevailed in Yellowstone that nobody knows within what range the grizzly population might be considered safe and stable. And if a safe and stable population requires, say, three hundred bears, and this ecosystem's long-term carrying capacity is only two hundred—*then* what? Because grizzlies' lives are so long and their reproduction so slow, the answers will require many years of research and monitoring.

For the other three areas considered as candidates for grizzly recovery—the Selway-Bitterroot, the Selkirks, and the North Cascades—no population goals have been set. Although data on the productivity of grizzly foods in these ecosystems are almost entirely lacking, it is believed that all three are sufficient in space, cover, isolation, and food for viable grizzly populations to exist. The recovery plan calls for population-limiting factors to be identified, but that's pretty hard to do where there are no populations worth speaking of. Habitat-limiting factors are significant mainly in the Selkirks, where logging is intense. Presumably, over the long haul, once recovery has been achieved in the Yellowstone, Northern Continental Divide, and Cabinet-Yaak populations, work can finally begin in earnest on these others. The way things are going, however, the wait may be long, if not endless.

One of the strongest criticisms of the grizzly bear recovery plan has been that it identifies only these six areas for grizzly restoration. Quite a few conservationists feel that many more pieces of ancestral grizzly range could support viable populations with only minimal management expense. In other words, if you released a sufficient number of wild grizzlies there, left them alone, and tried to keep people from killing them, they might well thrive. And if they didn't, it is argued, so what? There are plenty of wild grizzlies available for relocation from Canada and Alaska, so you could still try again, or even decide it was a bad idea and forget it. In *Where the Grizzly Walks*, Bill Schneider proposed a number of possible grizzly sanctuaries: the Gila and Aldo Leopold Wildernesses of New Mexico; the Blue Range Wilderness of Arizona and New Mexico; Rocky Mountain National Park, the Weminuche Wilderness, and the Flattops Wilderness, all in Colorado; the Bridger Wilderness of Wyoming, just south of Yellowstone (an area which a fully recovered Yellowstone population could begin to colonize on its own); the Anaconda-Pintlar Wilderness of Montana; and the River of No Return Wilderness in Idaho.

The government folks argue in turn that given the hard facts of limited financial resources and personnel, it makes sense to concen-

trate on the few ecosystems with the best prospects for grizzly recovery, fix things there, and only then turn elsewhere.

The recovery plan, with its emphasis on habitat protection, sets
up a reasonably good framework for the long-term survival of the
grizzly; but habitat protection will rapidly become irrelevant at current rates of man-caused mortality. The Endangered Species Act provides for a fine of up to twenty thousand dollars and a prison term of
up to one year for the illegal killing, wounding, trapping, or harass-
ment of a grizzly bear or for the possession, transportation, sale, or
receiving of grizzlies or parts of their bodies. It also provides for half
of any fine levied, up to a total reward of twenty-five hundred dollars,
to be paid to anyone who has provided information essential to the
conviction.

Yet federal prosecution has been all but nonexistent, and law
enforcement has been left almost entirely to the states, whose laws
are far weaker and whose handling of grizzly cases has been nothing
short of atrocious. The U.S. government has simply not supplied the
manpower necessary to enforce federal law. For all five and a half
million acres of the Yellowstone ecosystem, the Fish and Wildlife
Service until 1983 provided a grand total of *one* agent. Moreover, the
states are extremely jealous of their "rights" over "their" animals—a
jealousy with which the feds have been reluctant to tangle.

The result? Cases like these.

❨ In the spring of 1982, a man from Worland, Wyoming, led an
old horse up into the mountains of the Shoshone National Forest, shot it, and waited for the smell to draw in a bear. It would
have been legal for him to kill a black bear this way, but it was a
grizzly that came.

He killed it anyway. He cut off the head and paws, took
them home, and stowed them in the freezer. Thanks to a particularly quick and cunning bit of detective work, Wyoming
game wardens soon had wind of the man's achievement (the
states' failure is almost always one of prosecution, not investigation; many of the wardens are real go-getters)—not soon
enough, however, to prevent his returning to the dead horse and
killing another grizzly and this time, perhaps having learned
how much whole pelts are worth, bringing the whole thing
home, where, when the law arrived, it reposed in his garage.

Two grizzlies dead and in hand. This could have been a

solid federal case. But word had gone out from the U.S. Department of Justice that whenever there is overlapping state and federal jurisdiction, all prosecution, regardless of any disparity of penalties, should be conducted by the state. In any case, the U.S. Attorney for Wyoming was well known to regard mere wildlife cases as beneath his consideration.

Although the bears had been killed in the Cody district, it was somewhat mysteriously decided by the county attorneys that the trial would take place in the poacher's hometown of Worland. The investigation had been thorough, and the evidence was inescapable, but the local warden (to whom the evidence had been turned over by the investigating wardens) and the prosecutor failed even to confer beforehand, and the state's testimony was a hash of confusion.

If this had been a federal trial, the man could have been fined twenty thousand dollars for each of the two dead grizzlies, and sent to federal prison for two years. In the event, after serving four days in his hometown jail and paying a fine of fourteen hundred dollars—much less than a legal grizzly hunt in Alaska or Canada would have cost him—the poacher walked away.

In June of the same year, at the mouth of Gravelbar Canyon, also on the Shoshone National Forest, a Wyoming oil field worker set out the carcass of a Charolais steer as black bear bait, and killed an adult female grizzly who came to feed on it at dusk. Someone later saw the dead bear near the campsite, and reported it to Wyoming game wardens. The wardens retrieved the body, looked up the name of the hunter to whom the nearby bait had been registered, and arrested him. About a week later, he was tried in state court and fined eleven hundred dollars.

Meanwhile, only three days after the bear's body had been found, interagency team biologist Larry Roop was flying over Gravelbar Creek when he picked up the signal of a motion-sensing radio collar broadcasting in "mortality mode"—that is, indicating that the collar had been stationary an abnormally long time. Roop thought it possible that the bear, Number Sixty-three, had been feeding on the remains of the poacher's bait and had lost the collar. A trip to the site, however, failed to find it. Two weeks later, Roop tried again, and still could not locate the collar. Again in mid-July he searched, again unsuccessfully.

Again in August, Roop and his assistant Bill Rudd went in to try to retrieve the lost collar. The signal was strangely diffuse, and they could not home in on it. Finally, on a hunch, Rudd walked along the creek, and there, still partly submerged, lay the remains of Grizzly Bear Sixty-three, still wearing his radio collar. The reason for their previous inability to locate the signal was now clear: high water in spring and early summer had muffled it, and now, as the water level fell, the broadcast antenna had become partly exposed.

The carcass would normally have been demolished long since by scavengers and decay, but the icy waters of the creek had smothered its scent and slowed decomposition. Nevertheless the smell was overpowering. When an expert senior warden was called in to perform an autopsy, he had to stop several times to retreat upwind and recover, covering his face with his handkerchief.

Slice by slice, he cut the grizzly carcass to bits, and at last found what he was looking for: what looked to be a bullet hole in the skin of the neck, and a broken second vertebra beneath. The warden squeezed dozens of small chunks of the spongy rotten flesh through his fingers in search of the bullet which might match the rifle barrel of the perpetrator, but he could find none.

The investigators had not at first looked closely at the radio collar, but now they found that it had been cut halfway through, the knife having been stopped by the wire antenna imbedded in the leather. In the other side of the collar, there was a neat round bullet hole.

They felt certain that the man who had killed this grizzly was the same who had already been convicted of the first killing at the same place; the beginning of mortality mode in Sixty-three's radio signal corresponded with the date of that other killing. But they had no evidence beyond the circumstantial to link the man to this second bear.

They didn't have to say so, however. Yellowstone's sole federal agent worked with state agents in persuading the man that they had enough on him to send him to the federal penitentiary if he were to be tried before a jury, and after some hours they extracted a confession, in return for an agreement that there would be no federal charges and the man would not be sent to jail.

He was fined eleven hundred dollars for the killing of Number Sixty-three—the same fine he had paid in June—and was forbidden to hunt in Wyoming for one year.

(In October of 1981, a five-hundred-pound adult male grizzly was feeding on a moose carcass on the Gallatin National Forest near Cooke City, Montana, when he was shot in the back. The man who pulled the trigger claimed self-defense and was fined fifty dollars.

(After a whole string of such incidents in 1981 and 1982, there was a flurry of public indignation. The National Audubon Society began to offer a reward of up to fifteen thousand dollars for information leading to the arrest and conviction of grizzly poachers, and distributed posters to that effect to trailheads and campgrounds all over the Yellowstone ecosystem. Audubon also mounted an intense lobbying campaign in Washington. The Department of the Interior, partly in response to Audubon's pressure, formally petitioned the Attorney General to step up federal efforts to prosecute grizzly killers, and agreed to provide an additional law enforcement agent for Yellowstone and another for northwestern Montana. Wyoming outlawed baiting, and closed large areas to black bear hunting altogether. A number of Yellowstone Park rangers were deputized to enable them to make arrests outside park boundaries, where virtually all the illegal killing takes place, and the Forest Service also increased its backcountry patrols. And finally, in February of 1983, a tip from someone with his eye on that fifteen grand led to the first federal conviction of a grizzly poacher in Wyoming's history. It looked as though things were really starting to change.

And then . . .

(The really big federal case, the one that everybody in grizzly bear officialdom had his money on as the great precedent-setter, was to be the trial of a well-known Wyoming outfitter who had been suspected for years of killing grizzlies and whom at last they had nabbed dead to rights. In an extensive nationwide investigation, the Fish and Wildlife Service had found witnesses willing to testify against him, and the government was flying them in to Wyoming to swear that they had seen him kill two grizzlies near his hunting camp in the fall of 1982. But somehow —perhaps because one of the two federal judges before whom the case was to be tried had made it clear that endangered species cases were not of interest to him—the outfitter wound up, in the fall of 1983, coming to trial in his hometown *state* court, where even the maximum penalty would be far less severe than a federal sentence. The judge said, "If [those bears] had been in [the outfitter's] camp, which I am certain they had been in the past, tearing up his camp and stuff, he probably should have shot them then and there." He dismissed the charges, and accepted a plea of guilty for "cruelty to animals."

And so it goes. Of course it will never be easy, no matter how much manpower is brought in, to patrol country like the five and a half million rugged, remote acres of Yellowstone grizzly habitat, but the knowledge that an effort is being made, that grizzly killers *may* be caught, and that if so they *will* be in serious danger of a heavy fine and a federal prison term could go a long way. Even *one* really harsh federal sentence could make a vast difference. Only a few poachers are professional black-marketeers and prepared like other premeditating professional criminals to defy the law. Most grizzly killers are reckless opportunists, trigger-happy hunters, roadside vandals, or bear-hating outfitters or stockmen, and they are eminently stoppable.

The recovery plan tells us mainly *that* grizzly habitat must be protected, and leaves the *how* up to the management agencies. In the late seventies, well before publication of the recovery plan, a few enlightened individuals, led by Craig W. Rupp of the U.S. Forest Service, foresaw the need for detailed procedural means to grizzly recovery and began to develop an extraordinarily sophisticated set of grizzly management guidelines for use by the three states, five national forests, and two national parks within the greater Yellowstone ecosystem. The document that resulted has had decisive influence well beyond Yellowstone, and it is to be hoped that its influence will grow wider yet, for if there is ever to be a chance of integrating human land use with grizzly bear conservation, it will undoubtedly be in accordance with a model like that set forth in the "Guidelines for Management Involving Grizzly Bears in the Greater Yellowstone Area," whose principal author, Stephen Mealey, is pounding his fist on the table and thundering at his Yellowstone Institute seminar:

"Unless we believe it *can* be done, it *won't* be done! You'll see—this is a new era in wildlife management, and there's a cultural change now under way in our society that's going to bring the necessary public support. If managers carry out these guidelines, the Yellowstone grizzly *will* make it. Land use doesn't have to be harmful if it's done with sensitivity. Bears and humans have lived in close proximity for hundreds of years. It can be so simple."

Mealey goes on to explain the basic premise of the guidelines, which is to stratify the entire Yellowstone region into five categories of land use priorities, or "management situations," according to grizzly population and habitat conditions.

Management Situation One comprises the heart of grizzly habitat. All of Yellowstone Park falls into this category. In MS-1, all conflicts between grizzly bears and other land uses are to be resolved in favor of grizzlies' needs.

Management Situation Two tends to fall just outside of MS-1 areas. MS-2 zones are considered important but not essential to grizzly recovery, and although grizzlies must be considered in land use decisions, they do not have unequivocal priority here. If an MS-2 area is found to be more important to grizzlies than previously known, it must be reclassified into MS-1.

(Because Yellowstone grizzlies have recently been ranging farther and farther from the core of their old range, a good deal of MS-2 land may have to be reclassified. How thoroughly that job is done will be a good indicator of the U.S. Forest Service's commitment to grizzly recovery.)

Management Situation Three consists mainly of developed areas in the midst of grizzly habitat. Further development here is to be minimized, and the avoidance of conflict with grizzlies is of top priority.

Management Situation Four is potentially good grizzly habitat, and needed for recovery. The priority here is to maintain or improve that habitat and hope grizzlies come and use it.

Management Situation Five is rarely or never used by grizzlies, and not considered important to recovery.

As you can imagine, the drawing of the management-situation lines has raised a lot of dust. The quality of data fed into such a process, of course, has a lot to do with how well it is to work, and that quality has so far tended to vary rather widely from one management entity to another.

Between the Shoshone and the Gallatin national forests, for example, despite the fact that they share a common border, there are deep-rooted differences that illustrate well the gulf between high-minded bureaucratic intentions and their real-life outcomes.

Much of the Shoshone is classified wilderness, and the leading human use there is recreation, which is much easier to make compatible with grizzly needs than is resource development. Furthermore, the Shoshone is part of the Forest Service's Region Two, headquartered in Denver, which has an outstanding record (at least by Forest Service standards) in conservation. Region Two's director for wildlife, John Mumma, used to be supervisor of the Shoshone National Forest back in the days when Steve Mealey, then the Shoshone's chief biologist, was drafting the guidelines. Besides taking an active part in developing the guidelines, Mumma has long had a personal commitment to the grizzly bear. His successor on the Shoshone, Randall Hall, also showed courage and determination in standing up for the bear against demands by hunters, oil companies, and the Forest Service bureaucracy itself. After the rash of grizzly killings associated with black bear baiting, Hall threatened to close the Shoshone to bear hunting altogether unless the state of Wyoming did something about baiting; the state responded by banning baiting in much of the Yellowstone ecosystem and closing the rest to spring black bear hunting altogether. In October of 1983, Steve Mealey himself took over as supervisor of the Shoshone—one of the first trained scientists ever to reach so high an executive line position in the Forest Service.

The Gallatin National Forest, on the other hand, has traditionally been devoted to logging, mining, and livestock grazing, and the leadership of Region One, in Missoula, Montana, with which it is affiliated, has a reputation in wildlife conservation as bad as the Denver region's is good. The Gallatin was slow to respond to even such elementary grizzly-protection imperatives as bearproof garbage cans for its campgrounds, and their initial drawing of their grizzly management-situation lines was slow and stingy. The Gallatin's supervisor, John Drake, has said he is making a major effort to accommodate the grizzly—sharply cutting back the acreage available for logging, closing roads, even closing whole areas to human use. But the Gallatin continues to allow sheep grazing in its MS-1 zones, to open essential grizzly habitat to intensive timber harvesting, and to build miles of new road. When the Gallatin didn't like how some details of the interagency antipoacher patrols were going in 1983, they simply dropped out. And all this has been done, technically, in accordance with the Yellowstone guidelines.

As Mealey continues to his seminar, "Don't forget that one of the principal population-limiting factors for grizzly bears is the personalities of the people involved in their management. And keeping personality subservient to clear procedures is one of the areas where the guidelines can be most effective. These guys' performance is going to be measured in major part by how well they live up to the guidelines. Their asses are on the line."

Well, let us hope so. The philosophical distance some land managers must traverse to follow those guidelines faithfully can be a long one indeed. The Forest Service's history has been one primarily of resource exploitation, and their psychology has traditionally been rather ferociously utilitarian. Mealey has seen how far already from its past the Forest Service has come; he is himself the son of a career Forest Service official. He also sees the means of moving further and faster as best achieved in procedures and regulations. He wants, for example, to see a preventable-mortality ceiling for every national forest that has grizzly bears, and to make every forest supervisor's tenure dependent on his success in keeping grizzly mortality under that figure. Where the fire-breathers of the independent environmentalist movement might brand a given obstructionist bureaucrat as an irredeemable redneck, and despair of his ever changing, Mealey would build a structure around him that theoretically makes it impossible for even a thoroughly bad guy to behave badly. In that sense he is the classic liberal optimist, believing that man is perfectible by means of wisely modeled institutions.

Mealey's view will have an opportunity to prove itself in the next couple of decades, for it will be largely his ideas that govern how American national forests treat the grizzly bear. And it will be in American national forests that the grizzly will win or lose his race against extinction.

The special strength of the Yellowstone guidelines, and what makes them an essential companion to the recovery plan, is their specificity. Consider, as just one example of many similarly detailed procedures, the guidelines for timber harvesting in MS-1 grizzly habitat.

First, the likely effects of the logging on grizzlies must be evaluated by trained biologists. Timber on the national forests is almost always cut by private contractors, and the contract must specify that in the event of conflict with grizzlies, the harvest may be temporarily or even permanently halted. In some habitat types, timber cutting may actually be used to improve the productivity of grizzly foods, by mimicking the action of wildfire; the contract must specify techniques for doing so.

Cutting sites must be small and irregularly shaped. The cuts should not be larger than ten to twenty acres, and in those over ten, small islands of trees should be left uncut for their cover value in the newly created forest openings. The soil may not be scarified—that is, have its root system plowed up—because scarification inhibits the growth of the successional shrubs, grasses, and forbs that can be expected to burgeon after timber harvest. For the same reason, slash —the twigs, trimmings, and whatnot left over—should be spread out and burned, in order to reintroduce captured nutrients to the soil.

Wet meadows, marshes, bogs, stream bottoms, and all other moist sites—the most productive sources of grizzly plant foods— should be left altogether alone. Mature, nut-producing stands of whitebark pine should also be left alone. Garbage in logging camps must be kept strictly unavailable. Logging should preferably be done in winter, and must always be done at a time when grizzlies are not using the area.

The handling of logs and the building of roads must be done in such a way as to minimize soil compaction and other damage to vegetation. And probably the most important timber harvest guideline of all is the stipulation that all roads built for access to logging sites be restricted to that use alone during the harvest and be either closed or, preferably, obliterated afterwards. No matter how brilliantly you may have improved the grizzly habitat, opening it to motorized access can easily wipe out all your gains.

Forest Service profits on timber sales in grizzly country are then to be devoted to enhancing grizzly habitat, much of which in the Yellowstone area's national forests—after nearly a century of fire suppression, harmful logging practices, and livestock grazing—can use some help. Careful controlled burning can open up the canopy of the overrepresented mature forests and stimulate the growth of food plants. Old clear-cuts, especially those which were heavily scarified, can be replanted in native forbs, grasses, and berry bushes. Overgrazed livestock range can be restored. Damaged riparian zones can

be revegetated, which will result in stream stabilization and increased production of the moisture-dependent succulent plants so important to grizzly nutrition.

There are similarly specific timbering guidelines for each of the other four Management Situations, and there are equally stringent restrictions on grazing; trail building; road building; resorts, cabins, and other residential development; outfitter camps; garbage disposal; campgrounds and campsites; the disposition of road-killed animals; the storage of food; the handling of game meat; gas, oil, mineral, and geothermal exploration and development; and even the use of dogs.

All the snazzy guidelines in the world, however, will avail you nothing unless you have accurately analyzed the habitat to be affected and have accurately predicted the effects of the activity proposed. To that end, Mealey devised for the guidelines a rather fantastically detailed method for achieving real accuracy of analysis and prediction. Mealey's method is too complicated to cover fully here, but it is worth understanding how difficult, how time-consuming, and how costly this kind of thing can be.

First, you establish two sorts of overview: one by an *extensive* survey, with a general look at the topography, the vegetation, the climate, the wildlife, and the history of resource use in the whole area to be affected; and the other by an *intensive* survey of the specific site, noting grizzly habitat components and centers of activity.

From that information you make a map showing primary and secondary impact areas and the habitat components within them. Then within each habitat type—of which there may be dozens—you must lay out five or more sample plots, with special attention to microsites such as seeps. You sample and photograph the grizzly foods in each plot in spring, in summer, and in fall, and document actual use by grizzlies by searching for scats, tracks, diggings, and so forth. Scats are then analyzed for species content. Eventually, you arrive at numbers expressing food productivity for each season as well as three seasonal ratings of the plots' value as cover, as part of available space for the population as a whole, and for the overall naturalness of grizzly behavior in the area. These numbers then add up to a habitat-quality rating.

Then you have to start predicting the consequences of the changes foreseen, assigning "after" ratings to go with the already established "befores." Mealey cautions that this is the part of the process most vulnerable to human error, since "value anticipated" can be a rather subjective judgment, and, as he writes in the guide-lines in emphatic all-capitals, "ONE SEVERE NEGATIVE EFFECT MAY OFFSET TWO OR MORE POSITIVE EFFECTS."

Finally, you reach a range of scores that expresses and ranks the kind, duration, and magnitude of all possible impacts, including the affected seasons, the overall biological changes anticipated, and the likely effects on grizzly bear behavior and habitat.

If the total expected impact is negative—that is, if the proposed activity might jeopardize grizzly recovery—then you must consult with the Fish and Wildlife Service as required by the Endangered Species Act, in order either to redesign your proposal or to forbid the activity altogether. In these consultations there is customarily a lot of back-and-forth pushing and pulling by all parties. Of over five thousand such negotiations so far, only three have not been resolved—one of them the infamous case of the little snail darter versus the gigantic Tellico Dam.

The Yellowstone guidelines are certainly the most far-sighted, scrupulous, and comprehensive grizzly management scheme in existence. Having appeared in 1979, they have been available to federal land managers for some time, and with publication of the recovery plan in 1982 came a formal recommendation that they serve as a model for the protection of other grizzly populations; with no more than slight modification, they may easily be applied to any ecosystem where grizzly bears live. Yet not a single management entity outside of the Yellowstone region—neither national forest, national park, Bureau of Land Management district, state reserve, nor Indian reservation—has adopted the guidelines. Moreover, even within Yellowstone they are sometimes treated more as an obstacle to be got around than as a tool.

Why? The answer, no surprise, is a very human one: politics, pride, jealousy, turf. The Forest Service's Region One doesn't want to accept unchanged a system created by its rival Region Two. The Gallatin sees the guidelines as the handiwork of the Shoshone. Glacier Park doesn't want to ape Yellowstone. And, besides, doing all that stuff is *expensive*.

Everybody wants to write his *own* guidelines now, usually on the spurious grounds that "things are different here." The management of Forest Service Region One insists that because the long-range planning of each of its forests must be done in accordance with the National Forest Management Act of 1976, which requires that the welfare of threatened and endangered species not be degraded, each forest plan will necessarily include stipulations similar to those in the Yellowstone guidelines.

"Similar" is the rub. What actually happens is that every national forest ends up with its own set of rules, and consistency flies out the window.

The Kootenai National Forest, for example, includes some of the most severely threatened grizzly country anywhere—roads, mines, ski resorts, livestock, and intense backcountry recreation all pushing from all sides into an already degraded, long, skinny, and therefore highly vulnerable piece of grizzly habitat in the Cabinet Mountains. Under the guidance of wildlife biologist Alan Christensen, the Kootenai is now operating under probably the strictest and most complicated management rules anywhere. Grizzly habitat on the Kootenai has been mapped out in extremely fine detail, recognizing critical feeding areas, denning areas, movement corridors, and the need to maintain adequate cover. Grizzly habitat there has been stratified into five management situations similar in concept to those used in Yellowstone but expressing even more specific differences in habitat components. All of the Kootenai's resource exploitation is considered in terms of its *cumulative* effect on the grizzly bear population, rather than, as is sadly so often the case with other national forests, piecemeal.

Right next door, however, on the Idaho Panhandle National Forests, only two management situations have been delineated (although biologists there now say they plan at some time in the future to develop their own modified version of the Yellowstone guidelines), and the mapping of grizzly range shows only two vaguely drawn lines enclosing the presumed population center and a buffer zone around it.

This sort of splintering and redundancy may well be a built-in attribute of all highly specialized bureaucracies, and in cases where the desired ends are not yet clear, such a competitive myriad of experimental means may provide a variety of approaches from which the best may then be chosen. But in the case of the grizzly bear, the desired end has been clear for a good long while: recovery of threatened populations. And the means has been equally self-evident: protection of habitat and minimization of mortality. Furthermore, the fine details of the means to that means have been refined to universally applicable practicality in the Yellowstone guidelines and the recovery plan. Whether a tendency to administrative contrariety is innate in bureaucracy or not, it is certainly suppressible, as the NASA space program and any number of other concerted national efforts have shown.

At least since the late 1970s, a unanimity of conviction among the relevant government agencies and the American public has existed sufficient for the campaign to save the grizzly bear to have begun to take unitary shape. Yet bureaucratic obstructionism, personal egotism, and purposefully muddy thinking have kept that from coming to pass. If decision authority over factions in conflict could be achieved, saving the bear might be a relatively simple matter. But the structure of American government prevents the exercise of such centralized power except in cases of the deepest national concern, among which, alas, the endangered biosphere seems to figure less than large. Especially in the federal government, originally specialized agencies like the Departments of the Interior and of Agriculture (the respective parents of the National Park Service and the U.S. Forest Service) have grown to such vastness and complexity that the exercise of authority even only *within* them—never mind *between* or *over*—is severely limited. From one point of view, we might regard this phenomenon as a protection against rash action, a system of checks and balances. But it also entails the ubiquitous curse of great size and complexity—inertia. One would think that when at last an end and a means have been identified and the machinery put in place and started up, then that force would propel the engine of government inexorably forward toward its stated goal, steamrollering all obstacles. The problem with that view in the case of the grizzly bear is that the loudly proclaimed governmental unity of intent in fact masks a chaos of contradiction, confusion, and hypocrisy. There is more to government than what is structural and official; there are hidden agendas, deals, sub-rosa compromises, and, most powerful of all, a ponderous inertia within each agency of government to continue to behave as it has always behaved. And there is always that classically American unstated faith that our world and our greatness can expand indefinitely, no sacrifices will be necessary, we can have it all. Yes, save the grizzly bear—but also drill for oil in his habitat. Great, save the grizzly bear—but what a fine place this meadow would be for a few new condo chalets.

The question must be put to land managers over and over again: Are you willing to do what you must do to do what you say you wish to do? And if no one with the power truly to damn and punish is standing above the party so questioned, how pure is his heart likely to be, and how pure, in impunity, his conduct?

These are the ambiguous bureaucratic circumstances faced by a young biologist named Christopher Servheen, who has served since 1982 as grizzly bear recovery coordinator, a position technically within the U.S. Fish and Wildlife Service but in practice connected to every agency involved in grizzly recovery. All the agencies are theoretically bound by the strictures of the Endangered Species Act and such grizzly-specific expressions of its authority as the recovery plan and whatever management rules, like the Yellowstone guidelines, they may have pledged themselves to; but if any of them should fail to do what they have promised in writing or are obliged by law to do, Servheen does not have the power to make them do it. Central authority is not his. He must beg and wheedle and persuade.

Still, we all know that the authority written into a position can be quite different from that which its holder actually exercises, and Servheen's successes are a measure of his forceful personality and sometimes dogged persistence. When a state-federal clash was brewing over the question of black bear baiting, Servheen was able to convince Wyoming—which is sometimes fanatically jealous of its traditional prerogatives such as the control of hunting regulations—that the public would go along with radical changes. And he was right: despite the ugly portrait painted of them by some antihunting groups, sportsmen were in the main perfectly happy to accept stringent new restrictions on Wyoming black bear hunting, because it was made clear from the outset that the purpose was to aid the grizzly. Servheen also arranged for the Audubon Society reward to be administered through the Fish and Wildlife Service, and he has made sure that Audubon and other private conservation groups and the government are all working together, profiting from one another's expertise. On the Flathead Indian Reservation, he was instrumental in getting McDonald Peak closed from late July to early September, when grizzlies concentrate there to feed on estivating insects in the talus above eight thousand feet. This had been one of the most popular backcountry destinations in the Mission Mountains, but the public response, despite the loss, was positive. "It makes a tremendous difference," Servheen says, "for these agencies to see that the public will welcome restrictions as long as they understand the reason behind them—and especially if the reason is saving the grizzly bear. When the public hearings for oil and gas exploration in the Washakie

Wilderness were held, more than ninety percent of the testimony was opposed to exploration, and a lot of that was because of the grizzly bear—even though oil and gas would mean new jobs for the area."

Servheen has also increased coordination and communication among researchers; helped Glacier and Yellowstone parks at last complete formal bear management plans; been instrumental in Yellowstone Park's having established flexible seasonal closures of nearly twenty percent of its backcountry to human use, specifically to protect grizzlies; worked with state and local governments to reduce the garbage problem; put together interagency law enforcement efforts; called attention to the horrific problem of bear attractants in hunting camps; stepped up the government's public information activities; achieved timber-cutting limitations in grizzly habitat in northern Idaho; and arranged for an extensive population survey in the Northern Continental Divide ecosystem, where Montana's twenty-five-grizzly limit has been based on not much more than guesswork.

Servheen has also had his frustrations. The state of Montana has been as refractory about grizzly conservation as Wyoming has been helpful. In northwestern Montana, where grizzlies tend to be fairly small, black bear hunters mistakenly, or "mistakenly," kill a number of grizzlies every spring; in the spring of 1983, five grizzly bears died within ten days. Stricter regulations, such as closing seasonally critical grizzly habitat components to human entry during the spring black bear season, would affect hunter success only slightly if at all and would greatly reduce those "mistaken" grizzly killings, and all such a change would take is the stroke of an official's pen. But Montana has done nothing. Montana law also permits the sale of grizzly hides, claws, teeth, and other parts unless it can be shown, which is almost impossible to do, that the bear was killed illegally. Unless the merchandise has crossed a state line, which is also virtually impossible to prove, the federal government has no jurisdiction. Needless to say, under such circumstances, there are a great many more grizzly parts sold in Montana than could ever be accounted for by the official count of legally taken northwestern Montana grizzly bears—of which there are, you will recall, about a dozen a year. The town of West Yellowstone, Montana, continues to serve as an underground bazaar both for professional poachers and for those less than perfectly scrupulous citizens who find themselves with a dead grizzly bear on their hands, such as those who, say, shot a snooping bear "in self-defense" and had it turn out, *oops!* to be a grizzly. Despite several bills introduced to crack down on such trade, however, the Montana legislature has failed to act, and the Montana Department of Fish, Wildlife, and Parks, whose active support would probably insure passage of such a bill, remains silent. Servheen has also had a number of head-on collisions with Forest Service stubbornness. The Forest Service continues to resist committing money to research on human impacts on grizzly bears, and insists on allowing livestock grazing in much prime grizzly habitat. Radical action of the kind desperately needed to forestall a population crash in the Cabinet Mountains—namely, the introduction of more grizzlies from other areas—has not been forthcoming. Intensive recreational use of many Forest Service wilderness areas is often so heavily concentrated that it denies grizzlies use of critical habitat components altogether, yet forest managers have not moved to disperse or restrict backcountry use. And state-federal jurisdictional hassles and law enforcement problems seem interminably intractable.

Funny . . . having set out to get inside the grizzly bear, to concern itself with the bear's biology and being, to focus on the bear's profoundly nonhuman nature, this story now finds itself winding in ornate curlicue through the tangle of thoroughly *non*-nonhuman affairs encircling the grizzly bear. No thing to be understood without an understanding of its context? Yes, one supposes, even while worrying that the context may threaten to swallow up our hero the bear. Anyhow, so be it. If the grizzly bear cannot exist without the aid of people and their institutions, may we not think of them as literally inseparable from the grizzly bear's being? The bear is not part of us, then, but we are part of him.

And humanity is not a peripheral aspect, but central, the decisive part. Every grizzly bear carries our society inside him like a bomb, a ticking bomb, already well advanced toward blowing him off the face of the earth, and continuing relentlessly to tick toward ignition unless we intervene to disarm it.

It is worth thinking deeply about what the cost of that pacific intervention might be. From the most distant perspective, we may say that the ongoing civilizing of the planet—the growth of technology and of sheer human numbers—alone must doom the grizzly bear. Which is to say that only regression, or plague or holocaust, can save him. Certainly it is hard to imagine a world supporting four times its present human population and also the grizzly bear. But the point where the last wilderness must be subdued, its mountains mined, its trees cut down, its valleys filled with settlement, is still, thank God, a good long way away. At the moment, civilization can still afford the wilderness and its shaggy royalty.

Why, then, have the relevant institutions behaved, until it was almost too late, as though we could *not* afford the bear? The principal reason is probably simply momentum: we had struggled for so long —for millennia—to subdue the wild, to harvest, to use, to remake what after all refused to yield to our pride. In the wink of history's eye, however, the wilderness yielded, bowed its head in abject submission; and we, like other fighters drunk with victory, just kept on pummeling the loser. Then suddenly the frenzy dissipates, and we step back and take a look—not a little horrified—at the carnage we have wrought. This is the subtext of the Endangered Species Act: oh, earth, what have we done?

With that law and what it stands for, the nation accepts responsibility for reform of its own behavior and for reparation of the biosphere which that behavior has damaged. What, then, we must ask, is the cost, in dollars and convenience and social welfare, of preserving the grizzly bear and a wild world sufficient to support him? What must be sacrificed in board feet of timber and so in the cost of new buildings? What increase will there be in the price of oil and natural gas if we forgo the deposits that lie beneath the grizzly's kingdom? What would the setting-aside intact of grizzly bear habitat do to the cost of beef and lamb and wool and silver and copper and real estate and elk-hunting trips and downhill skiing?

Not very damned much, that's what.

Then why not just do it? If it's really so cheap—and at the national level it is—why not lock out the timber companies, the oil industry, the stockmen whose animals graze on government lands, the miners, the developers, and all the rest?

Two reasons. The first goes to the very structure of our social and governmental organization: modern societies seem capable of establishing institutions virtually overnight, but incapable of fundamentally changing them once they are in place. The preservation of grizzly habitat is in many ways in direct conflict with the grand old Forest Service ideal of multiple use and sustained yield of natural resources. But the Forest Service is required by law *both* to protect grizzly habitat *and* to continue multiple use of *each* national forest. The idea that some forests might be devoted, say, to wildlife and scenic values and recreation while others might be intensively tree-farmed seems to be institutionally inconceivable. In this light, the fantastically complex analysis and stratification of grizzly habitat outlined in the Yellowstone guidelines may be an example of a basically bad thing done very well. Obviously it would be far simpler, and probably much less costly to the nation as well, to keep out the mining and timber companies and real estate developers and turn all the currently occupied grizzly habitat over to the bear. But short of revolution—and nothing seems a less likely text for one—it cannot happen. Full protection of grizzly habitat can be done only in national parks, not in national forests. Then how about turning a few national forests or parts thereof *into* national parks? Most of the Shoshone, for example, and much of the Bridger-Teton would make dandy additions to Yellowstone Park, and the Bob Marshall Wilderness is certainly suitable for joining up with Glacier. But, well, ha. Try it.

The second problem at least *ought* to be a little less intractable: special interests. These break down easily into two categories, the big and the little, both of which should be eminently attackable on their own respective territories, namely, in Washington, D.C., and in grizzly country itself.

The really big special interests, the ones who can wield real power at the national capital, are old hands at getting a good deal from government. They have often grown up in symbiosis with, if not indeed as parasites on, the agencies meant to regulate them. Personnel move easily back and forth between private and public positions of power—a fact excellently exemplified in the current chief of the Forest Service, a former executive of Louisiana Pacific and a noted anticonservationist who has gutted the industry-restricting regulations that had grown out of the National Forest Management Act of 1976. There is nothing in the Forest Service's official creed to suggest that that agency should favor timber companies over backpackers, or mining over botany. That's just how it is—mere historical reality. The officially proclaimed purpose of the relation between agency and industry is to maximize the commonweal's share in private profit making, and to realize the greatest good for the public interest, but only the very naïve dream that it really works that way. Just consider that the U.S. Forest Service employs about five hundred wildlife biologists and *six thousand* foresters.

Nevertheless, incremental progress has been and still can be made on the bear's behalf against the likes of the timber industry and the National Woolgrowers Association and Asarco. For one thing, environmental virtue must now at least seem to be part of every industry's credentials, and all of them pay at least lip service to preserving the grizzly bear. For another, the growth of independent conservationist lobbies—which are sometimes seen as special interest groups but in fact usually work for the welfare of all the people—has put young muscle and good brains up against the despoilers, and indeed without them the grizzly might already be gone from the West.

The little special interest groups are mainly those which have been close enough to the agencies for long enough that the two have begun to grow roots into each other. Undoubtedly it must be hard to grow up on a ranch abutting Forest Service land on which your grandfather and your father and you have all grazed cattle and *not* to think of that government land as a little more yours than, say, some Florida tourist's, and never mind what the law says. Tourists come and go— for that matter, forest supervisors come and go—but the rancher and that government rangeland stay, and stay together. The cowman and the district ranger may shoot pool at the same bar in town. The foreman on the seismic-exploration crew, if he thinks his guys aren't getting a fair shake, can sit on the ranger station's doorstep until he gets action—not that he'd really have to, since he and the Forest Service folks know one another already, and naturally they make an effort to get along. The seismic crew may want to do something that's not so good for grizzly bears, but the grizzly's partisans unfortunately aren't camped out on the doorstep to stick up for him. No, sticking up for the bear is left to the ranger, and under the circumstances it may just be a little easier to get the seismic guy out of the office with a mumbled okay so the ranger can get on with his work. Meanwhile the local outfitters may have two hundred thousand dollars apiece sunk into their backcountry hunting camps, and they may get three thousand dollars per dude for a nice ten-day hunt, so it's very much in the outfitters' interest too to get along with the rangers who issue their permits. Those environmentalists making noise back east about hunting camp restrictions—shoot, *they* don't hunt, most of 'em, and *we* don't even *know* 'em. Besides, sometimes the little local interests have unexpectedly big-time pals, sometimes even in the District of Columbia. That unkempt old sheepherder strolling into the Sportsmen's Café when the rangers are having coffee may need a bath and look the very image of the impotently suspicious rural isolationist, but between him and his old buddy the United States senator back in Washington and their mutual old buddies the National Woolgrowers he may have the power to make even Regional Foresters think twice about pulling certain sheep-grazing allotments out of grizzly habitat. Besides, the Forest Service *likes* its forest users. Multiple use is what it's all about, and you can't keep your multiple uses in harmony unless the users like you and cooperate with you—right?

Ross and Emery Davis's family has been running sheep up here in the Conant Basin for five generations—since long before it became part of the Targhee National Forest, and long before the country east of the ridge was Grand Teton National Park. Yellowstone Park, on the other hand, had been protecting and producing grizzly bears to eat Davis sheep for a century, and for a century the Davises had been killing them with impunity. Then the Endangered Species Act came along, and suddenly grizzlies were worth more than wool and lamb. And now it was a federal crime to kill grizzly bears.

Yet grizzlies all around Yellowstone continued to die by the hand of man—shot, or poisoned—and a wildly disproportionate number of those deaths were occurring on or near the Targhee National Forest's sheep-grazing allotments, where not only the Davises but a number of other livestock owners pastured their herds.

In a study prepared for the Targhee's management in 1978, Forest Service biologist David Griffel wrote, "It was obvious that the herders were not cooperating fully in monitoring efforts. There were several cases when the herder provided erroneous information concerning sheep kills, and cases when the herder refused to communicate in any way."

The Yellowstone Interagency Grizzly Bear Study Team's 1979 report stated:

> Sheepherders openly admit they will kill any bear they see, whether it is killing sheep or not. Sheep are currently grazed on approximately eleven percent of the study area [that is, of the entire Yellowstone ecosystem]. Thirty-seven percent of the known grizzly mortalities have occurred on this land during the last two years. The number of unreported deaths is unknown, but information sources indicate this number could be substantial....
>
> From 1970 through 1975 there are records of twenty bears killed on sheep allotments. Since 1975 [when the grizzly bear

was declared a threatened species under the Endangered Species Act] there have been *no* officially reported grizzly bear mortalities on sheep ranges. Two of our instrumented bears have been killed [between 1975 and 1978] on sheep allotments. One was found dead after a nearby sheepherder had been shooting at disturbances in the dark, and the other was shot from the road while the sheep were being moved off the forest, although he was not molesting sheep at the time. Information gathered by undercover agents and volunteered by sheepherders indicated that at least three other grizzlies and possibly as many as *fourteen* have been killed in the past two years. . . .

If our most optimistic population estimate of three hundred fifty bears [a figure the study team later revised radically downward] is used with our most conservative estimate of sheep-connected mortality for the last two years, we have lost approximately 1.5 percent of the population. If we take the most pessimistic population estimate of eighty-four or less, with the highest mortality estimate of seventeen, we have lost about twenty percent of the bear population over the last two years.

In his 1980 report to the Wyoming Department of Game and Fish, Larry Roop wrote, "This area has been one of the most serious, constant, long-term drains on the grizzly bear population since the beginning of this study. There were two known grizzly bear mortalities from sheepherders in the Targhee during 1978. One of these was discovered only because it was a radio-collared bear. The other was discovered by a researcher in a sheepherder's camp. Because of the discovery the researcher was threatened and was unable to collect the skull for study. . . . There were four grizzly bear mortalities strongly suspected, but not confirmed, in the Targhee National Forest during 1979. All of these losses were associated with sheep grazing."

In a 1981 study, Forest Service biologist Philip Lee wrote, "The Interagency Grizzly Bear Study Team estimates an average of eleven grizzly bears have been killed per year in the greater Yellowstone area since 1976. Less than 0.5 percent of the sheep using the study area were killed by grizzly bears, [yet] more than ten percent of the entire grizzly population in the ecosystem were killed after livestock conflicts on the Targhee—or possibly ninety percent of the bears using the forest during this period. (The Targhee makes up only four percent of the total ecosystem classified as Situation One.)"

Dick Knight of the study team has been arguing strenuously for years that the Targhee allotments in prime grizzly habitat should be closed down altogether, and in its evaluation of the Yellowstone guidelines the Fish and Wildlife Service did the same.

But in high mid-August of 1981, leaning back in his saddle as he neared the escarpment above Grizzly Creek, Targhee National Supervisor John Burns—new in the job, it should be noted, since the days of runaway grizzly mortality—sounded the note of doubt that can be heard as a relentless pedal-point through all the crashing discords of grizzly bear argument; his manner was taciturn, his voice mild, almost bland, his words slowly and cautiously chosen: "My judgment is that these figures are very inflated, for several reasons. The first is that most rumors and barroom tales tend by their nature to be exaggerated or unbelievable. The interagency team and the law enforcement people treat each of these stories as a statistic, so the purported incident gains credibility and acceptance. In fact, many of these tales are concocted simply to get a rise out of the feds. Much the same is true of early bear kill statistics reported to us by sheepherders. Also, there's a motivation there to look good with the boss, so one needs to realize that herders are prone to exaggeration. Then too, they enjoy spinning tall tales for their occasional visitors.

"I make no attempt to justify actions taken here in the past, but I want it understood that the Targhee National Forest is *committed* to protecting the grizzly. It's our legal responsibility, and we take it seriously. This is our plan, which, by the way, has now been approved by the Fish and Wildlife Service:

"First, we've closed down several grazing units that have had a history of conflict. Others will be closed permanently if there's so much as one incident. The unit up at the head of Conant Basin, which has been a source of trouble in the past, will be closed after August 15 —after only ten days of grazing—or as soon as grizzlies come into the area, whichever comes first. When sheep are about to go into a unit, it will be surveyed for signs of grizzly use, and if there is any the sheep won't be allowed in. If a bear comes into the unit later, then the sheep will have to be moved out. The herders are going to have to move their camps every two or three days, and teepee out with the bands. Basically, wherever there's a conflict it will be resolved in favor of the bear, and grazing will stop. Most important of all, we've got a full-time biologist up here all the time monitoring the herds and living day and night with the herders."

Isn't all this rather an expensive solution? Wouldn't it be simpler just to stop grazing altogether in Situation One? And hasn't the herders' behavior amply justified that?

"Well, we're working on some areas at lower elevations, outside of Situation One, to improve them for sheep, and I think eventually we'll be able to keep grazing out of the high country. Also, these guys have been up here all their lives. There's a tradition involved. And, especially now that Wyoming has passed a law to compensate stockmen for their losses to bears and other game animals, I believe we're going to be getting a lot more cooperation. Emery Davis has been consistently willing to work with us. I have Emery's assurance that his people will not shoot grizzlies. This represents a genuine willingness by him to solve the problem, and it's the key to a long-range solution. Sure, the monitoring program is costly, and we'd save a lot if the area were simply closed to grazing. However, my feeling is that the grizzly will make it only if the uses of the forest are dovetailed with the needs of the bear. We have to make the uses *compatible*, not mutually exclusive."

Emery Davis's camp that August looked like something out of a particularly realistic hard-grit Western movie set in the mid-1800s: mobs of sheepdogs frisking among the tethered horses, a big cast-iron pot for lamb stew, the traditional sheepman's pyramidal canvas tee-pees, and dirt—dirt everywhere. No, not quite everywhere. There was one item in all the camp that was not covered with dust: a spotless, gleaming, scope-mounted, high-power rifle. The herder never let it lie far from him. Davis—who with his red suspenders, generous spill of belly, and gap-toothed grin would fit right into the movie—was friendly, hospitable, and very cautious. After all, his visitors, the ranking brass of the Targhee National Forest, had the power to wreck his life.

The young monitor reported that everything was going great. There hadn't been a grizzly in the area all summer.

Back at base camp, district ranger Dan Schindler and district biologist John McGee, both of whom had been instrumental in devising the new grazing plan, were talking quietly in their tent. A few others were still sipping coffee down by the fire. It was the last evening of the new Targhee supervisor's visit to the sheep allotments in grizzly country. Only the faintest remnant of daylight glimmered in the Western sky. Then, from over the ridge in the next creek drainage, where another band of sheep than Emery Davis's biologist-guarded one was pastured, a rifle shot cracked, and then another, and then three rapidly more, and then the wilderness silence returned.

Schindler and McGee, talking, had not heard the shots, but when told they were unconcerned. "He could have been shooting at anything," said Schindler.

"Might have been a coyote," said McGee.

"Might have just been target practice."

In the dark?

"It could have been anything."

SEPTEMBER

W HAT grizzly bears do not do can be as intriguing as what they do, and their occasional refusal to do the expectable "natural" ursine thing also offers striking clues to their intellectual capability.

Recall, first, the grizzly's postglacial evolutionary heritage: indomitable monarch, climax carnivore, the biggest, the brazenest, the meanest bully in the countryside, the terror of pocket gopher and stone age man alike. Remember how when four-footed prey and beached marine carrion grew scarce in primeval California, grizzly bears would cruise into town to devour hapless tribesmen and their dogs.

Why, then, are the grizzly and her cubs digging for the starch-rich but decidedly low-calorie roots of Cous biscuitroot (*Lomatium cous*) tonight at the edge of an alpine pasture on which six tons of mutton bleat in the moonlight? The answer is probably some knowledge, perhaps not firsthand but passed along from their less law-ramparted foremothers, of the possible untoward consequences. What their innate bearhood dictates is simple and clear: meat is good; kill it if you can. And as for *can*, well, nothing could be easier. All that's needed to render a domestic sheep edible is a brief untaxing chase and a medium bop on the head. But somehow the mother bear knows that trouble would follow. Obviously such knowledge is not inborn, so where did she get it? Has she remembered her earlier cub's sudden death on the cattle ranch and extrapolated from that the thought that all livestock is to be avoided? Or did she learn from her mother to leave sheep alone, and is there then something like a cultural tradition at work?

If the latter case has played a part in her self-restraint tonight, we should consider what happens to cultural traditions when their realism wanes. Clearly, many human traditions hang on for a long time after their usefulness is lost, but it seems reasonable to assume that after a while the principle of natural selection will weed them out. Once we begin to understand the weather, for example, we no longer try to make it rain by sacrificing virgins. By the same token, if genuine complete protection of grizzly bears is accomplished—if their killers actually go to jail, and sheepherders at last so truly fear the law that they no longer even shoot over the heads of grizzly bears —then wouldn't it figure that grizzlies will eventually lose their fear of killing sheep?

No big deal if so, most hard-line conservationists would say: those range-maggots have no business in the wilderness in the first place, shearing the alpine flowers down to the bare dirt and robbing good forage from bighorns and grizzlies. But few of those conservationists are likely to have thought further, to the possible consequences of total grizzly protection over the long term, when more than domestic sheep may have outlasted the bear's stigmatic fear of armed retribution.

Consider the story of Number Fifteen. Old Fifteen—so monikered because in 1976 he became the fifteenth grizzly to be captured, marked, and studied by the Interagency Grizzly Bear Study Team— was a well-known bear around Yellowstone, and what both officials and biologists like to call a good bear. That is, he stayed out of trouble with people, made an honest living, and was almost eager to jump into researchers' traps. Even good bears, of course, have their occasional brushes with people, and so it was that in 1971, when still a cub-of-the-year, Fifteen was first trapped at Yellowstone Park's Pelican Creek campground. He and his mother may have been there scouting for garbage, or they may have just been innocently passing through and have been drawn to the trap by the scent of the bait. Whatever the case may have been at Pelican Creek, Fifteen was soon, like almost every other Yellowstone bear in those days, well acquainted with the pleasures of dining on garbage. The park's dumps had been closed by then, but there was still plenty of garbage to be had around the town of West Yellowstone, Montana, and Fifteen was a regular fixture there, easily recognizable because of a large bald scar on his rump. Fifteen was captured three times in 1974 in and near garbage at West Yellowstone, and after the third time he was tranquilized, bundled up, and transported clear across the park and into the remote backcountry of the Shoshone National Forest. Upper Sunlight Creek and its environs were excellent grizzly habitat, and Fifteen stayed put. He denned not far to the southeast that winter, on Rattlesnake Mountain, his den door actually within sight of the town of Cody, Wyoming, and he was observed in the Sunlight area again in the summer of 1975, but eventually a yearning for his old home must have gotten to him, for in 1976 he was caught in the interagency team's trap near the Gallatin National Forest's Rainbow Point campground on the shore of Hebgen Lake, a good ninety-five airline miles west over several rugged mountain ranges from the point to which, two years before, he had been moved.

Even in his young adulthood it was obvious that Fifteen was going to be a really big bear. He was a superb predator, killing elk even in their midsummer prime, and the good nutrition showed. When he was trapped again in May 1977, in his first year as a full-grown adult, he already weighed four hundred pounds, and by that September, when he was captured yet again, he weighed nearly five hundred.

Through much of this period, Fifteen was wearing a radio collar and providing information for the grizzly bear study about his home range, movements, habitat use, and general way of life. He was an extraordinarily vigorous bear, always one of the last grizzlies to den up in fall and one of the first out in spring—a fact that probably reflected his exceptional predatory skill, which allowed him to obtain food when other grizzlies, more dependent on vegetation, would have to be hibernating. In 1978, for example, he had emerged from his den by the first of March, and at midmonth, when many other bears were still asleep, he was seen feeding on the carcass of a large bull elk.

Fifteen also always maintained a lively interest in garbage. His home range included several large and busy campgrounds, as well as a number of summer cabins near Hebgen Lake, and the researchers had good reason to believe that some local residents were actively feeding garbage to bears. Fifteen's day beds were often found close to the town of West Yellowstone. Nonetheless, he never got into trouble with people. Despite considerable livestock grazing within his home range, the only time Fifteen was known to have fed on domestic animals was when an algae bloom on Hebgen Lake was responsible for the deaths of many cattle who had drunk from it and he made use of the carrion. And he had never been an aggressive bear: the study team's tests showed that when he was in the trap and so could be presumed to be under some degree of emotional stress, Fifteen's blood carried exceptionally low levels of catecholamines, the family of chemicals usually associated with aggressiveness.

He was almost friendly. Like other bears who feed on garbage but never kill livestock, Fifteen knew that he had little to fear from the hand of man—and often something to gain. In August of 1978, for instance, at a time of year when carrion is scarce and elk, in their sleek prebreeding puissance, are almost impossible for a grizzly to catch, Fifteen was caught in the study team's trap near West Yellowstone four times within eighteen days: the allure of the meat used as bait was so powerful that he had apparently lost all fear of the trap, and, because he had spent most of his life near human settlement and its nourishing refuse, man-scent, far from scaring him away, may even have acted as an additional attractant.

For the most part, however, Fifteen resolutely avoided direct encounters with people. As one of the principal study animals for Bart Schleyer's master's thesis on grizzly bear daily routine, Fifteen was often radio-tracked at close range on the ground by Schleyer and his associates, and there were occasional unavoidable meetings. On July 28, 1979, just one day after he had been captured and fitted with a new radio collar, Fifteen met Schleyer head-on in dense lodgepole forest, and the bear's reaction, in this circumstance in which many another grizzly might have reflexively charged, was to turn tail and flee. Three days later, Fifteen moseyed back to Schleyer's camp at night and slowly circled it until he was quite close. Hearing tree limbs cracking in the darkness, the biologist whistled. Fifteen replied with a deep, rolling growl, and Schleyer clambered up a tree. The bear continued to roam peacefully around the area for several hours, showing no interest whatever in the treed man, and eventually he ambled off. The next day, radio-location from the air showed that he was over ten miles away. In all, over the two years of his field work, Schleyer spent three hundred forty-eight hours tracking and observing Number Fifteen at close range, and the bear was frequently known to be near other people, unbeknownst to them—fishermen, backpackers, and so forth—and never once did Fifteen display the least hint of aggression.

Fifteen was captured again in 1980 by the interagency study team, and twice in 1981. In August of 1982, when he was trapped yet again, his weight was nearly five hundred pounds, and within *six weeks*, when he was captured once more after he had been feeding on cattle carcasses along the South Fork of the Madison River, his weight was up to six hundred eight pounds. To forestall the possibility of trouble with live cows from this awesomely large grizzly—although he had never shown any inclination to kill cattle—officials moved Fifteen well into Yellowstone Park, to the Blacktail Deer Plateau. The taste of beef apparently lingered tantalizingly in his mind, however, for within two weeks he was back on the South Fork, now up to six hundred thirty-five pounds. On October 14, when he spotted Bart Schleyer and an assistant at a distance of about fifty yards, Fifteen scared the daylights out of the biologists by charging fast straight at them—already too close for them to try to scale the one tree at hand—but they quickly realized that the bear's ears were erect and tilted forward, a sure sign of strictly nonhostile curiosity, and in any case Fifteen had almost immediately (probably as soon as he had recognized them as human) executed a fast right-angle turn and was loping away. When Schleyer located the bear's day bed nearby, he found two large scats in it containing melon seeds and plastic bags. The next day, Fifteen was trapped and again shipped off to Blacktail Deer. It was the nineteenth time in his eleven years that Fifteen had been caught in a trap reeking of man. In the light of subsequent events, researchers agonized that their own activities may have contributed to Fifteen's habituation to people, but any such contribution was surely insignificant compared to that made by garbage.

In May of 1983, probably in a fight with another male over mating prerogatives, Fifteen lost his radio collar, and the study team lost contact with him. He was spotted once that spring with an elk kill along Gneiss Creek, near Yellowstone Park's western boundary, an important elk wintering ground and Fifteen's usual spring neighborhood, and the study team's pilot saw him again in the same area in June, copulating with a female grizzly. The pilot estimated his weight at about four hundred pounds—a normal weight loss, since it is in mid-June that carrion and prey availability declines sharply, fruits and other high-energy vegetable foods are not yet available, and grizzly bears are paying off the last of the metabolic deficit of the past winter's hibernation. Because it is the height of the mating season, male bears' testosterone levels are very high, and elevated testosterone is classically associated with increased appetite in all mammals. That factor, combined with the decline in caloric value of his diet, undoubtedly made for a very hungry and highly stressed bear. Under the circumstances, it was only to be expected that Fifteen would head toward West Yellowstone, prowling for garbage.

About five-thirty in the morning on Thursday, June 23, 1983, an enormous, rangy grizzly bear broke into an ice chest that had been left out overnight on a picnic table at the Bakers Hole campground on the Gallatin National Forest just outside the park, three miles north of West Yellowstone. The victims of the burglary reported it and were issued a citation by the Forest Service for improperly making food available to bears.

On Thursday night, at the condominium development known as Yellowstone Village—where, to officials' despair, bears have been openly fed time and time again—a bear got into some dog food.

On Friday morning, June 24, a longtime summer resident was awakened by a commotion outside her cabin near Hebgen Lake, ran out onto the porch, and saw a large bear going through the garbage can below. Fifteen stood up on his hind legs and took a violent swipe at her, but luckily the porch was some ten feet up, a height to which he could almost but not quite reach. The woman had seen many grizzlies before, but this one, she felt, was by far the most aggressive she had ever encountered.

That night about ten-thirty, at another cabin on Hebgen Lake, a large grizzly bear got into the garbage bags. The cabin's occupants had been leaving their garbage out on the porch all spring, but this, they said, was the first time they had had any problems.

About midnight, at the Rainbow Point campground, barely two

hundred yards from the cabin on the lake, a camper saw a very large bear moving through the campground toward the southwest—the direction of Yellowstone Village, where, sometime the same night, the garbage dumpsters were overturned and rifled.

From about twelve-thirty to one-thirty in the morning, dogs at another cabin nearby were barking continuously. A large bear had stolen their food from the cabin porch, and had overturned an old empty refrigerator in the yard.

Earlier that evening, about eight-thirty, William Roger May, a twenty-three-year-old shipbuilder from Sturgeon Bay, Wisconsin, and his friend Ted Moore, also from Sturgeon Bay, had arrived at the Rainbow Point campground and, in the gathering darkness, had cooked a dinner of steak and corn on their charcoal grill and had a couple of beers. Then they had done the dishes and, as the Forest Service recommended, stowed all their gear in their car. They had set up their large canvas tent—a relatively new one, free of food odors—and, about eleven, they had gone to bed.

About two-thirty in the morning, the tent began to shake. They had heard shouting and an exuberant ruckus from some people nearby earlier in the evening, and Moore's first thought was that it was some kind of prank.

May had been sleeping with his head and neck pressed against the wall of the tent, and now, it is thought, something bumped against his neck. The next thing Moore heard was May screaming. The bear's first—and perfectly natural—reaction to bumping something animate with his nose was to bite it and hold it still and investigate. What he bit, through the wall of the tent, was Roger May's neck. The carotid artery was severed by that one bite, and blood gushed forth.

Whatever may have been a bear's learned reticence and caution, the immediate presence of a wounded and bleeding animal, particularly if it is struggling to escape, sets in motion an ancient genetically programed sequence of predation.

The bear, still holding Roger May by the neck through the wall of the tent, began to pull, and his strength was such that the canvas was rent, and the bear pulled May through the hole thus created. The tent collapsed.

Moore struggled out of the wreckage of the tent. The moon was full, and the sky was clear, and Moore could see May clearly on the ground about ten feet away, and the bear standing over him. Seeing

Moore, the bear grabbed May by the ankle and dragged him about thirty feet away. Moore reached into the collapsed tent, took an aluminum pole, and ran at the bear, brandishing it. He threw the tent pole at the bear, and the bear withdrew into the shadows.

May could still speak, but he was obviously gravely injured. Moore returned to the tent to search for his glasses and car keys. When he emerged, his friend was gone, and the woods were silent.

The bear had carried May only about twenty feet farther away, but he had gone into shadowed brushy timber where he could not be seen, and had now begun silently to consume his prey.

A few other campers, who had heard May's brief screaming, arrived to offer help, and they and Moore wandered terrified through the campground calling, "Roger! Roger!" Someone telephoned the sheriff in West Yellowstone, and the bear's reaction to the arrival of the police car with its loud siren and flashing lights was only to drag the body a little farther into the woods. This was known because the drag marks and bear tracks across the campground's dirt road were found on top of the tracks of the police car's tires. Throughout the shouting and flashlight-shining and siren-wailing, the bear had not abandoned his kill and had continued to feed.

An investigative team began to form early that morning. Dick Knight, head of the Interagency Grizzly Bear Study Team, flew over the area to see if any of the study's radio-collared bears were around, and none was. The site of the killing was roped off, and investigators began to reconstruct the scenario. Both the Rainbow Point campground and the nearby Bakers Hole campground were evacuated, and all trails on the west side of Yellowstone Park were closed. By late afternoon, thirteen bear traps had been set, some at the campground, some along the road, and some at Yellowstone Village.

The investigative team gathered that evening at the district ranger station, and at midnight they began to check the traps. Those at Yellowstone Village and along the road were empty. Barely ten feet from the spot where Roger May's body had been found, there was a bear in the trap—a large grizzly with a bald scar on his rump. Fifteen.

They tranquilized Fifteen with a dose of Sernylan. They took scrapings from his claws and around his muzzle, clipped hairs from his paws and face, and collected about three pounds of fresh scats, in which what looked very much like human hair and skin could be seen. Dick Knight took these samples, along with the samples of the victim's hair and blood, to Bozeman, Montana, from which they were in turn flown on to Missoula, where the state crime lab was calling in (it was a Sunday) a hematologist, a hair expert, and a pathologist. Meanwhile, in Bozeman, Ken Greer, of the interagency study team, had already looked at hairs from Fifteen's scats under the microscope and was sure they were human. Soon the state lab had matched up hairs from the victim with those from the scats and confirmed that they had come from the same individual. Fifteen was injected with a massive drug overdose, and he quietly died.

Everyone's first thought was to try to find what must have driven the bear crazy enough to do such a thing. His body was sent to Bozeman, where Ken Greer performed a detailed autopsy. Fifteen's weight was down to four hundred and thirty-five pounds—from the previous autumn's six hundred plus—but that was normal for this time of year, and the bear was in perfect health. The investigation showed that Roger May and Ted Moore had followed all the rules for staying out of trouble with bears—clean camp, no food in the tent or anywhere else around camp, no provocative behavior whatever. Gradually, the plain fact had to be faced that neither Roger May nor Grizzly Bear Fifteen had done anything *wrong*. Tragedy to be tragedy must be avoidable; this was just a case of bad luck. Wherever there are people and grizzly bears in the same place, it can happen, and, mercifully rare as such encounters may be, they will always happen.

"The incredible thing," Chris Servheen, the federal grizzly bear recovery coordinator, later said, "is not that it happened, but that it doesn't happen more often."

And why doesn't it happen more often? What could be easier prey than a person? Certainly a backpacker is easier to catch and kill than an elk, and there are more of them too.

The answer is fear. Most grizzly bears have learned that people are not to be killed, and those few who do not learn virtually always pay with their lives. The minuscule number of grizzly-caused human fatalities have all resulted from situations where, through a disastrous confluence of circumstances, bear instinct has suddenly overwhelmed bear learning—where the basic drives governed by the brain's limbic system, such as feeding, sex, and aggression, momentarily override the inferential, synthesizing, and ultimately inhibitory activity of the cortex. Even Fifteen, if he had even a moment to think about it, never approached a human being with malign intent.

The only villains, if there must be villains, in the sad story of

Roger May and Grizzly Bear Fifteen, are the people who despite years of warnings made their garbage accessible to bears. Most of them knew it was wrong, and dangerous, but they liked seeing bears. It was garbage that drew Fifteen into human precincts, and it was garbage that accustomed him to not minding being near people. Perhaps if Yellowstone Village and the summer people on Hebgen Lake had kept their garbage secure, Fifteen would never have been in the neighborhood in June of 1983. Perhaps if he had not been feeding on garbage year after year, Fifteen would have been too wary of people to have come snooping around a campground. But the area where Roger May died is good grizzly habitat irrespective of garbage, and certainly

as long as there are both people and grizzly bears in the same place they will occasionally come into contact, and while careful precautions, as Yellowstone Park's great success in recent years suggests, may minimize bear-caused human injuries and deaths, we cannot hope that they will never happen.

Let us circle back now to the question that prompted this brief biography of Fifteen. Might it be that grizzly bears' reluctance to kill people is a moribund cultural tradition, surviving from the days when retribution was automatic and inevitable, when indeed innocent grizzlies were often slaughtered just for the hell of it, and every grizzly bear knew that people and firearms went together? If so, what may we expect to happen with long-term total protection? Yes, Fifteen was caught and killed, and most other man-killing grizzlies have met the same end. But suppose one got away—say a mother, who then taught predation on humans to her cubs. Suppose that, gradually, a few grizzly bears learned how easy it can be to kill and eat people. If enough of them began to do it, would there not be an immediate collision between the law, which forbids endangering a population of a threatened species, and the human outrage that would cry out for capital revenge?

This may sound like a preposterously hypothetical question. After all, you are still much safer camping out in grizzly bear country than you are driving to it in an automobile. (From 1978 through 1982, for example, of Yellowstone National Park's approximately eleven and a half million visitors, about twenty-six hundred people were injured seriously enough in various mishaps to require medical attention; there were about twenty-three hundred traffic accidents; and twenty-six people died in drownings, automobile wrecks, thermal burns, and climbing accidents. Of the twenty-six hundred personal injuries, five were caused by grizzly bears, two by black bears, and three by bears whose species was not determined. Roger May, in 1983, was the first person killed by a Yellowstone grizzly in over ten years.) Nevertheless, some bears in Yosemite and Glacier national parks seem to be learning that if you charge a backpacker, the first thing he's likely to do is drop his pack, and voilà! you have something good to eat. How big a step is it, ask, in the mind of a bear, from armed robbery to outright murder, especially when the rewards for the latter are so much greater?

Bears are obviously able to understand the distinction between acceptable and unacceptable predation, but it is equally obvious that some of them will break the rules if they can get away with it. Thus in Yellowstone we have both stock-killing grizzlies and those, like our protagonist, who spend their lives feeding peacefully alongside peacefully grazing cattle and sheep. It might be thought that the sensible Darwinian thing for *every* bear is to kill all the livestock he can get hold of, and people too: they're much better food than biscuit-root and spring beauty, and certainly such behavior would be consistent with the grizzly's evolutionary heritage of omnipotence and his genetic predisposition to carnivorism. But the fact is they don't do it. As long as they associate certain activities with the likelihood of human retribution (and it is not clear exactly how they learn this, only that they do), grizzlies are fully capable, given a moment to reflect, of making the necessary discrimination. Of course there will not always be that crucial moment to reflect, and so neither livestock nor man will ever be perfectly safe in grizzly country.

Nevertheless, as long as attractants are also minimized, a system of punishment *can* keep danger to an acceptably low level. But for such a system to work over the long haul, grizzly populations obviously must be secure enough to sacrifice the occasional miscreant. Unfortunately many are not. If there were to be some sort of epidemic of grizzly attacks in Yellowstone—which, in the case, for example, of a series of severe drought years, is not inconceivable—what people would regard as appropriate retribution could well end up killing so many bears that the population would be reduced beyond hope of recovery. To the other compelling arguments for grizzly recovery, therefore, we may add that of human safety.

How much control of delinquent bears, in the end, can we hope for? There are a number of research projects on what biologists call aversive conditioning recently completed or still under way, and the results so far have not exactly been encouraging.

Take, for example, a study by Bruce Hastings, Barrie Gilbert, and David Turner in Yosemite National Park. Yosemite's black bear problem is horrendous. The bears there have learned to open jars and to pull down food bags from specially constructed, supposedly bear-proof suspension systems, and sometimes they literally chase people out of their campsites at mealtime. So savvy have Yosemite's black bears become that they know that only a closed container is likely to hold food: uncapped bottles and backpacks with flaps and zippers open are rarely messed with. *Sixty-one percent* of Yosemite's back-country visitors in 1979 had some kind of encounter with a bear.

The author of this book and a friend, in the summer of 1981, had barely arrived at a high-country lake in Yosemite and leaned their packs against a boulder when a good-sized black bear came sauntering out of the woods and, with barely a glance at the people, made a beeline for their packs. Shouting, arm-waving, tree-limb-brandishing bothered that bear no more than a muttering panhandler slows down a Manhattan chairman of the board. The bear wasn't aggressive; it was just as if the people weren't there. As the bear sidled ever nearer and the packs' two defenders were losing their nerve and ready to give up their goodies—which would have meant giving up their whole trip—two headbanded, no-shirted young Californians burst over the hill yelling, "There's that son of a bitch!" and hurling brick-sized rocks at the bear. This seemed perhaps excessively provocative of a dangerous animal, but the bear took it sufficiently meekly to withdraw, still none too hurriedly, to the upper limbs of a large pine tree, from which, seated upright on one branch with his chin resting photogenically on his paws on another branch, he continued a placid vigil for nearly an hour—thus denying the dust-covered and exhausted backpackers their swim in the lake. The bear finally moseyed nonchalantly off, but the night was punctuated with yells and potbanging throughout the echoing mountains as the bear visited first one and then another and another campsite, raising perfectly fearless hell wherever he went.

So Hastings's study focused with some intensity on ways of discouraging such rampaging ursine vandals. If things ever got half this out of hand with a grizzly population, clearly it would be disastrous. To avert a bloodbath you would have to eliminate either people or grizzlies from the area altogether. (Perhaps it should be reemphasized here that one does not chuck stones at a *grizzly* bear, *ever*, even if he is on a beeline for one's pack.) Hastings first tried sticking lithium chloride pellets—an emetic—in hot dogs and leaving them around a campground, and, um, as he puts it, "No definite effect was documented."

Then he tried booby-trapped food sacks: "A plastic bag with one liter of two percent ammonium hydroxide was placed in a counterbalanced food sack 2.5 m. above the ground. A string was left dangling from the food sack for easy access by the bears. A balloon was also placed in the stuff sack for a twofold purpose, that of providing a loud noise and of producing a full appearance to the sack. . . . The bears usually avoided touching the aversion sack and exposing its contents. However . . . this did not alter the normal food-obtaining activities of the bears; there were no significant differences in bear activity, interactions, or damages after the aversion sack was used compared with the same measures before the treatment."

Next Hastings tried upping the concentration of ammonia and the number of food sacks. This time the bears occasionally touched the sacks, but only thirteen percent of the balloons were ever broken. Still, bear activity at the particular campsites where the ammonia bags were mingled among real food bags did decrease moderately, leading Hastings to conclude, in wonderfully poker-faced biologese, "These data indicate that this technique might be employed to pressure problem bears from one campground to another."

Grizzly bears' response to such deterrents as electrically charged wire fences has been similar. Usually they will manage simply to find a way around the painful obstacle, but if they really want what's on the other side, they will virtually walk through fire to get it. "You have to understand it in terms of the history of the species," says Dick Knight, leader of the Yellowstone grizzly study. "Grizzly bears have evolved not to care very much about pain unless there's really damaging injury involved, and their hide is so tough they're very rarely injured under natural circumstances. Once they've identified a high-energy food source, they're just programed to go after it, and the only thing that will stop them is fear of being killed. If they have to go through some electric shock or chemically induced nausea or whatever you want to throw at them, that's okay. They'll do it."

It has been almost unanimous popular wisdom that keeping bears and people apart is the only real way to keep people safe from bears. But a study by Katherine McArthur Jope in Glacier National Park has found precisely the opposite: "Most hiker injuries have been inflicted after the hiker was charged by the bear . . . [and] charges occurred primarily on trails with little human use. The findings of this research, together with records on human injuries in the park, suggest that habituation of grizzly bears to high numbers of hikers in their habitat may reduce the rate of injuries resulting from fear-induced aggression." The apparent contradiction, however, may be less deep than one may at first suspect. Much of Glacier Park is either extremely heavily vegetated in the forest understory or else rugged, steep, rocky, and open—the first a situation in which bears and people may easily surprise one another at extremely close range, and the second, in open alpine country, one in which grizzlies are naturally nervous and aggressive because of the lack of visual cover into which they can quickly disappear. Thus, in both situations, whatever aggression occurs is more likely to be *fear-induced* than, say, related to food. If we could leave out the food-getting issue—that is, in an ideal world where campers never littered and all garbage dumps were walled off like prison yards—then a comfortable proximity of grizzlies and people might well be manageable. But as long as food and people remain closely linked in the minds of grizzly bears, neighborly relations are bound from time to time to be strained. Moreover, as long as illegal killing remains a serious threat to grizzlies, any loss of fear of humans will expose more bears to the deadly trigger-happy few. Nevertheless, increasing grizzly habituation to people is probably inevitable as long as backcountry recreation in grizzly habitat continues to increase, and it is in dealing with this inevitability that Jope's study will doubtless prove invaluable. In showing how clearly grizzly behavior distinguishes between fear-induced aggression and that which is instrumental, or goal-oriented, it is further testimony to the subtleties of judgment grizzlies are capable of and to the wisdom of the choices they will make if, first, their innate aggression-alarms are not set off and, second, they have not been allowed to become garbage addicts. As long as they perceive people as bell-wearing, predictable, harmless, ungenerous with food, and unacceptable as prey, grizzly bears are—even at close quarters—going to leave us alone. Well, okay . . . most of the time.

Surely the romance of the grizzly would be less potent if the bear were not dangerous to us. Of the deep change in human attitudes toward nature that was at the heart of the Romantic movement, Kenneth Clark, in *Animals and Men*, wrote, "Man in his relationship to animals began to sympathize with the ferocity, the cruelty even, that he had previously dreaded and opposed."

What Clark called "this new religion of violence," as exemplified in Delacroix's savage "lion-hunt" pictures—"episodes in a war between men and animals in which, for the first time in art, the outcome is uncertain"—continues albeit confusedly to inform our love of the likes of lions and tigers and grizzly bears. Perhaps the primary element that confuses our sympathy is the human overreadiness to identify animal violence with human anger. Clark's "cruelty even" puts the finger on the most vulnerable spot of the Romantic fallacy—the centrality of individual human consciousness—for the evidence is that cruelty is a distinctly human idea and would be unfamiliar to grizzly bears or indeed to any other wild beast. A truthful and truly sympathetic human membership in the community of nature would demand that we distinguish between those aspects of violence which we know we share with our fellow creatures and those which may be uniquely, tragically our own. In instrumental aggression such as predation, it may be that the concomitant elevation of such brain chemicals as epinephrine produces a subjective response in the mind of the grizzly in some way similar to the excited, hypervigilant fight-or-flight emotion that is a component of human anger, but the apparent utter placidity of the predator once his kill has been made, or even once the kill has been missed, suggests an important difference. The best candidate for an analogue of human fury is probably the aggression of mother grizzlies defending their young, but the fact that removal of the threat to the cubs seems always to result in immediate extinction of the mother's aggressive behavior does not harmonize well with the rhapsodic and somewhat self-perpetuating passion that we experience as anger. Mother grizzlies whose young have been threatened do not stalk and ambush the perpetrators as human mothers are wont to do.

As for cruelty—the idea is too uniquely human to waste much time getting animals tangled up in it. We say that nature is cruel, but what we mean is that if we behaved in such a way *we* would be acting cruelly. For a valid human ethics with respect to the wild, the distinction is crucial. Nature does not provide us with exculpatory examples of cruelty. By the same token we have no business inculpating nature's violence. Acts of ignorant barbarity like Yellowstone Park's slaughter of wolves in the early twentieth century no longer, thank goodness, seem even conceivable, but we still have some distance to go toward an honest recognition that there is no pattern in nature for human evil.

It is, then, in supreme innocence of us—whom she knows only as alien beings inconveniently at large in her realm, to be avoided with cool xenophobic self-possession—that the bear chooses the path she will travel, and the way she will live. What she does not do and where she does not go are determined largely by her rigorous avoidance of the two creatures capable of harming her or her young, man and the adult male grizzly bear. What she does do and where she does go are at bottom very simply decided, almost entirely by nutritional needs. At certain times there are other influential factors at work—the cubs' education, the need for cover, the regulation of her body temperature, the imperatives of the mating season—but all of these can be summarily subordinated, should the need arise, to that single-minded drive for food.

We must not, however, fall into the romantic-nostalgic trap of thinking that ultimate causation somehow "solves" the grizzly bear "puzzle." No more than infantile sexuality explains the variety of adult neurosis, no more than the selfish gene can account for the variety of lifeforms, does the ceaseless hunger of the grizzly bear give adequate meaning to the full variety of her behavior. It is essential to our understanding that we keep constantly in mind the nutrition-centeredness of her motivation, but it is far from sufficient. The wonder of her existence resides not in her most basic drives but in their expression. Occam's Razor (which holds that "entities ought not to be multiplied except from necessity") has done great service in the physical sciences, but it has also, as in the naïve behaviorism that reduced much animal study in the middle years of the twentieth century to mechanomorphic absurdity, far too often shaved biology to an impossibly fine point.

In *Animal Thought*, Stephen Walker quotes what has become known as Lloyd Morgan's Canon, the early modern behaviorist reincarnation of Occam's Razor: "In no case may we interpret an action as the outcome of the exercise of a higher psychical faculty, if it can be interpreted as the exercise of one which stands lower on the psychological scale."

To this Walker responds, "It is debatable . . . whether parsimonious explanations, especially of biological and psychological phenomena, are necessarily the best ones. Applied to human actions, the Canon would require us always to assume that people act from the most straightforward and least intellectually demanding motives. This might be a useful palliative against the urge to search for deep and dark explanations every time someone forgets a name, or misses a bus, but it would surely be unwise to assume that the simplest explanation of a politician's promise, or a child's tears, is always true. Similarly, because all animals feed, and move, and fight, it does not follow that the mechanisms which control these actions in the lowest and simplest species are the only ones at work in all the others."

Quite right. But where does this leave us? Well, humbled, for one thing. There is so much we cannot know because we cannot even think of what questions to ask. When we see the bear sitting on her haunches at the top of a cliff looking out over a sea of forest and meadow, and we ask, "What is she doing?" the only available empirical answer is "Nothing." But that seems woefully unsatisfactory. Can we say then that she is thinking? Surely her brain is not so unlike ours that her consciousness can simply be turned off when she is evidently awake and aware. But *thinking*? Thinking *what*? Can man hope ever to know?

For the moment we can only wonder, and observe. As our observations ramify and perhaps begin to interconnect, at least an external reality may gradually take shape. And must suffice.

This morning, in this season of abundance, there are berries ripe in the streamside glades, pine nuts piling up in the high-mountain whitebark woods, and a hundred patches of harvest in between, of ground squirrels, mountain-ash fruit, angelica, melica, mushrooms, clover. But what are the mother grizzly and the cubs intently gulping down? Grass. They have moved downslope from the alpine sheep pastures to a sidehill park in which a patch of springlike green denotes a seep, where the grass remains soft and succulent. Succulent, yes, but in comparison with other available foods, such as berries or nuts or rodents, much inferior. *Why* then? Well, here we are again. We can only describe, and wonder, and guess.

Even as fruits and nuts and small animals mature in September and the Yellowstone ecosystem seems to overflow with late summer's bounty, the distribution of foods is changing fast. This is a dry season, and a time when many plants have finished their protein-producing cycle and are already returning to subsurface quiescence; of many only the indigestible cellulosic aerial structure remains. Perhaps grizzly bears now must choose to live in areas where sufficient variety and abundance of food are relatively concentrated—a requirement which might eliminate many seemingly good, if wide-spaced, feeding sites. In areas where food resources are concentrated, energy conservation could have a significant additive effect on good nutrition, and so not traveling far to feed on higher-quality foods might compensate for the lower quality of food immediately available. Perhaps, as the bear's metabolism begins to accelerate in preparation for the weight-gaining binge that always prefaces the winter, certain micronutrients become more important determinants of feeding strategy—and so perhaps this hillside grass is providing something for the bear and her cubs which we have no notion of. Even in the glory days of the Trout Creek dump in Yellowstone Park, grizzlies always supplemented their garbage diet with a wide variety of natural foods; a need for nutritional diversity may be why.

Yet although the complex configuration of the vegetation mosaic may account for a short-term restriction of grizzly movements, September can also be a time of long-distance travel. For some grizzlies, these movements may actually amount to a formal seasonal migration, repeated year after year: certain individuals seem to maintain quite discrete summer and fall ranges, connected by a narrow, unvarying corridor. Especially in drier years, the high elevations which, as the last snowbanks melt away, have continued to produce young and succulent vegetation well into August may in September turn suddenly dry or cold or both, desiccating the green plants and forcing grizzlies to head for creek bottoms, riversides, and other low-elevation wet sites in search of roots, berries, grasses, and forbs. This is often also the time of year when young grizzlies, especially young males, may try to colonize new range, setting out headlong cross-country into parts unknown. And with the first chill winds of the high country's early autumn comes another kind of movement which can have a decisive effect on the whereabouts of grizzly bears: the mating season and migration of the elk.

Dust whips into plumes across the sagebrush tablelands, gold in the slant light of sunset. Above the gunmetal sheen of Pelican Creek floats a serpentine gauze of mist, through which a flight of white pelicans takes wing for Mexico. Above the Marsward horizon the sky is vertically bisected, the left half limpid evening-blue, the right half white with the heavy smoke of lodgepole wildfire.

Yellowstone's grizzly bears are still widely scattered, some high in the mountains harvesting the late fruits of wild rose, mountain-ash, red-osier dogwood, twinberry, bearberry; some at low elevations digging in the glacial deposits of the wide river valleys where the soil is moist and friable, for ants, pocket gophers, and the roots of cow-parsnip, yampah, loveroot, biscuitroot, buckwheat; still others following the ridgelines to the stands of whitebark pine between eight and ten thousand feet, where the poor little squirrels are still diligently hoarding nuts for the delectation of their ursine murderers.

The five herds of Yellowstone's roughly twenty-five thousand elk have begun to break up into small groups and drift downslope toward the rutting grounds and greener pastures. The older bulls, alone or in loose aggregations, are the first to move, closely followed by the cows, also singly or in small groups. Groups of fifteen-month-old spike bulls—the original stag parties—mill sullenly behind, trailing the groups of cows and their calves-of-the-year. "A lot of spikes," writes Dick Knight (who has studied elk as well as grizzly bears), "are sexually mature but don't know what to do about it. They are similar to a twelve-year-old boy who has fantastic, uncertain dreams of sex but isn't even sure how to ask for a date. They will be off in the brush rehearsing their lines, usually a monotonous, single-noted whistle ending in uncertainty." Two-year-old males, usually called raghorns in Yellowstone, are also restless with vague endocrine stirrings and still too immature to know how to act on them. They prance and caper and try to move in on the cows, seeming to invite rebuff from the older bulls and indeed, when they come too near, receiving it, in the form of low-headed bluff charges from the reigning old magnificently antlered bulls. Young cows, who come of sexual age later than the males, pace docilely amidst the cow-and-calf groups, watchful and timid. The three-year-old bulls are sexually capable now, and from time to time they try to urge a lingering cow away from her sistership, but they are rarely successful; most of these young bulls' time is spent lunging fiercely at one another, as it were in rehearsal for the battles royal of ruts to come, or bashing the daylights out of small trees.

The great old bulls have since August been scraping the tattered velvet from their almost absurdly splendid antlers—thrashing the willows and firs till the antlers' tines are slimed with blood, and continuing to rub and polish them until the bases turn a hard rich walnut brown and the tips shine ivory white. A very small percentage of the males will do almost all the inseminating, and the display alone of these ponderous ornaments is a prime determinant of breeding success, for large antlers are a sign that a bull not only is in good condition but also has been able to afford a lot of grand excess—that he is, in short, rich. The massive antlers of a dominant bull elk are a good example of that occasional profligacy in nature which derives from the relative expensiveness of eggs and cheapness of sperm: the males in their strutting glory may look like kings, but it is the females who do the choosing, and it is female choice that has accounted for the evolution of what otherwise is something of a severe inconvenience. The antlers do have some physical utility—as weapons in the highly ritualized fights between bulls for mating supremacy—but their principal value is as symbols of potency, acting both to intimidate male competitors and to stimulate the fancy of potential members of the harem. The size of the antler rack seems to be related directly to the overall physical condition of the bull and to levels of testosterone, and it is therefore an accurate indicator of qualifications for fatherhood. Every year anew, a significant portion of an adult male elk's nutrition goes toward creating these otherwise useless appurtenances. Apropos of most of them, one is tempted to think of an ill-paid clerk who spends half his income on flashy clothes and still doesn't get the girl.

Dressed for success, then, the bulls drop virtually every other consideration in favor of the promotion of their own exhibitionist splendor—their tawny hides sleek, their fat reserves at the annual maximum, their necks swollen, their gonads in an uproar. Almost their every moment is devoted either to challenging other bulls in possession of harems of fertile cows or to gathering and defending harems of their own. They do not select for individual cows, but go indiscriminately for numbers, trying to capture entire already existing herds of females—for it follows from the egg/sperm model that whereas females will try to choose the *fittest* mates, males will try simply for the *most*. What works best is wryly reminiscent of human male machismo: showing off, foppery, bullying, fighting.

Especially at dawn and dusk, when courtship is most active, the bulls are ceaselessly, restlessly bugling. The bugle of the bull elk is one of the characteristic and most thrilling sounds of the Rocky Mountain West—and rather a challenge to describe. In *The Elk of North America*, Olaus J. Murie has at it thus: "Sometimes the rutting bull produces a roaring sound that at a little distance reminds one of the hoarse bellowing of a domestic bull. It is as though his voice, wearied by frequent use, stuck on a low pitch and failed to rise to the high, clear notes. Normally, however, the call begins on a low note, glides upward until it reaches high, clear, buglelike notes, which are prolonged, then drops quickly to a grunt, frequently followed by a series of grunts. The call may be very roughly represented thus: '*A-a-a-a-ai-e-eeeeeeeee-eough! e-uh! e-uh!*' At close range the low notes are clearly heard. They possess a reedy, organlike quality that changes rapidly as the high note is struck. A deep resonance from the capacious chest accompanies it all. At a distance the low, hoarse notes are lost to a great extent and the high bugle notes are especially clear, giving rise to the impression of 'whistling.' There is much individual variation in the pitch and character of the bugling. This is especially noticeable when three or four bulls in the same vicinity are heard in close succession."

The bugling of the elk is a signal that the rut will soon be on in earnest—that, to the exclusion of almost every other consideration, the attention of all will be devoted to the rituals of courtship and male battle; that the large and therefore many-eyed and therefore well-protected female herds of summer are dispersing into smaller groups; that the calves-of-the-year are now less zealously guarded by their mothers; and that the subadult and other lonely bulls are so thoroughly self-absorbed in trumpeting their pompous amour-propre through the canyons as to have little thought for danger and little energy for escape. It is a signal which every meat-minded Yellowstone grizzly bear knows well.

In the last light of afternoon a pair of trumpeter swans is mirrored in the stillness of a backwater slough of Pelican Creek, among shimmering rings of rising trout. A lek of gray-winged olive mayflies rises and falls above the willows, and above the mayflies swallows wheel and softly call, and above the swallows sail the night's first nighthawks into clouds of caddisflies. The distance-muffled yips of coyote pups and the slow deep *hoo-h'hoo* of a great horned owl come faintly from Astringent Creek's headwaters. The wind has fallen silent now, and the valley's few backpackers gather at the points of light that are their modest fires. A dappled packhorse dongs his bell and clanks his hobble-chain. Light snow, the autumn's first, begins to fall.

Not five miles away, in the dining room of the Yellowstone Lake Hotel, the human swarm is clanking silverware, making new friends, airing old grudges, calculating the day's miles per gallon, planning tomorrow's drive to Jackson Hole, reading *David Copperfield* or the matchbook cover, eating chicken teriyaki or surf-'n'-turf, listening or not listening or trying not to listen to two musicians saw and clink listlessly away at what seems once to have been a Mozart duo for violin and piano; and, surely, somewhere in this throng, some few at least of these visitors to the national park must be talking about what is out there in it.

What, one wonders, is the Lake Hotel dining room's human swarm's relation to the park, to the ecosystem it enshrines, to its strenuously intercontentious yet ultimately harmonious *being*? It may seem unfair to ask for a single expression of that relation; we are talking about individuals, whose thoughts about where they are are bound to be highly various. Yet there must be a relation between the mass of the citizenry—in particular the visitors themselves en bloc, who are the core of the park's constituency—and their national government's stewardship of the place. Alas, this crowd seems, frankly, rather oblivious: at least to the misanthropic temperament of the ecophile it comes easy to think how pathetically little the vehicle-imprisoned visitors ever really get from being here—some scenery, some geysers, some elk or bison seen from the roadside—for a few evenings' eavesdropping ascertains that nearly all the talk at these tables is of how far, how fast, how big, how . . . nice. And the impassioned ecophile aches to bellow in their faces, "*Nice? Nice?* It isn't *nice* at all! Nature is not *nice*—any more than *God* is *nice*." And so, hotly, forth. From which sort of ungentle adjuration it is but the shortest of rhetorical steps to, "You people don't belong here. Get out."

Which will hardly do. First of all, the ecophile should remind himself, among the obdurate zeroes here there are a scattered few nonzeroes who hew faithfully to what he regards as the correct ideological line, and the kind of dogmatic "qualifications" that flow naturally from his dreams of selective exclusion might well end up disqualifying *him*. Second, he should remember that we live in a largely urban, highly technologized society increasingly alienated from the processes of nature and therefore ill equipped to know even where to start thinking about the likes of ecology. Third, philistinism and democracy go hand-in-hand, and that's that—would he like to try another form of government? Fourth, the Americans here, the ecologically aware and the motor-numbed alike, happen to own the place. Fifth, a lot of these folks may be getting a great deal more out of being in Yellowstone than mere eavesdropping reveals: this kind of thing does not lend itself easily to talk; most people are uneasy talking about spiritual experience, and it rarely comes up over dinner in hotel restaurants. Finally, he should probably face the fact that it is not altogether healthy that he likes bears better than people.

Still, even when we put all the typical nature-lover's classic misanthropy aside, it is hard to escape the conclusion that the citizenry's conscious relation to the park is inadequate as a mandate for stewardship. What must be preserved and how that must be done to keep the park alive are not likely to be realized by most of the park's constituents. What *is* Yellowstone National Park? Even that must elude most of us. Yet Americans are deeply, and no doubt rightly, reluctant just to "leave it to the experts." In a democracy in which recondite technical expertise becomes more and more essential to managing institutions, this dilemma becomes more and more pervasive. Its natural consequence has been the growth of intermediaries—special interest groups, the press, a book like this—which act to channel, edit, and shape information flowing in both directions. Since they are neither expert nor elected, the question of these intermediaries' accountability is a difficult one, but it is usually adequately resolved, informally, in their simply maintaining believability on both sides of the relation. Their authority rests not so much on their individual unimpeachability as on the public's and the experts' corporate synthesis of the information they have set in motion; there is, if you will, a kind of natural selection at work. Certainly falsehood is sometimes not rooted out thereby; but it is hard to imagine a universally effective truth-policing system that would not partake of the censor's own biases, and who then would police the censor? Thus box within totalitarian box, and no thank you. Meanwhile, the present discordant welter of strident conservation groups, scandal-happy and eternally oversimplifying journalism, and importunate books must suffice to keep the park and the people aware of each other's deeper needs— one medium explaining why the photo shop and gas station at Fishing Bridge ought to be torn down to restore critical wildlife habitat, another insuring that when park officials try to shirk their responsibility the public is watching, and another perhaps just pointing into Pelican Valley and saying, "Look there."

Well, do look there. You will recall that it is dusk, and light snow, the autumn's first, has begun to fall. From the timbered valley edge steps an elk, a bull, head high as bulls' heads are held only in the rut. He lowers his head then, extends his neck, curls back his lips, and bugles. From across the creek, in shadow, another bugle replies. Twenty yards out into the open, the first bull stops and looks back over his shoulder, and the first of his cows appears. Five more follow, timidly bunched up, their long ears swiveling. The bull bugles again, opening the preorbital glands beneath his eye sockets and releasing a heavy scent of musk on his breath; the intensity of this scent, like that of his other pheromones, is an indicator of rank. At the end of the bugle, the bull coughs harshly and sprays urine forward onto his belly, lowering his head at the same time in order to spatter his newly beshagged neck. The bull's thick woolly mane—another ornament, like antlers, grown specially for display in the rut, and acting as a carrier and broadcaster of pheromonal stink—is urine-stained nearly black.

A little farther out into the sagebrush-covered tableland of the valley margin, he pauses at an elk-sized mudhole, his alone, kept vegetation-free year after year by the passionate wallowing of succeeding generations of rutting bulls. He steps in, and rolls about like a beast possessed, his testicles swollen and now fully descended in accordance with hormonal changes brought on by the shortening length of day, his erect penis spurting acrid scent all over him and into the mud. He sloshes his mane repeatedly through the noisome mire, and walks back to the edge of the woods to rub the clotted musk-mud off on his own scent-trees. Somewhere in the shadows across the valley, the bachelor bull who answered his bugle enacts the same scent-advertising ritual.

In the gait of elk in breeding season there is a lordly stateliness that quite belies their vulnerability. The herd moves slowly, as though on parade, as the bull circles them in a fluid high-stepping trot, keeping them grouped tightly together, his neck stretched forward, his ivory-tipped crown held high. When they reach the slow-flowing weed-thick stream, the bull is the first to cross. On a gravel bar in midstream he turns to survey his harem. One by one in single file, the cows enter the water.

Now the bachelor bull makes his appearance, emerging from a copse of spruce at the far edge of the creekside meadow, bugling belligerently. He too moves slowly, waving his antlers from side to side.

The two bulls recognize each other, a fact they signify now by nodding stiffly, like duelists. They are almost exactly the same size, and probably the same age, and so they will fight. (Greatly unequal bulls do not trifle with physical engagement: the clearly dominant one simply chases an inferior intruder away, hissing mightily the while.) They approach each other with averted eyes, only their quivering hackles suggesting that they are at all aware of each other's presence. As they come near, the two bulls turn aside and stand like mirror images, heads high, each attempting to display his greater size and superior condition. Still parallel, they walk stiff-legged side by side, in perfect step, for perhaps a hundred yards, their every muscle straining with suspense—for either may suddenly turn on the other now. But these bulls, probably because they are so equally matched, continue to parallel-walk for minutes on end, as the cows watch intently from the willows nearby. Again the bulls bellow, and turn, and now face off.

They come cautiously together with lowered heads: antlers are constructed so as both to engage one another easily and to disengage easily, but they are powerful weapons, and neither bull will risk unnecessary injury in a preemptive charge. They lock antlers carefully, plant their feet firmly, and—shove. There is no attempt to inflict damage: this is simply a test of strength. When one bull wishes to withdraw temporarily from the fray, he pulls back and averts his eyes, and the other, also mildly looking away, waits quietly. Again they engage. For nearly half an hour, groaning occasionally from the strain, they lean into each other with equal might, barely moving, until finally, weakening, they begin to move each other back and forth, first one and then the other starting to buckle at the knees and then just in time recovering.

At last the challenger stumbles, and draws back. He lowers his head near the ground, extends his muzzle, drops his ears, and makes rapid chewing motions with his jaws—a display of abject submission. The battle is over. The victor utters a staccato series of hoarse, loud barks, and the defeated bull, seeming to droop all over, makes his way slowly back to the timber whence he appeared. The winner looks scarcely better, standing with all four legs spread shakily apart and gulping air like an asthmatic.

For sometimes as long as six weeks, bulls in possession of breeding herds must undergo these exhausting challenges over and over again. Besides the cost in sheer fatigue, there is the constant danger of injury should locked antlers slip, which they not infrequently do; and despite their highly evolved symmetrical design, sometimes the antlers of sparring bull elk will not disengage, and the two die of starvation locked together. The privilege of elk fatherhood is dearly bought.

Each victory buys a little more of it. There is in fact some evidence that the sight of battle alone acts on the cows as a sexual stimulant. It seems in any case to have done so on these: one in particular, her tail sticking out straight, her vulva red and distended, looks to be distinctly in the mood. During the rut, there are anestrous periods between twenty-one and twenty-eight days long, at the end of which a cow reaches a peak of receptivity which is advertised both by the change in her nether parts' appearance and by the emission of bull-enchanting pheromones, so that copulation will occur as near as possible to the moment of ovulation.

The bull approaches the cow, his dangling, lapping tongue clearly signaling his intentions. If the cow were not near her peak of receptivity, she would move rapidly away, but this one stands her ground, gazing back over her shoulder at her suitor. He licks her flank, her croup, her back, her withers, her head; they touch noses. He bugles quietly, and begins slowly and repeatedly to lap at her vulva. Older and more dominant bulls seem to take their time at this, which probably aids them in passing their genes along, since such foreplay calms the cow and makes more certain a successful completion of the mating act.

Now the bull lays his chin flat on the cow's rump and gently slides his forequarters forward and up, his front legs dangling awkwardly on either side. The copulation is brief. Afterwards, the cow moves a short distance off and licks her own flanks, and then the mounting sequence is repeated. This continues through several more episodes of approach and copulation. One study of the Tule elk of California, whose mating habits are virtually identical to those of Rocky Mountain elk, found that an average of about six separate mountings preceded actual ejaculation. If the egg is successfully fertilized, a cow's estrus ceases immediately. She will remain in the harem, but the bull and she will no longer pay each other the slightest attention.

The next day, there is another fight to be got through. It is clear from the challenger's looks that this battle is much less equally matched than yesterday's: on the intruding bull's back the still falling feathery snow melts almost instantly, which indicates the poor condition of his pelage, which in turn indicates poor nutrition; on the dominant bull's back, with its healthily growing insulative underfur, the snow accumulates. The fight is quickly over, and afterwards there is another cow to be serviced.

Another small cow-calf herd, presided over by what looks to be an eminently challengeable younger bull, has entered the valley, and the dominant bull naturally must try to take advantage of this opportunity to enhance his holdings. So still another battle looms, this one not so easily to be dismissed. Should he be successful in expanding his harem, the big bull will have to expend still more energy keeping them all together and, since a larger harem is all the more desirable, he will have to defend it against increased numbers of challengers. The toll of such continuous days of nothing but fighting and fornicating mounts rapidly up. As in other fields, there can be such a thing as being too successful. Businessmen who overdo achievement risk heart attack; elk, grizzly bear attack.

As the days grow shorter and the nights more chill, the grizzly's way of life begins to anticipate the implacable demands of the approaching winter. She is entering the stage known to biologists as *hyperphagia*—meaning simply that she eats so much it's incredible. When autumn takes hold, the grizzly's demand for calories will at least double and perhaps even triple as she begins to store fat for hibernation. To aid in digesting this massive intake of food, she also drinks huge quantities of water—a factor that may help determine the descent from the mountain heights which seems always to characterize this period in the grizzly year. Besides bringing them into the proximity of abundant water, the altitudinal migration of autumn provides grizzly bears with access to the steadily diminishing moist sites and warmer microclimates where green vegetation and late-ripening fruits may remain; migration downslope also brings bears to the valleys where the elk rut and tire and grow careless.

Autumn nutrition can be a decisive determinant of grizzly bear population dynamics, for several reasons. Even if spring and summer foods have been plentiful, inadequate fat buildup in fall may result in premature exhaustion of the fat-dependent metabolism of hibernation and so lead to depletion of muscle tissue in late winter, leaving the bear dangerously weakened at the time of emergence from the den in early spring, when food abundance is lowest. Spring starvation, therefore, can be a significant source of mortality. Some bears whose fall nutrition is exceptionally poor may starve even during hibernation itself.

Furthermore, physical condition at the time of denning in late fall has a direct effect on the fecundity of pregnant females. There is persuasive evidence that in pregnant bears, whose fertilized embryos are still in a state of suspended animation and not yet attached to the wall of the uterus, an internal assessment of their own physical condition takes place in the early stages of hibernation, and if that condition is insufficient the blastocysts will not be implanted, and no cubs will be born. There is also some evidence, admittedly less clear, that *selective* abortion may sometimes take place—sacrificing one or two blastocysts (perhaps somehow identified in utero as inferior?) in order to improve the viability of the one or two retained. Such a process could account for the findings of several studies that litter size is strongly correlated with autumn food availability.

In cases of borderline nutritional insufficiency, the blastocysts may be implanted, but the cubs born that winter are likely to be undersized and to have strikingly poor chances of survival. In his study of black bears in northern Minnesota, Lynn Rogers has found that cubs weighing less than four pounds at the time of emergence from the den—a puniness that has occurred only in winters preceded by a food-poor fall—are four times more likely than heavier cubs to die before they are weaned. Those cubs whose mother was poorly nourished during the fall prior to their birth but who nevertheless manage to survive infancy continue to be smaller than other bears of the same age, and they are much more likely to die before reaching the age of first reproduction.

The influence of nutrition on the population dynamics of grizzly bears has been observed in detail in Yellowstone, by Frank and John Craighead and their associates, by Dick Knight and the Interagency Grizzly Bear Study Team, and by a good number of other population experts on the sidelines analyzing and reanalyzing both the Craigheads' and the interagency team's data. A comparison, by the interagency team's Bonnie Blanchard and Dick Knight, of population parameters for the periods 1959–1967 (before the abrupt closure of the park's garbage dumps and the resulting sharp reduction in the availability of high-calorie grizzly food) and 1974–1979 (after) showed that the average age of first reproduction had risen by a full year, from 4.5 to 5.5, and that the average litter size had declined from 2.2 to 1.9 cubs. Another analysis, by Joel Varney and Frank and John Craighead, also showed a steep drop in the Yellowstone grizzly's reproductive rate after 1968. Whether this decline is to be attributed to lowered nutrition as a result of the dump closures, to increased mortality, consequently lower population density, and in turn decreased breeding opportunity, or to other factors altogether remains a hotly disputed question. A climatic analysis by Harold Picton, as we have seen, has identified a long-term drying trend in Yellowstone's weather, and he proposes that its influence on the availability of *natural* foods may be a sufficient explanation of the decline in reproduction. Several critics of the Craigheads' population modeling argue that lower density has little effect on breeding opportunity and moreover should increase access to food, which should lead to a density-dependent improvement in reproduction. Another recent reanalysis of the Craigheads' and the interagency team's data suggests that the decline in reproduction was under way *before* the dump closures, and that an improvement in Yellowstone grizzlies' ability to exploit natural foods, combined with their apparent colonization of previously unoccupied or seldom-visited range, may be pushing population parameters back upward. Dick Knight believes that Yellowstone's grizzlies have recently been using food sources which they may have neglected or underutilized under the regime of the garbage-dump welfare state. Grizzly predation, particularly on elk, has shown encouraging signs of becoming more and more common through the past ten years, and Knight says, "I think these bears may really be learning something."

Irrespective of their interminable disagreements on the population question, all the scientific observers of the Yellowstone grizzly bear agree on one point: no matter what the food situation and population status are now, no matter how much grizzly nutrition might be improved in the years ahead, no matter even if such improvement could raise the Yellowstone grizzly's reproductive rate to the highest ever known, this population cannot much longer sustain the rates of habitat loss and man-caused mortality which it has undergone in recent years.

One solution for the double problem of low reproduction and high mortality was proposed by Frank Craighead in his 1979 book *Track of the Grizzly*, and reiterated in a written statement he submitted as testimony to a field hearing of the U.S. Senate Committee on the Environment and Public Works held at Cody, Wyoming, in 1983. "Formerly," wrote Craighead in his book, "the earth-filled garbage dumps served to 'zone' grizzlies away from people during the busy visitor season. . . . Baiting, the strategic placement of animal carcasses to attract grizzlies, is a tested and workable technique. It might only be needed temporarily, but could also be a continuing management tool. This should not be considered a 'supplemental feeding' of grizzlies (which is not needed) but a means of concentrating and keeping grizzlies in areas where there are no people." In his congressional testimony Craighead added, "It seems to me that when ecosystems are so altered that they can no longer adequately fill the needs of a species, some degree of management by man must fill the void."

In an article in *The Atlantic* in 1983, writer Alston Chase took the idea still further, advocating a formal program of supplemental feeding of Yellowstone grizzlies with the carcasses of "surplus" elk and other ungulates, and claiming that "the present grizzly habitat in the park is deteriorating. There may simply not be enough food to keep a fragile population from perishing." Chase was wrong both about habitat deterioration in the park and about food availability (the let-burn wildfire policy is improving both, for one thing), but he rightly pointed out that the principal argument against supplemental feeding is philosophical, and he rightly identified the source of the philosophical obstacle as the Leopold Report, which, you will recall, advocated at least an illusion of pure wildness as the ideal for ecosystems of the national parks. Craighead's idea of an ecosystem "so altered that [it] can no longer fill the needs of a species" and other of his published remarks indicate that he too believes the Leopold ideal to be fundamentally unattainable.

That is the first and more dangerous of two implicit philosophical assumptions underlying Frank Craighead's and Alston Chase's proposals. While it is certainly true that man's influence on the Yellowstone ecosystem has been substantial, it does not follow that *minimizing* human influence is an invalid ideal for management of the national park. Let us consider an analogy: the influence of venality and violence on the history of the United States has also been substantial, but it does not follow that the pursuit of justice is an invalid national ideal.

Our analogy leads straight to their second implicit assumption, that protecting the grizzly bear outside of Yellowstone National Park is a hopeless cause. The law is written, and stands. Most of the administrative procedures necessary to enforcing it and to protecting grizzly habitat are in place, and need only adequate commitment from the government—which, however slowly and inefficiently, does respond to public pressure. And public pressure continues to mount. The law *can* be enforced; man-caused mortality *can* be minimized. To claim that the park is the only place where the grizzly can survive is to abandon the surrounding national forests and private lands to the developers and the outlaws.

"Is there any park in the country," wrote Chase, "big enough to be a natural ecosystem for all the species it contains? According to a report of the First World Conference on National Parks, held in Seattle in July of 1962, 'few of the world's parks are large enough to be in fact self-regulatory ecological units.' "

As those who drew its boundaries could not at the time have known, not even Yellowstone Park is that big. No single piece of earth can be a perfectly self-contained ecosystem. There are always migratory birds, wind-borne seeds of exotic plant species, fadings-off from one biotic zone to another. Isle Royale National Park, in Lake Superior, which is the subject of especially intense biological scrutiny because it is a large, relatively isolated wilderness island and is there-fore as good a candidate for a self-regulatory ecosystem as can be imagined, has in fact been changed radically in the last century by outside but largely natural forces, notably colonization by moose and wolves from Canada; the incompleteness of its self-sufficiency does not diminish but rather enhances Isle Royale's ecological interest. Ultimately, only the planet as a whole can be thought of as a truly self-regulatory ecological unit—and even that distinction, in the light of recent theories about the influence of asteroid impacts on mass extinctions, may be seen as rather too strict. The point here is that ecosystems are *defined* by people, not merely identified; they are not so much things as ideas.

In his widely used basic textbook on biology, Clyde Herreid has written that an ecosystem is "a term that can be applied to any rela-tively isolated unit of organisms and their environment that you wish to study. It may be as small as a puddle or as large as the entire earth." How then shall we define the Yellowstone ecosystem? A full answer to that question is beyond the reach of this narrative, but surely one element in a reasonable definition would have to be "where the Yel-lowstone grizzly bear lives."

And that means not only the whole national park but also sub-stantial portions of the five national forests contiguous to it. If we take the Yellowstone grizzly's range as fundamental to our definition of the ecosystem, then we find that a very great number of the most complex processes of natural communities can be observed within the borders thus delineated. Here live not only grizzly bears but popula-tions of elk, moose, bison, bighorn sheep, mountain goats, cougars, wolverines, black bears, coyotes, pronghorn antelope, mule deer, beavers, bobcats, and many smaller mammals; countless bird species, many of them rare and vitally dependent on the sanctuary provided here, including bald eagles, peregrine falcons, ospreys, white pelicans, trumpeter swans; as well as innumerable associations of plants and fishes and invertebrates. Study of the mechanics of those populations which are isolated and an understanding of the relationships between nonisolated populations and those of adjacent ecosystems can yield invaluable information for generations to come. Within the Yellowstone grizzly bear's world there is probably a greater diversity of life being lived under natural conditions, relatively free of human modification, than anywhere else in the United States outside of Alaska. As an ecological laboratory, it is without parallel in all of North America. If we were to draw our ecosystem borders around only the national park, and leave out that other fifty percent of these five and a half million acres which is taken in by the national forests, that would no longer be even close to true. The Yellowstone ecosystem as we know it would be shattered.

That fact puts a heavy burden on the U.S. Forest Service, whose historic tradition is so severely at odds with the ideal of nonintervention in natural processes. Nevertheless, if this great wild place is to remain *itself*, if it is to endure as the home of the wild, free Yellowstone grizzly bear (and not of some half-tamed man-fed facsimile thereof), then that ideal must be central to land management throughout the ecosystem. Of course there will always be some human influence; some outright manipulation, such as reestablishment of a timber wolf population, will be necessary to right old wrongs and restore biological wholeness; and with upward of two million visitors a year, some negative human impact on natural processes is simply unavoidable. But if we abandon the ideal of minimizing man-caused degradation, we imperil Yellowstone's very meaning, which after all is *nature:* nature undefiled: a setting to awaken atavistic memories of the many-powered and mysterious world that filled the hearts of our ancestors with holy awe: the wild. We have set this land apart because we hallow it and the creatures who live here, and we hallow it and its creatures because they are wild.

Perhaps some day the whole Yellowstone complex will be wilder yet—automobiles left outside, livestock banished from the mountain meadows, the condos and Grant Villages bulldozed and their sites regreened with native vegetation, the animal and plant populations of the entire ecosystem altogether naturally regulated. That last item would require the end of sport hunting on most or all of the land comprising the area's five national forests—which seems, to say the least, a remote prospect. But aren't there, really, plenty of other places to shoot elk? Wouldn't that sacrifice be worth the benefit of seeing just this one place, this magnificently vast and unique island of wildness in a sea of technological civilization, enacting the immemorial processes of earth's history? The ideal solution would be for Yellowstone National Park to gobble up the rest of the ecosystem and double in size—but, as was concluded in the last chapter, well, ha.

Still, there are a few encouraging signs of movement in the right direction. A Forest Service man, no less—a biologist on the staff of the Bridger-Teton National Forest named John Weaver—has proposed that the five national forests of the ecosystem band together to institute a Greater Yellowstone National Wildlife Area, in which wildlife values would predominate in all management decisions, and human interference in natural events would be held to a minimum. Weaver's idea is hardly likely to elicit a boisterous chorus of yea-saying from the upper levels of his agency, but the kind of thinking it represents is heard more and more, higher and higher up. Steve Mealey, principal author of the Yellowstone grizzly management guidelines, himself a biologist and a dedicated conservationist, took over as supervisor of the Shoshone National Forest in the fall of 1983 and immediately began making courageously loud noises about new breaks for grizzly bears. Earlier that same year, in an interview with CBS News, Mealey's boss, Rocky Mountain Regional Forester Craig Rupp, said, "What we've been saying for years is, 'What's the impact of protecting the bear on man's activities?' That has to be reversed. We have to start talking about what the impacts of man's activities are on the bear. The bear has to come first." Now, when words like that come out of the mouths of United States Forest Service brass, it's hard not to think that things are changing.

In the meantime, it may be remarkable but is nonetheless the case that with the sole exceptions of the lack of the wolf and the precarious condition of the grizzly bear, Yellowstone is about as healthy an ecosystem as you can find anywhere. Despite its yearly millions of visitors, despite the mining and timbering and road building and poaching and development that are even now gnawing toward its heart, Yellowstone remains one of the precious few places in the entire temperate zone where the primeval stories of life still tell themselves over and over, from generation to generation, unedited, unexpurgated, unimpaired—and can, if we will it, do so forever.

With the waning of the rut, the breeding herds of elk and their frustrated and fatigued hangers-on begin to move along their ancient migratory routes, straggling through the early snows toward lower, warmer, drier range. Some bulls whose breeding has been success-fully completed now leave their harems and take cover in heavy tim-ber to recuperate. Others form fidgety all-male bands and cower together in the open. Those subordinate males who have failed to mate are exhausted after weeks of ineffectual courtship and fruitless combat, and are probably suffering from what in a person would amount to pathological depression. Since the beginning of the rut, many of the larger bulls have lost a hundred pounds or more, and it is the biggest who are now most vulnerable.

As they move through the dense spruce-fir forest in the failing light, the members of the traveling cow-calf herd can locate one another by the characteristic knuckle-cracking of each individual's leg joints. When one member stops, the whole herd freezes, instantly alert.

There is a sudden crashing in the undergrowth, and the eyes of the herd fix on the spot in the terrible darkness from which the noise is coming. One dominant cow struts forward in the stiff, short gait of emergency preparedness to gain a better view, but she cannot, and so utters the sharp bark of alarm that sets the herd to immediate mass flight.

The grizzly races after them through splintering fringewoods and into a hoarfrosted meadow, but none of the fleeing elk falters, and the bear quickly gives up the chase. The elk run no farther than over the first ridge. The standard predator's test has been conducted, and they know that the bear will make no further attempt on them tonight. But the cubs bound after and then past her and over the hill, impatient excitement ungovernable, burning with hunger for more of the blood and meat they have come so to relish in the last few weeks. The astonished elk bolt again, and again escape.

The cubs return obediently at their mother's call, but tussle rest-lessly with her, too fired up to settle down; she too, cuffing them irritably away, flipping over stones in halfhearted quest of grubs, is full of pent-up nervous energy. There is an awesome courage and incaution coursing through these bears' blood now. Some of the very chemicals believed to trigger and maintain hyperphagia—the family known as endogenous opiates—also act to blunt perception of pain and to lessen inhibition and fear, in the same way in which opiates operate in man. Chases they would try at no other time of year, risks they would not dare, they now undertake without hesitation.

In the timber from which the elk cows and calves were first

driven by the grizzlies, a lone young bull has lingered, one of the estrous cows' failed supplicants, as weak in spirit as in body, bedded down in a patch of thick vaccinium and hoping no one notices.

With a shift of the wind, however, the mother grizzly jolts as though with electric shock and streaks for the scent in the trees, with the cubs in furious pursuit. The elk has barely time to rise to his feet before they confront him. The predictable course of action for any prey animal in his poor condition and hopeless situation would be to break and run—and probably be overtaken from behind and killed forthwith—but this elk, for reasons that must remain his own, lowers his antlers menacingly and does not move.

Such an imperious gesture of defiance, despite its unlikeliness, would normally end all contention right here. But this is fall, and in their restless hyperphagic agitation all three bears attack at once, the mother dodging left, the two cubs right, and the elk is thus paralyzed by indecision for the critical split second. The mother bear rears up on her hind legs, reaches across the elk's rump, and drags him to the ground. She claws and bites into his flanks, spilling blue guts into the crimson huckleberry leaves. At this point, a prudent predator would stand aside and let the loss of blood finish the job, but the mother grizzly, mad with hunger and the taste of gore and the time of year, goes for the throat. By no means dead yet, the elk whirls and catches the side of the mother bear's neck with a single antler tine, and now her blood mingles on the forest floor with his. *Her* wound, however, will heal.

At dawn a subadult male black bear out on a routine prowl, also incautious owing to his own hyperphagia, digs through the blanket of duff beneath which the grizzlies have buried their kill. A big mistake. They kill and eat him too.

OCTOBER

A cloud consumes the mountaintops. It seethes down through the high defiles of naked rock, shrouds alpine glacial basins from the season's last life-lending light, and makes of serrate cliff-edge krummholz edgeless disembodied green-gray shapes afloat in a shapeless white-gray nothingness. Like a jaded fury avenging summer's innocence it searches through the canyons destroying all it can freeze, reaching inside the few remaining living forbs' cell walls to explode them from within, leaving behind only their purged and crumpled skeletons. Gaining speed and spitting snow as it descends, it shrieks through the pines and thunders over the lakes and buries the grassland flats, whiteness bearing darkness. Beneath a soft white pillow early winter smothers the last gasp of autumn.

The storm settles in for a grim gray week of wind and cold. A few warm days may yet return and briefly dispel the killing ice, but the killing has been done. Throughout the high country, all the common, easy grizzly foods are gone. Succulent green plants are dead. Marmots have rolled themselves into chill, barely breathing balls in burrows under the talus. Ground squirrels too are already hibernating. Pocket gophers, although they remain active all year, will not be seen again until spring, having moved their operations to well-provisioned winter quarters in tunnels deep beneath the thickening snow and soon-to-be-hard-frozen topsoil. In much of the dense, damp dirt best suited to the growth of underground plant foods, roots and tubers and rhizomes will soon be so securely frozen in they might as well be encased in stone. But the migrant herds of elk are still on the move, toward a fate that will provide a last burst of calories—and peril—for grizzly bears.

To reach their winter range, as we have seen, the elk move down. Because Yellowstone Park is basically a high-elevation plateau ringed with still higher mountains, many of the bands of elk must funnel through a relatively few negotiable passes and out-flowing drainages as they leave the refuge of the national park and cross its invisible borders into the lower-lying national forests. And hard against those borders, clustered around the traditional elk migration routes, are truly enormous numbers of big-game hunters. Within the typical six weeks of elk season there may be as many as fifty thousand hunters in this ecosystem, as many people as visit the backcountry for all other reasons combined the whole year long. One small elk herd, numbering six to eight hundred, winters entirely within the national park, along the Firehole and Madison rivers. Roughly eight to ten thousand members of the northern herd—somewhat more than half—will also winter in the park. The remaining ten to fifteen thousand Yellowstone elk must run a gauntlet of flying lead.

The gutpiles left behind when killed elk are field-dressed and the "walking carrion" of the weak and wounded are a grizzly bear bonanza. Exploiting it has required very little if any change in the ancestral movement patterns of many Yellowstone grizzlies: a number of them have always traveled outward and down from the high plateau at this time of year, seeking green plants yet unfrozen, fruits still unshriveled, and the inevitable casualties among the migrating ungulates.

What is new is the huge associated concentration of humanity—with scope-mounted high-powered rifles, itchy trigger fingers, and, far too often, bountiful and unsecured bear attractants all over their very campsites. There has long been a lot of blustery saber-rattling on the part of the Forest Service about cleaning up backcountry hunting camps—it is the Forest Service which issues the permits, and can revoke them—but to this day not a few of the camps look as if they had been designed for the express purpose of bringing people and grizzlies together for a spot of trouble. The worst, as a rule, are the camps kept in the same place year after year by scofflaw outfitters who think they own the wilderness and all that dwells therein. The bad outfitters are far outnumbered by the good ones, but there are nevertheless enough of the former to have done a great deal of harm. Remember that even an infrequent reward—sometimes even only one —can bring a grizzly bear back and back and back.

Some of these camps have to be seen to be believed. There may be pellets of horse feed strewn across the ground, and hundreds of pounds more of it in unprotected sacks. Often there is a cook tent redolent of bacon grease and peanut butter and steak, with ditto within; sometimes there is good food free for a bold bear's taking right out on the dining table all night long. Despite the Yellowstone guidelines' strict stipulations about keeping game meat out of reach, enforcement has been so spotty and some hunters and outfitters are so heedless (and, one might add, so stupid) that it is by no means rare in this season for Yellowstone grizzlies to feast on nocturnally filched haunch of elk. One well-known Jackson Hole outfitter lost a pack horse to a grizzly a few years ago when one of the guides in his employ left the poor horse tied to a tree overnight already packed with a load of meat! (The interagency grizzly study's report for that year commented drily, "This horse may have died at any rate, since eight days elapsed before the owner of the horse could find where it had been tied.") And the garbage that builds up in some of the worst-kept camps would do justice to a small-town dump. At that congressional hearing in Cody in 1983, several outfitters were heard grumbling that Yellowstone Park ought to reopen its garbage dumps to relieve grizzly pressure on hunting camps—but as long as even only a few of them are as liberally and reliably festooned with garbage and other attractants as they are today, you could bury Mount Washburn six feet deep in filet mignon and fill Yellowstone Lake to the brim with honey and there'd still be grizzly bears in those camps. The elk migration routes where the hunting camps are concentrated are by definition autumn grizzly habitat. There were grizzlies there long before there were outfitters and sportsmen. The bears might therefore be said to have a prior claim.

Even as they descend to the outlying lowlands to feed, Yellowstone's grizzlies may feel the first urgings of an imperative from far behind and above them, for soon, high on steep slopes of the remotest mountains, they must prepare their winter dens. These early stirrings are almost certainly instinctive; all grizzlies, even cubs, begin at this time of year to engage in seemingly random and purposeless digging. Even grizzlies in zoos, who know perfectly well that a nice snug den will soon be provided for them, start clawing at the walls and floors of their enclosures. Biologist Charles Jonkel and his colleagues once dug a winter den for an orphaned grizzly cub, and the result looked, at least to human observers, like as cozy and authentic a den as any bear could dream of, but the cub wouldn't have it. She left the man-made den immediately, and insisted on digging her own.

The timing of individual grizzlies' movement from their late-season feeding grounds to their denning areas often varies widely, according to a number of factors both physiological and environmental.

Pregnant females are almost always the first grizzlies to den—and in spring, by then mothers with newborn cubs, the last to emerge. According to the interagency study team's data, the mean den entrance date for pregnant females in Yellowstone from 1975 through

1980 was October 26, while for all other Yellowstone grizzlies it was November 12. The mean emergence date for females with new cubs was April 13, compared to March 27 for all others.

For male and nonpregnant female grizzlies, the most important contributors to the likelihood of earlier or later denning seem to be nutritional status and food availability.

Bears who reach optimal fatness early tend to give up hyperphagia abruptly, despite continuing availability of food, and travel straight to the subalpine zones where they will select a den site. They may prepare their dens right away, but, although food is now scarce or nonexistent at the high and early-winterstruck altitudes of the denning areas, the bears often remain outside for quite a while— sometimes three weeks or more—eating little or nothing, plodding around in a logy languor that seems already halfway to hibernation. As with other mammals, the number of a grizzly bear's fat cells seems to remain constant throughout his adult life: "optimal fatness," therefore, must refer not to the number but to the size of the cells. Ralph Nelson, the world's foremost authority on the biochemistry of bear hibernation (it is from his work that most of this narrative's information on the subject has come), believes that when the fat cells reach a certain size, they may emit some substance which triggers the unique physiological processes that induce hibernation. He cites studies showing that one such chemical, isolated by dialysis from the blood of hibernating ground squirrels, woodchucks, and arctic marmots, will send ground squirrels injected with it into deep hibernation even in summer. Like insulin, Nelson notes, the substance is biologically identical across phylogenetic lines. As of this writing, he is hot on the trail of an analogous trigger substance in bears. In observations of a captive black bear, Nelson found that over the course of six years the bear grew from two hundred to four hundred fifty pounds but lost almost exactly the same amount of weight each winter; although plenty of food remained available to the bear in late fall, he never overate—that is, never stored more fat than the particular amount necessary to sustain him through the winter—a strong indication that the storage of a specific (and lifelong constant) amount of fat is sufficient to induce hiberation. In his work with black bears— in whom the mechanisms of hibernation seem to be the same as in grizzlies—Nelson has already shown that predenning lethargy does indeed exhibit many of the biochemical characteristics of full hibernation. The sluggishness and anorexia of bears just out of the den in

spring are a manifestation of the same sort of "walking hibernation"
—except, of course, that the process is moving in the other direction.

For less than optimally roly-poly grizzlies, the simple sequence
of travel to den sites, den construction, fat-induced lethargy, and
finally denning and hibernation is likely to be complicated by environmental factors. For these individuals (and in bad years this may mean
the whole population) it is advantageous to stay in food-rich areas as
long as possible. Sometimes, depending on such factors as the severity
of the weather, snow accumulation, carrion availability, and the previous summer's productivity of food plants, these bears may be able
to find whitebark pine nuts, carcasses, roots, or other food sources at
high elevations near potential denning habitat. At other times the
only available food may be far from their winter homes, most likely
in the lowlands. In either case, some bears may eventually reach a
state of fatness sufficient for their metabolic autopilots to take over
and the classic sequence to be performed, although den selection and
construction may have to be hurried and the period of predenning
lethargy may be short or nonexistent.

Other grizzlies, however, may never reach optimum fatness before the onset of full winter makes travel so difficult and food so hard
to find that any further effort will result in a net loss of energy; these,
of course, are the last bears to den. Since their fat cells have not
reached the full size at which the trigger substance would be automatically released, there must be other influences involved in the induction of these bears' hibernation—perhaps temperature, photo-
period (length of daylight), the darkness of the den, the absence of
food, or some combination of these and other factors. One older
study claimed to show that the removal of food in fall was also sufficient to induce hibernation; but that was before Nelson's work, and
the amount of that bear's fat deposition up to that point was not
measured, and, since the bear was in captivity and therefore had
presumably been dining royally, he may have been ready to hibernate
anyway. Certainly a bear whose food is taken away in midsummer
will not start hibernating; he will simply starve. Which is not to say
that the sudden loss of food after denning may not be *a* factor. Anyway, however they do it, many suboptimally fat bears do manage to
achieve hibernation, although, as we have seen, pregnant ones may
fail to bear young or may give birth to cubs with poor prospects of
survival, and other bears, especially if their spring food supply remains poor, may fail to breed or may still starve.

And a few poorly nourished grizzlies may never manage to achieve hibernation: they lie curled in their dens waiting for a sleep that never comes, and, poisoned by the bodily wastes which the processes of hibernation normally would metabolize, die in early winter. A few others may begin hibernation successfully but then run out of fat—the fuel of hibernation—later in the winter. Such bears might then emerge to wander dazed through the foodless snowscape until they starve to death, or they might just stay in the den, consuming their own vital tissues and poisoning themselves with urea until they too die.

Other factors besides those associated with the physiological induction of hibernation sometimes affect the timing of den entry. The Craigheads' study in Yellowstone, for example, found that grizzlies living under similar environment conditions (elevation, vegetative type, weather, and so forth) would often *all* hole up for the winter during the same heavy snowstorm. The bears seemed to sense the oncoming snow well before its advent was apparent to human observers; perhaps they could feel the falling atmospheric pressure. Sometimes even under clear blue skies, they would head straight for their dens regardless of whether they were near their den sites or out foraging somewhere far away, and, sure enough, heavy snow would follow—obliterating their tracks, the den openings, and all evidence of their tenancy. The biologist Ian McTaggart Cowan has pointed out that the hunting practices of some of the Indians who came to hunt in the Yellowstone area—who prized grizzly claws as symbols of their prowess and who knew that a bear in the den is at his most vulnerable—might have exerted a strong selective pressure for such behavior. Furthermore, as Frank Craighead has noted, Yellowstone's black bears—who were not subject to intense hunting pressure from prehistoric man—don't make a habit of denning during snowstorms. Of course, there may be a whole complex of other factors involved, but evasion of possible threats is certainly suggested by such behavior as denning during snowstorms. In New York, where the Indians actively pursued the black bear, Stuart Free found another evasive denning strategy: the black bears he observed "would walk up to a den site, go in, then back out stepping in their own tracks for twenty yards or more, then leap perhaps fifteen to twenty feet to the side and then continue to . . . another site and then do the same thing." In his remote study area in Canada, Art Pearson found that the timing of Yukon grizzlies' den entrance was *not* correlated with snowfall. Some of the enormous grizzlies of the Alaska Peninsula den up early, long before the snow flies, while others can be found still fishing for salmon until late December.

When grizzlies den may be highly variable, but *where* is not. Although a natural chamber such as a cave or a hollow tree may once in a while meet their strict requirements, grizzlies almost always dig their own dens, for they have very particular ideas about what is suitable.

Throughout grizzly country, from Wyoming to Alaska, the most constant characteristic of den sites is the angle of the slope in which the dens are dug—nearly always between twenty-five and fifty degrees from the horizontal, with by far the majority clustered right around thirty degrees. The reasons are simple: such slopes are steep enough that there will be plenty of soil or rock overhead to form a nice thick den roof that is unlikely to collapse, and they are still shallow enough for the den opening to be clogged and covered by a heavy blanket of snow, which both insulates the den and conceals it.

Another consistent characteristic of grizzly dens is their aspect —that is, orientation. Grizzly bears seem to have an uncanny foreknowledge of the direction from which the prevailing winds of winter will blow, and, since snow tends to blow off the windward side of the mountains and accumulate on the leeward side, it is in the lee that almost all grizzlies dig their dens. The compass orientation of that lee may vary from place to place even within the same locality, according to topographic and microclimatic factors, but den sites are reliably found where snows are deepest. In Yellowstone, for example, where the prevailing winter winds and snowstorms blow strongly from the west-southwest, most grizzly dens are dug on northern slopes— although, probably owing to the extreme irregularity of the terrain here, which could account for a good deal of refraction of the wind, a substantial minority of dens are found at other aspects. In Banff National Park in Alberta, where the winter weather rolls in from due west and meets a simple north-south mountain chain, almost all grizzly dens are dug in east-facing slopes. In some areas where winds are variable and snow depths relatively constant, such as the Mission Mountains of western Montana, grizzly dens may be found at any aspect—but, again, always beneath deep snow.

How do they know where that deep snow is going to be? At least some of grizzlies' ability to select den sites is probably instinctive, since orphaned cubs-of-the-year have been known to den successfully.

Some small areas seem to be used intensively for denning year after year. Once in a while, an old den will be reused, but in most grizzly denning habitat the soils are such that the dens collapse after spring thaw. Several active dens may sometimes be found clustered within a few hundred yards of one another—suggesting perhaps that off-spring return to localities where they and their mother denned in earlier years, or perhaps that young grizzlies learn about such sites from their older compeers, or perhaps that certain kinds of places simply ring an innate chime of recognition. It is also true that older and more experienced grizzlies tend to pick better sites and dig better dens than the young, despite the fact that cubs (except for orphans) are assiduously instructed by their mothers through one or often two cycles of denning. Subadult grizzlies are sometimes found frozen to death in poorly constructed or poorly sited dens from which the snow cover has been blown or melted away, but grownups virtually never are.

Elevation is another den site characteristic which is highly uni-form within a given ecosystem but which may vary considerably among biogeographic provinces. In Yellowstone, den sites range from six thousand five hundred up to ten thousand feet above sea level, and nearly half are clumped between eight and nine thousand feet. In the Canadian Yukon, most dens are found near four thousand feet; in Alaska's Brooks Range, about three thousand; on Kodiak Island, about eighteen hundred; and on the Alaska Peninsula, about thirteen hundred. The narrow altitudinal range of the denning zone in all these localities admirably exemplifies the grizzly's ability to come up with local solutions to local problems, for there are few characteristics of climate, geology, and vegetation in common among these areas, yet in each the bear over the centuries has quite specifically defined the best denning habitat, and within each community there is little variance from the established norm.

A consistent combination of certain features seems to character-ize the locations of grizzly denning zones throughout North America, and in a given locality that combination can generally be found only within a narrow range of elevations. Other characteristics, such as forest canopy cover, may change greatly from place to place, but the following seem to be the basic invariables. The geology must be such that the soil is diggable but still firm enough not to collapse even through rapid fluctuations of freezing and thawing, which are occa-sionally inevitable. The vegetative cover must provide a network of deep-reaching roots to stabilize the soil that forms the den roof, and the plants' aboveground parts must be sufficiently strong and reticulated to stabilize and hold the snowpack. The weather must be cold enough winter-long that even during a warm spell, such as that brought on by a thermal inversion, the covering of snow will not melt through and thus expose the den opening, for the loss of the snow barrier could have several untoward consequences: chilling meltwater could trickle into the den chamber; freezing air, especially if the weather were to get really cold before it snowed again, could also destroy the snug warm microclimate which forms in a perfectly snow-sealed den; and the den could be easily seen, and so would be vulnerable to predators (not only people but also wolves have been known to kill hibernating bears in their dens, and newborn cubs would be in particular danger from their conspecific male elders, who typically emerge earlier and for whom in earliest spring food is in critically short supply). And, finally, the den site must be remote enough to minimize the possibility of disturbance.

As you may imagine, that last requirement is getting harder and harder to meet in a lot of grizzly country. In this regard, for once, Yellowstone's troubles are rather less than those of other areas: most Yellowstone grizzlies den well within the protected confines of the national park, and the rest tend to den very high in the remotest mountains of the adjacent national forest wilderness areas, where the brutal terrain and winter weather are simply too treacherous for much of anybody to brave. Outside the national parks and the ruggedest wildernesses, however—in northern Idaho and western Montana, for example, and in an astonishing number of places in Canada and the far North—increasing winter logging, winter exploration for oil and gas, and winter recreation are bringing more and more people and their chain saws, bulldozers, trucks, helicopters, dynamite, snowmobiles, and blaring stereo tape decks into previously silent and pristine grizzly bear denning habitat, and some of the bears have shown themselves to be highly vulnerable even to disturbances which might seem to us quite mild, and even at some distance from their dens.

Unlike deep hibernators such as ground squirrels and marmots, bears are relatively easily roused from their winter sleep. But the awakened grizzly is a groggily docile Dr. Jekyll to his ferocious midsummer Mr. Hyde. In all their years of observation of grizzly denning, although individual hibernating bears' response to disturbance varied quite a bit, the Craigheads and their associates never once knew a bear to defend his den. On the contrary, they found, a grizzly disturbed either during the predenning period or in hibernation is likely to abandon his den altogether. If the season is still early enough, or if another suitable site should luckily happen to be available not too far away, the bear may succeed in digging a new den and finishing the winter in good shape, but in areas of hard-frozen ground or very deep snow—both, as we have seen, conditions which normally obtain all winter long throughout eligible denning habitat—the grizzly bear who has abandoned one den will probably never find another. Thus, as encroachment on denning zones increases, will a few more grizzly bears die.

The rules of den construction vary just as little as those of site selection. First, if local food availability or his nutritional state permits it, the typical grizzly likes to move to the den site early—in Yellowstone, the usual range is between eight and twenty-two days prior to final entry—and take his time digging the den, foraging a little in the immediate vicinity, making minor improvements in the den, collecting and arranging his bedding till it's just right, and generally winding down, in the classic pattern of predenning lethargy.

In Yellowstone, as in other heavily forested areas, the final choice of the exact den site is usually on the upper one third of a steep slope and directly beneath a large old tree, most often a whitebark pine or a subalpine fir, whose bole and root network will help forestall the danger of a collapsed ceiling. The commonest understory plants at the site are *Vaccinium* species—huckleberry, grouse whortleberry, and the like—which also have strong root complexes. These are also the usual vegetative cover in nontimbered denning habitat. The bear begins by burrowing straight into the slope, tunneling either horizontally or at a slight angle upward, flinging a stupendous shower of rock and root and rubble out between his legs and down the mountainside. The first two to six feet of excavation form a passage barely big enough for the bear to squeeze through. At the end of this tunnel, the grizzly then digs out a larger space, which will be the bedroom.

The sine qua non of den construction is heat conservation, so the sleeping chamber is usually only big enough to accommodate bedding and tightly curled-up bear (or, for mothers, bears), with just enough room left over to change position comfortably in. About twenty percent of Yellowstone grizzly dens have the tunnel sloping slightly upward toward the bedroom—which, since heat rises, is an excellently efficient configuration for conserving warmth. A few unusually large dens may have a raised sleeping platform at the back, serving the same purpose. Other grizzly dens may have an elbow or some other change of direction in the entrance passageway, an arrangement that would limit air circulation and thus also conserve heat. Like almost everything else about these idiosyncratic creatures, grizzly bears' dens are sometimes inexplicably eccentric: Jack Lentfer and his associates, in their work on the Alaska Peninsula, found one den formed entirely in the snow with an S-shaped tunnel nineteen feet long, a small alcove, and then a cone-shaped boudoir six feet across and nine feet high!

The basic excavation of the den usually takes only three to seven days, but grizzlies may spend much longer than that collecting and arranging their bedding and otherwise fussing with the details. Although the Yellowstone interagency study has found a few cases in which grizzlies seemed not to have provided themselves with any bedding at all, these may just be rare examples of inexperience or incompetence. Because in order to avoid disturbing the animals the researchers wait to investigate the dens until after emergence in spring, it is also possible that those bears had simply cleaned all the bedding out of their dens before the biologists got there: the Craighead team in the sixties had two study bears who did precisely that. In any case, most grizzly bear dens are elaborately upholstered, and this too is a heat-conservation tactic. The Craigheads found that Yellowstone grizzlies usually chewed off spruce and fir boughs (cushier than pine or deciduous shrub branches)—sometimes felling whole trees like beavers to get at the soft stuff up high—and then made shallowly cup-shaped beds that ranged from three to fourteen inches deep. One of their female study bears normally used conifer boughs for her bedding but then when she was pregnant made a much softer bed of moss and grass, and the Craigheads speculated that that variation might be routine for pregnant grizzlies. Dick Knight's interagency team, however, in a more recent study with a considerably larger sample size, concluded that Yellowstone grizzlies' choice of bedding material was related only to what was available near the den, without any particular selectivity. Farther north, where beargrass is common in grizzly denning habitat, that seems sometimes to be the mattress of choice.

Anyway, however carefully or randomly it may be chosen, bears' den bedding does its job beautifully, trapping and warming dead air in the many small pockets its springy construction creates—just like a goose-down sleeping bag. The Craigheads once built an artificial den for a young captive black bear and placed a telemetric thermistor in the midst of the (nonartificial) bedding and inserted another thermistor surgically in the bear's abdominal cavity, and they found that with the hibernating bear's internal temperature averaging about ninety-six degrees Fahrenheit and the ambient temperature well below freezing, the microclimate created by the bedding stayed between eighty-three and ninety-seven degrees. Thanks to its architecture and its insulation, then, a bear's winter home is a remarkably cozy place.

In the final days before entering the den, a grizzly bear's feces become loose and watery as the last of his food is scoured from the bowel. Some bears seem then to ingest a variety of indigestible material, which will form a kind of plug, sometimes as long as three feet, in the lower part of the large intestine. These anal plugs are often found just outside vacated dens in spring; some are composed mainly of hair, some of sand, some of pine cone pieces, and still others seemingly just of dead cells sloughed off from the walls of the gut. No one has any idea what purpose such a plug may serve.

And now, in this deep dark hole in the ground, something of a miracle begins to take place. To appreciate just how miraculous bear hibernation really is, it will serve us well to go into some detail.

Any animal, to stay alive, needs to keep building itself anew all the time. The substance of the living cells that make up the organism must be constantly replenished. Most cells have a far shorter lifetime than the organism of which they are part, and when they die they must be replaced. If we don't eat or drink, we quickly come to lack the simple proteins and the water which nourish living cells and from which new tissues must be built, so we waste away and die. In addition, many of the chemical products of the protein breakdown that characterizes the creation, the replenishment, and the death of cells happen to be poison, and that is why if our bowels or our kidneys are blocked, we die in a hurry. Yet a hibernating bear, sometimes for as long as seven months, does not eat, does not drink, does not defecate, does not urinate.

Bear hibernation is a phenomenon radically different from the winter sleep of other hibernating mammals. A hibernating wood-chuck's body temperature falls from ninety-seven to less than forty degrees Fahrenheit, he breathes only once about every six minutes, and his heartbeat drops from a hundred beats a minute to four. When he and other small hibernators are in that condition, they are virtually impossible to arouse. If you pull a hibernating woodchuck out of his burrow, you can roll him down the hillside like a bowling ball, and he will remain nearly as insensible as one. But these same so-called deep hibernators must also rouse themselves every few days to move around and, usually, to urinate, and many must also eat, drink, and defecate, or they will die of starvation or uremic poisoning just as surely as we would if we gave up eating, drinking, and elimination. In these periodic arousals, the animals wake up fully, their body temperature rises all the way back to normal, their heartbeat and respiration speed back up, and their whole metabolism is little different from its fully active summer state. The energy cost of such frequent and radical metabolic recoveries is high, and, although the stored fat of a few species of small hibernators may be sufficient to sustain them through the winter, most must keep substantial caches of food nearby or must even venture out into the cold cruel winter to forage every time they awake.

Bears, on the other hand, once they have sunk into hiberation, are there to stay (with the exception, of course, of those few individuals with inadequate fat stores). Because bears' body temperature falls so little—a maximum of about twelve degrees below their summer normal of a hundred and one—they are quite easily roused to a state at least approximating full consciousness, and can then, as long as they have a moment or two to get their bearings, escape danger or defend themselves, but if you leave a hibernating bear alone he is unlikely even to lift his head for months. His self-sufficiency is complete.

We can only speculate, so far, about how the unique mechanisms of bear hibernation may have evolved, but Ralph Nelson's work has led to intriguing suggestions that somehow, in the random variation of genes over the generations of early bears or their precursors, certain of the basic biochemical processes of starvation may literally have been reversed. Such a case must be extraordinarily rare indeed, in which a seemingly unfit individual—a starving one—contributes a crucially advantageous adaptive characteristic to a species' evolution.

A starving animal undergoes a high rate of what is known as

protein catabolism—that is, the breakdown of the complex proteins of its living tissues into simpler compounds, many of which are poisonous and so must be filtered out and eliminated as waste. Protein catabolism of exactly the same kind also takes place in a hibernating bear, but black bears—and presumably brown (including grizzly) bears as well, and probably polar bears too—have evolved additional pathways of protein *anabolism*—that is, the synthesis of complex proteins from simple compounds, or the exact reverse of *catabolism*. These anabolic pathways take the products of protein catabolism out of the usual waste channels—resorbing them straight through the walls of the bladder and the bowel—and then break these wastes down further, combine their components with other substances derived from the catabolism of stored fat, and create living tissue all over again. This state of simultaneous protein catabolism and anabolism is unknown in any other animal. There is a phoenix inside a midwinter's bear, creating new self from the ashes of the old.

Although the hibernating bear does not urinate, he does lose a good deal of water as vapor in his exhaled breath. But more water is produced in the fat breakdown that fuels the bear's metabolism, and the waste matter that is resorbed for protein anabolism also contains water, which, once its poisons have been purged by the kidneys, broken down, and resynthesized into living cells, can then be recycled. Throughout the winter, therefore, the water content of a hibernating bear's red blood cells, plasma, and other tissues remains perfectly balanced.

Because the bear's fur has more than doubled in insulative value during the fall, having grown especially thick on his back, sides, and neck—precisely the parts which will be exposed when he is curled up nose-to-tail in the classic hibernating position—and because the den maintains so cozy a microclimate, and because so large a curled-up animal's surface-to-mass ratio is so low, only a small amount of well-insulated bear surface is available to radiate into an already warm and well-insulated environment the large amount of inner bear warmth: thus his body temperature falls very slowly, finally reaching a low of perhaps eighty-nine degrees in the coldest part of the winter. The Craighead team found that a hibernating bear's temperature tends to fall as the ambient temperature falls and to rise when it rises, but when the bear's body temperature falls all the way to eighty-nine, it will immediately shoot back up to about ninety-one and a half, even if the outside temperature continues to fall—a fact suggesting, they wrote, "a spontaneous arousal mechanism . . . [which] may serve as an alternative to the regular periodic awakening that occurs in other mammalian hibernators."

The hibernating bear's heartbeat also slows down gradually, from a summer-sleep normal of about forty beats per minute to only eight or ten; for a short while each day, however, the heart rate rises back to about forty—perhaps due to another spontaneous arousal mechanism insuring that the general metabolic slowdown does not go too far. The bear's consumption of oxygen falls by half or more. There is also a substantial decline in the amount of carbon dioxide lost in the breath—conveniently making all the more carbon available for protein synthesis.

While body temperature declines and heartbeat and breathing slow down, protein turnover—both destruction and creation—is speeding up, toward a rate three to five times that in a nonhibernating bear. This protein metabolism generates quite a bit of heat—perhaps enough, Nelson has speculated, to be a significant contributor to the relatively high body temperature of hibernating bears as compared to that of other hibernators. The high rate of protein turnover also keeps a lot of amino acids tied up that would otherwise find their way into the creation of the body's most plentiful deadly waste product, urea. Nelson has hypothesized that a decline, presumably hormonally regulated, in the production of certain enzymes also helps hold down urea formation. Urea is precisely the substance which the hibernating bear's major unique anabolic pathway is designed to turn back into useful proteins, but the energy expense of doing so is high, so any suppression of urea production is advantageous—prevention, in short, being cheaper than cure. Thus, less poison than usual is produced in the first place, and what is produced is transformed, dross into gold. Natural alchemy: by winter's end the bear actually has a lower concentration of urea in his blood than he has at summer's height.

Despite a whole winter of inertness, the hibernating bear suffers no muscle atrophy, nor even cramps. Somehow, he loses no calcium from his bones. Although the concentration of cholesterol in his blood is double his summer normal (and double that of most human Americans), his arteries do not harden, and cholesterol stones do not form in his gall bladder. (In fact, a bile juice produced by hibernating bears, known as ursodeoxycholic acid, has been used to dissolve gallstones in people, obviating the need for surgery.) Although the bear's kidneys have been continuously refiltering the bodily wastes produced by the threefold to fivefold increase in protein metabolism, he will never have developed a kidney stone. A pregnant female will also have given birth and nursed her rat-sized newborns up to five pounds apiece or better at emergence time.

Keeping all that fine-tuned machinery running smoothly costs a hibernating four-hundred-pound grizzly bear about eight thousand calories a day—and yet the bear does not lose an ounce of lean body mass. Although the experimental evidence is for male bears, it is believed that even a parturient mother, gestating her fetuses, giving birth in midwinter, and then suckling her fast-growing young for as long as three months in the den, probably loses lean tissues only to cub production. A hibernating bear's entire weight loss is in fat. Indeed, when a bear emerges from his den at winter's end, he often has a substantial amount of fat still in reserve, to tide him through the food shortage of early spring. All this without a bite to eat all winter long. It is surely as splendid a miracle as nature performs.

But to achieve it, the mother grizzly and her cubs must first survive the big-game hunting season. On the resolute purposefulness of their prehibernation hyperphagia and the mother bear's certitude of where it may best be indulged, therefore, a certain restlessness obtrudes. She knows what a rifle can do; she has seen rifles kill. And she knows how to read the signs of rifles' and riflemen's propinquity.

They are hardly difficult to read. The country is full of commotion. Along the little dirt spur roads gouged through what until not so many years ago was logjam-clotted and therefore untrammeled riparian habitat for grizzly bears each autumn, now pickup trucks, horse trailers, campers, off-road vehicles, motor homes, cars, and even dirt bikes swarm up the twisting creek bottoms toward the trailheads, where they join more of their ilk tilted into ditches, nosed into roadside deadfalls, clustered in the gravel turnouts. Three times each day, the hearty shouts of hail and well-met sportsmen feeding drift on the wind through the timber. At dawn and eventide, when the migrating elk venture warily out to meadow edges to graze, the mountains ring with gunfire. Gutpiles, carcasses, wounded prey, horse feed, left-out leftovers, riverine still-green grass or not, this is no longer a healthy place for a grizzly bear to be, and the mother and her cubs decide it is time to pull out.

Back up the canyon, then, the bears move into the regions of snow, clinging to the midnight shadows under heavy brush and timber, avoiding their accustomed easy trails, stopping and listening to the slap of playing cards and the laughter of men from a tent three miles downvalley, and then padding stealthily on until the forest thins and the alpine snowfields shine before them in the moonlight. Here they wait until an hour before first light, when the moon is down and they can move with some sense of security into the unbroken whiteness of the snowfields. They are traveling fast now, in a steady lumbering lope, far from any cover, until at last they crest a saddle at ten thousand five hundred feet and, as though they actually know they have reached safety, dawdle down the other side into the national park.

Later that morning, trudging through deep powder snow on his cross-country skis, Bart Schleyer picks up the signal from the bear's radio collar, too faint to pinpoint her location but still easily identified by its assigned frequency. He greets that static-clouded, barely audible click with a sigh of fervent relief, for it means that one more mother grizzly bear—most precious of all of Yellowstone's bears—is safe.

Schleyer radios his discovery in to the park's Lamar ranger station, and the rangers telephone the Interagency Grizzly Bear Study Team's Larry Roop in Cody. By afternoon, aloft in his light radio-tracking plane, slammed up, down, and sideways so gut-wrenchingly by the wind he can barely write, Roop has located the bear and her cubs where they are bedded down, invisibly, in an island of timberline krummholz. And another heartening dot—grizzly bear alive—goes on the map.

A look through only a few of Roop's copious notes from an earlier hunting season may help us appreciate just how good that little dot feels:

An unmarked 250–300 lb. adult female was shot on September 13 by a bird hunter near Eagle Creek, north of Gardiner, Montana, in the Gallatin National Forest. The bear was shot at point blank range with a shotgun. The hunter's dog harassed the bear and it charged the hunter. Authorities determined that the bear was shot in self-defense and no charges were filed. The female may have been accompanied by cubs.

On September 23 a young male grizzly was shot by a bow hunter in the Hilgard area of the Gallatin National Forest, Montana. Bullets were also later found in the carcass. The grizzly was mistakenly shot as a black bear and the individual was fined $500 by the State of Montana for taking a protected animal, but $400 of the fine was suspended because the individual reported the incident.

A 500 lb. adult male grizzly, bear no. 46, was shot on October 1 near Cooke City, Montana, in the Gallatin National Forest. Charges of taking a grizzly bear without a license were filed by the State of Montana. The case is pending and the individual will reportedly plead self-defense. Since the bear was shot from behind and the bear was shot while feeding on a dead moose, authorities can find no justification for the shooting of the bear.

10/2 One lg. ad., golden with black hump and legs, hunters killed elk and went for pack horse, when they returned 30 mins. later bear was feeding on elk, bear refused to leave, they left elk for bear and returned later for antlers.

10/6 Camp damage by one or possibly 2 different grizzlies, a private hunting party's camp and an outfitter's camp damaged, groceries scattered, camps unoccupied.

Bear no. 22, a 300 lb. adult male grizzly, was shot by a hunter on October 8, near Camp Monaco in the Shoshone National Forest, Wyoming. The State of Wyoming has turned the case over to federal authorities and charges are pending against the individual. The hunter is pleading self-defense. Bear no. 22 . . . was shot over the gutpile of the defendant's elk.

10/10 Camp damage, tracks, sow (f.f. width 136 mm) and 1 or 2 ygs. (f.f. width 109 mm). Camp vacant at time. Bears had been into camp only 2–3 hrs. earlier. Tents torn, groceries scattered, cooler torn open, tack tent ripped open and horse cubes eaten.

On October 15 radio-collared bear no. 26, a 300 lb. adult female, was found dead along the highway approximately 3½ miles north of Gardiner, Montana. The bear had apparently been struck by a large vehicle and dragged along the road. Later autopsy revealed the bear had also been shot.

10/21 One ad., hunter was treed by grizzly while hunting elk on foot.

While checking campsites in the Thoroughfare and upper Yellowstone after outfitters had vacated the sites, U.S. Forest Service personnel discovered the remains of bear no. 49. The bear carcass was found on November 3, but it had apparently been dead for some time. It lay only 50 to 100 ft. from the corral of a recently vacated outfitter's camp. A field autopsy revealed what appeared to be shotgun wounds. . . .

11/19 One med. size subadult, est. wt. at 200 lb., attacked and mauled hunter, cause of attack unknown, uncollared bear.

And so, on and on, it goes. In the interagency study team's 1982 report, Dick Knight wrote: "Since 1975, 95 grizzly bears have been fitted with radio collars and monitored for varying lengths of time. Of these bears, 37 were known or suspected to be dead at the end of the 1982 field season; 84% of these deaths were man-caused. Only 38 of the total 95 bears were known to be alive at the end of 1982."

The big jet floats through the overcast toward the airport butte above Billings, and slithers to a stop in slashing rain. Good, thinks the high-school teacher from Minneapolis. This will be snow in the high country. Good tracking.

This is to be his first elk hunt, his first foray into the Western wilderness, his first experience with a professionally outfitted and guided expedition. Driving south toward Cody, seeing the snow-streaked escarpments of the Beartooth Plateau fading up into the clouds, and, farther on, as the weather begins to break and the distant saw-edged peaks of the Absaroka Range glint white and black through tattering mists, he feels his pulse race in response to the awesome sheer scale of this landscape, so brutal, so *wild* in comparison to the intimate horizons of the grainfields and pastures and woodlands of his wonted Midwestern whitetail deer countryside. He remembers reading recently what Theodore Roosevelt once wrote of this place—

"There is no more beautiful game country in the United States"—and, peering up into the glaciers and crags and cliffs, he reflects that it is more than just beautiful: it is also scary.

Over a glass of Yellowstone bourbon in the bar of the Irma Hotel —which, having as always done copious research, the teacher recalls old Buffalo Bill himself built—the man is full of deep thoughts about the glories and myths of which he is about to partake. He is that rare sort of hunter for whom the experience is almost spiritual, an engagement in a harmony more ancient than his race; in true wilderness for the first time in his life, in pursuit of the magnificent Yellowstone elk, he will, he senses, more truly now be in touch with his ancestors than he has ever been.

When the outfitter comes to pick the man up at the hotel next morning, he strides across the lobby toward the teacher with a solemn scowl beneath his Tom Mix black ten-gallon, and from beneath his long black soup-strainer mustachios comes a bitten-off "Howdy." The outfitter gravely shakes the Minnesotan's hand, leads him in silence out to the sidewalk, and there introduces him to his fellow hunters—a deeply tanned Californian in mirrored sunglasses and shiny new Hollywood-cowboy clothes, and three fat, florid brothers from Cincinnati. "You ride with me," the outfitter tells the Californian. "That's my blue truck there," he says to the man from Minnesota. "You follow me."

The blue truck exhales an asthmatic plume of blue smoke, the teacher's rented Toyota falls in behind, the Cincinnati brothers' gold-flecked van smoked with plexiglass heart-shaped bubble-domes set into its hindquarters brings up the rear, and the votaries of Nimrod are off.

The trailhead is a dusty congeries of horses and leather and canvas and rope and groceries and duffel bags and monogrammed suitcases and rifles and ammo boxes and feed sacks and cases of beer. One party besides their own is packing up to head in, and two others have just come down from the mountains. The incoming dudes lounge uncertainly at the fringes of the action, eyes on their gear, creases in their jeans. The outgoings, grimy and gregarious, pitch in with horses and unpacking, not only in sporting camaraderie but also, doubtless, in eagerness to get to their cars and the soonest possible hot shower. The other parties' wranglers and outfitters go about their labors with systematic deftness and a constant peppering of sarcastic repartee, while the teacher's own outfitter is roaming about aimlessly and silently, hefting the weight of his clients' gear and frowning, hacking off a strip of leather from a jumbled heap of sorry-looking tack and flipping it into the woods, rummaging through the safe box in the back of his blue truck and emerging with nothing in hand.

While the black-hatted outfitter and his young wrangler wrestle with hitching up a packsaddle on an old swaybacked roan, the teacher eavesdrops a bit on two of the other outfitters, who have stepped behind a horse trailer.

"I wonder how much longer that son of a bitch is going to keep getting away with this," one is saying softly. "Have you seen that camp of his up on Sunlight?"

"I sure don't think he gets too many repeaters," replies the other.

"Well, I don't know about that. He gets a pretty high success rate."

"Yeah, don't he, and *how?*" Neither man has to speak further; they both know he means illegally, and probably sometimes inside the national park.

"Would you look at that now?" the first man whispers, peeking around the corner of the trailer. Both bow their heads laughing as a pannier crashes to earth and splits a seam, debouching cans of fruit cocktail, lima beans, Spam.

Meanwhile, the brothers from the gold-flecked bubble-domed van have found seats on the sidelines and are already, at ten-thirty in the morning, passing a bottle of Canadian Club. The Californian approaches the Minnesotan and proceeds without preliminaries to expound on his past sporting exploits—he has steelheaded in British Columbia, angled for sheefish and shot Dall sheep in interior Alaska, stalked stag in Scotland, even blown away a wildebeest in Botswana. He regularly flies to Texas for a quick weekend at one of those guaranteed-hunt game farms where beaters drive within sure-shot range the likes of oryx, Cape buffalo, zebra, and kangaroo.

At the same time, across the clearing, another group's outfitter is busily introducing his clients to one another and to their wrangler and guides, and keeping up a lively conversation all around, telling them about his most recent hunt and what to expect on this one.

The Californian decides it is high time there was a little bonhomie in their own group, and with this in mind he approaches their own outfitter, who is pulling on a cigarette and staring morosely into the forest. The Minnesotan can hear the man trying to engage the outfitter in reminiscence of an earlier time when they hunted together from the same camp on upper Sunlight Creek, but what few replies he elicits are grudgingly wan and short, and the Californian returns to the teacher's side.

"Jesus," he hisses.

"What?" inquires the teacher.

"I couldn't even get the man to talk to me. I mean, I *know* this guy, I've hunted with him before, and he was never rude like this. Rough character, sure, but not like this. And then finally he tells me. His wife just left him. Last week. While he was out with the party just before us."

It is hard to like the look of any of this.

A blizzard sweeps in from the southwest, and the Absaroka's western slopes receive a fresh two feet of snow. Then there comes a day of warming and sun, and then a blazing-starred night of ten below. Result: an adamantine glaze of crusted ice, and therefore exceedingly difficult access to pine squirrel nut-caches for the grizzly bears. The mother and her cubs must again traverse the alpine pass and descend to the outlying eastward drainages where the snow is shallow and uncrusted, and food and danger are both abundant. The evening ground-breezes sluicing upcanyon are an overrich broth of aromas—man-sweat and smoke and steak and horses and leather and apple pandowdy—all foreign yet also, at least to the mother bear, familiar, all perilous but tempting, all signifying easy food and easy death. This is a moment to rend the ursine soul, when being a grizzly bear means having to choose between an ancient, naught-fearing, expansive self—risking a sudden and violent end—and a restricted, calculating, modern self—taking the chance of insufficient winter fat stores and eventual starvation.

As in human dilemmas, the accessibility of immediate reward can be decisive. The bear and her cubs travel slowly, with the utmost caution, along only the ruggedest ridgelines and only at night. From the ridge above Silvertip Basin, high in the headwaters of the North Fork of the Shoshone, they scent a gutpile at sunset, but they wait till three in the morning to drop below to feed on it, on the outskirts of a slumbering camp. While their mother feeds voraciously, the cubs wander from her side, enter the camp, and sniff along the edges of the tents. They catch the scent of fresh meat and follow it, but it leads only to game bags tied high on a line between two trees, out of reach.

They linger long moments at the cook tent, snuffling hungrily at a spot in the dirt where a pan of bacon grease was spilled a week ago, but still they find nothing to eat. The mother bear, her nose twitching in dread, must now also enter the camp to fetch her feckless young: she whacks each cub hard on the head and without pausing further races at top speed for the heights; the cubs, having smelled their mother's rage and fear, need no more instructions, and they bound along behind.

Lighting the gasoline lamp above his outdoor work table in the predawn darkness, the cook of the Silvertip Basin camp sees the grizzly tracks and kicks them illegible before the rising hunters may know, and he reflects how glad he is that *his* camp—unlike some others he knows of, unlike for example that pigpen up Sunlight—follows the rules.

The district ranger from the Shoshone National Forest telephones grizzly bear study team biologist Larry Roop at his office in Cody to report that a camp near the head of the North Fork of the Shoshone had two grizzly cubs in their tack tent night before last, rifling a sack of horse feed. When the outfitter shouted and clapped his hands, the cubs fled only a short distance, and he had to fire several shots over their heads to set them running. The next morning, the outfitter found the tracks of a larger grizzly nearby, presumably their mother.

The forest ranger wants Roop to trap the bears and transport them into Yellowstone National Park.

Roop points out that the hunting camp the bears visited is in Management Situation One under the Yellowstone guidelines, which set forth specific standards for the control of nuisance grizzlies:

> In Management Situation One areas, a grizzly bear will be determined to be a nuisance if either or both of the following conditions apply:
> A. the bear uses unnatural food materials (human and livestock foods, garbage, livestock carrion, and game meat in the possession of man) *which have been reasonably secured from the bear*, resulting in habituation of the bear and/or human injury or loss of human life;
> B. the bear has a history of aggressive (not defensive) be-

havior towards man which constitutes a *demonstrable* immediate or potential threat to human safety.

Roop makes it clear that neither of these criteria applies, quietly emphasizing that horse feed left in a tent on the ground is not exactly "reasonably secured." (He is too polite to say that it is tantamount to a full-page ad in the bear-wanted section.) Furthermore, Roop tells the ranger, this late in the year a great deal of grizzly habitat in the park is no longer usable, and the success of transplants, always poor at best, is poorer now than at any other time.

The ranger relents. Regs are regs. But neither he nor Roop is very happy about not being able to take action. Both suspect that this may not be the last they hear of that grizzly bear family this fall.

The same afternoon, Roop flies along the ridgeline that divides the drainages of Sunlight Creek and the North Fork of the Shoshone River, and it is not long before he picks up the mother grizzly's radio signal. A horseback party of elk hunters can be seen threading through sparse timber on a snow-patched spur ridge to the north. The snow has melted from the grassy main divide, and there Roop spots the bear and the two cubs, digging busily—probably, he thinks, for yampah roots—and keeping carefully to the south-facing slope and thus out of sight of the men below. The three grizzlies look up only briefly as the familiar plane buzzes over, and with a melancholy murmur Roop adds another dot to the map.

When Roop flies back down the ridge a quarter of an hour later, the mother bear is leaning back against a sun-warmed rock, front legs limp at her sides, chin on her chest, and the cubs are nursing.

Base camp on Sunlight Creek, after a week in the backcountry, has settled into weary routine. There seem to be no elk at all in the vicinity. The cuckolded outfitter's dejection is so intense that, as a black hole in space acts on nearby matter and light, it sucks all available cheer into an inaccessible other dimension. The three brothers from Cincinnati were the first group to spend two nights at the spike camp up on the edge of the alpine, where one of them (they don't know which; all were firing, and all, probably, drunk too) wounded a scrawny young bull, which it took their guide another whole day to track down and dispatch, the three Ohioans having unsportingly

withdrawn into deeper consultation with their Canadian Club. The weather then turned suddenly warm, and their elk had to be packed out and sent to the freezer right away, so there came to camp no game meat to fire the venatic fancy. Next it was the Minnesotan's and the Californian's turn at the high-country spike camp, and they and the outfitter spent two and a half long days riding the ridges, glassing distant hillsides, and getting off not a shot.

They still all ride out from the base camp mornings and evenings to reconnoiter, flesh willing but spirits weak. There remain the empty hours of midday to while away. The guide and the outfitter usually take to their sagging white canvas wall tent. The three brothers from Cincinnati drink and play cards with taciturn earnestness, each from time to time growing red in the face, slapping down his hand, and stalking off for a nap. The Californian each day takes his horse and his tripod-mounted spotting scope and searches diligently for game. Once, he sees a magnificent seven-by-seven bull—that is, one with seven tines on each antler, a real trophy—but by the time he and the outfitter get within range the elk is gone. Another time, he thinks he sees, so far away that even at the highest magnification they are little more than specks, a mother bear and two cubs, one brown, one blond. The Minnesota teacher has spent a couple of chilly afternoons close to the stove in the cook tent with the wrangler and the cook, the son and daughter of the outfitter; the rest of the time he has spent trading.

In John G. Mitchell's *The Hunt*, he reads and rereads a quotation from the *Meditations on Hunting* of José Ortega y Gasset:

> To the sportsman, the death of the game is not what interests him; that is not his purpose. What interests him is everything he had to do to achieve that death—that is, the hunt. . . . Death is essential, because without it there is no authentic hunting; the killing of the animal is the natural end of the hunt and the goal of hunting itself, *not* of the hunter. . . . To sum up, one does not hunt in order to kill; on the contrary, one kills in order to have hunted.

Yes, the teacher muses: without death no authentic hunting. It is all very well to talk about the pleasures of the place, the ritual pursuit's own validity, the mysteries of the hunting instinct—but unless I actually kill game what will all this have been but a waste of time? He feels with chill clarity the primal urge mounting within himself to kill something. He regards it with a certain detachment, as though it were not exactly part of him; yet of course he knows that it is. When a hawk flew over yesterday, he felt an undeniable if quickly shame-stanched flood of desire to take a shot at it. Ortega is right: there must be death.

Another afternoon and evening tense and frosty above what the outfitter has said is a heavily used elk trail, another hearty dinner in unhearty company, another night of the Californian's snoring and the crackling of fire in the little pot-bellied stove and the flapping of tent walls in the mountain wind, and the Minnesotan rises before dawn to make the most of the next-to-last full day of the hunt. At first light, he and his partner have already taken stands on opposite ridgelines, and the outfitter has ridden to the head of the creek to flush game down the drainage through the timber and out into the open below their positions. But not one of the Yellowstone ecosystem's twenty-five thousand elk happens to have been in that valley this morning.

They ride all day in spattering snow, pausing only to glass the landscape for telltale lines of tracks. They see none. Again in the late afternoon they take stands, and again the outfitter rides high along the ridge and then down the valley to drive elk toward them, and again there is nothing.

As they ride back toward camp in the leaden dimness of an overcast dusk, the outfitter reins in his horse, lifts his black hatbrim with an index finger, turns in the saddle, and, pointing earthward, says, "Well, now, take a look at this here." The hunters dismount and there, in the dusting of snow which has only since sunset begun to coat the trail, are the tracks of a lone and, says the outfitter, very large elk.

It is too dark to pursue the elk, but there is good reason, the outfitter assures them, to hope he will still be in the area tomorrow morning.

It has been a long, hard day. The kids and the young guide have already gone to bed. As the rest of the party, worn out, not saying much, all skunked again, sit around the fire after dinner, the whiskey flows apace, and a heavy torpor descends. There is a loud crack of breaking sticks from somewhere in the circumambient darkness, and all freeze.

Between two trees not twenty yards away, incredibly, a six-point bull elk is staring transfixed at the fire. The outfitter is the first to see him, and for the first time on this trip he smiles. He reaches in slow motion behind him for the teacher's seven-millimeter magnum and slides it to him inch by inch across the ground. The hunter lifts the rifle slowly to his shoulder, and through the scope he can see nothing. Then the elk turns his head slightly: his eyes flare orange with reflected firelight; and the teacher, drawing and slowly exhaling a long deep breath to steady himself, puts a slug neatly between them. The elk crashes a few steps through the brush, and collapses. Things like this just don't happen. But this did.

A whoop of pure joy breaks forth from the outfitter, and there are handshakes and back-thumping and at last something like real fraternity all round. A feverish happiness aches in the teacher's gorge. Until this moment he had no idea this would mean so much. He loves this elk he has killed as he has never loved another of the many animals he has shot, he does not know why, and with the possessiveness that only love can fire to this heat, he *owns* this elk.

The elk has fallen in thick doghair lodgepole pine from which the carcass cannot be dragged. Field-dressing a seven-hundred-pound elk in such a place, at night, especially when you are exhausted and half drunk, is not an easy job. Nonetheless, although his son and the guide, awakened by the shot and the party's subsequent outburst of glee, have risen and offered to help, the outfitter is determined to do it himself, and it is midnight before he has finished; he concludes that quartering the elk can wait till morning. There is a sturdy limb exactly above the spot where the elk went down, just high enough that when the men hoist the carcass's hind feet up to it the antlers graze the huckleberry underbrush. On the ground beneath, the viscera steam in the lamplight.

It is about two hours before dawn. After a long day and most of a night of profitless scrounging for roots in the avalanche chutes and talus slides of Dike Mountain, a single whiff of meat on the wind gusting up from Sunlight Creek is enough to galvanize the mother bear's nerves. She leads the cubs straight to the edge of the camp from which the odor is issuing, and pauses, uneasy. She stands up; sniffs; listens. All quiet. All clear. Once more, hunger has overcome a grizzly bear's better judgment.

The cubs by now weigh nearly a hundred pounds apiece, and their mother, her predenning fattening nearly complete, is approaching four hundred, but the elk carcass is so securely tied that even together they cannot pull it down, so they turn to the gutpile and polish that off. Then the mother grizzly chews a leg and shoulder free from the carcass and drags it into the gully of a trickling side stream, where all three bears have at it.

The cubs begin to squabble over a particularly toothsome morsel, both tugging at it angrily. The female cub wrests it away, and her brother cuffs her hard on the side of the head. She lets out a piercing yelp of complaint, and their mother admonishes them with a deep growl to behave themselves.

"Aw, *shit*," cries the outfitter from his sleep, his hand already reaching for his rifle.

The teacher also bolts awake at the cub's loud yelp, and then hears the mother grizzly's growl. He wriggles out of his sleeping bag and takes up his magnum.

The moon is bright, three-quarters full. The two men meet at the disfigured carcass of the elk.

The mother grizzly and the male cub leap from the gully and vanish into the timber, but the pale golden female, distinct against the streamside wall of Engelmann spruce, hesitates before fleeing, to snatch up the contested bit of meat. Three shots sound in rapid succession.

The teacher believes that the one he fired missed, but he cannot be sure.

The outfitter nudges the small bear's body into the brush as, stunned awake by the riflefire, the blinking other members of the party approach. The two men turn to stare into their flashlight beams.

"Those doggone black bears are the bane of my existence," the outfitter chuckles in a tone of ardently forced joviality this group has not heard from him before. "I reckon we missed the little son of a bitch, don't you think?" He shoots a quick, searching look at the teacher, who may not know much about bears but is pretty darn sure, because he saw the humps on their shoulders quite plainly, that that was a family of *grizzly* bears. And he knows that either he or the outfitter or the two of them together have killed one of the cubs. He knows you can go to jail for that. A poster he remembers seeing at the trailhead said the Audubon Society was offering a fifteen-thousand-dollar reward for information leading to the arrest and conviction of anyone who has illegally killed a grizzly. Whether or not his own bullet actually hit that bear, the teacher knows he is guilty. He *feels* guilty—of a crime indubitably and entirely of passion. He feels that no law, no certainty of punishment, could have stopped him, so passionate was his possession of the game he had killed. But he does not ask himself if a gentle hand of discouragement on his shoulder, such as a wise outfitter might have applied, might not have kept him from firing. He does not ask himself if the bears might somehow not have been drawn into the camp. He does not even ask himself why the elk was not quartered and hung out of reach. He feels bad for having killed a legally protected animal, but he has not the least notion of how much the loss of this single female cub may mean to the Yellowstone grizzly bear population. He figures there must be plenty more; the outfitter indeed has said there are. Still, he has never committed a serious crime before. He wonders for a brief moment, with a bitter inward laugh, if he could collect the reward for turning himself and the outfitter in.

"I guess we did. Miss, I mean." He does not think to contest the outfitter's crucial "we."

"Let's get that elk into camp, what's left of him," the outfitter is saying, his hands outstretched, his torso bent tensely forward, his whole body seeming to urge the party away from the scene of the shooting. "We better go ahead and do some butchering and get this meat hung up, in case that little bear decides to come back."

Once all the others are safely back in bed, the outfitter returns to the body of the female grizzly cub. He stuffs rags into the gaping exit wounds left by the two-hundred-grain slugs from his thirty-ought-six. He wraps the body in a tarp to keep his clothes from getting bloodstained, takes the bundle in his arms, and struggles a quarter-mile into a tortuous deadfall where the duff on the forest floor is several feet thick. He shovels out a hole, drags the cub's carcass in, and covers it up. It has begun to snow heavily now, and by daylight, in the extremely unlikely event that anyone should bother to worm his way into this tangle, the grave will be invisible.

While the rest of the hunters are saddling up in the watery pre-dawn dimness, the teacher slips off to the place where he saw the outfitter first shove the little bear's body out of sight. There remains only a patch of congealing blood. If he had harbored a doubt, it would now be dispelled: this must have been a grizzly bear. And now he has a secret which he can never reveal.

The outfitter comes quietly to the teacher's side and tells him he'd be glad to have him come along on another hunt next fall, on the house.

Off and on for two weeks now, the mother grizzly has been preparing her winter den, beneath the roots of a lightning-scarred whitebark just below timberline on a steep north-facing slope along the spine of the Absaroka, ten thousand feet above sea level. She has bored in through the entanglement of taproot and lateral roots and stone and half-frozen mud, biting, clawing, shoveling, raking, and smoothing till the entrance tunnel was clear and firm; she has excavated the hibernaculum itself beyond, deeper into the hillside, tugging out loose rocks in the walls and biting off protruding roots until the bedroom was neat and secure; she has searched the forest nearby for last summer's new-grown soft tips of fir boughs and carried them in dozens of loads into the den, where she has formed them into a thick, shallowly concave, heat-trapping nest. Traveling back to the new den now, the bear and her surviving cub pass by the site of the den where the cubs were born last January, now collapsed and nearly obliterated by the summer rains. The new den is barely half a mile farther on. It is literally astride the drainage divide: snowmelt at its mouth next spring may flow west into the Lamar and Yellowstone rivers in Yellowstone National Park, or east into Sunlight Creek and the Clark's Fork of the Yellowstone in the Shoshone National Forest.

The mother grizzly spends a day and night rearranging the bedding, perhaps because now there will be one fewer cub to house for the winter. And now there is nothing more for the two bears to do but wait for sleep to overtake them.

Larry Roop radio-locates the bear one last time, and spots her and the cub sunning themselves on the spill of excavated rubble below the den entrance. He flies past several times to see if the missing cub may be merely out of sight. He plots the den location on his map, and writes in his notes: "10/26. Possible mortality, cub. Check in spring." Of the cub's death at the hunting camp nothing more will ever be known.

Twenty miles north, Roop spots a very large dark brown grizzly feeding on the carcass of an elk in the snow. He catches a glint of orange at the bear's neck—a radio collar—and quickly searches the frequency band to see if the collar is transmitting.

It is. Roop can hardly believe the number he sees on his receiver's digital readout: it is old Number One, who had seemed in July to be starving, who had nearly died just from the administration of his usual dose of Sernylan, and for whom he and Steve Mealey had both, in the presence of the entire Yellowstone Institute seminar, confidently if sadly predicted an imminent demise.

Roop circles back for a closer look, and the grizzly stands up tall and peers back at the airplane. Old Number One is as fat as a pig. The biologist laughs aloud.

In dendritic clusters along the oceansides, along the Great Lakes shores, along the great rivers, miles-wide brilliancies shine deep into space; scattered among them, thousands more, lesser versions of the same, spatter the continent; between them all, all night, pulse filaments of moving light. The whole vast constellation—cities, towns, glittering web of highways—hums, grinds, roars. And above the electrified nightscape hangs a dim and sour haze, the airborne waste of that combustion of long-dead plants which engenders all this motion and light.

The sun rises on an America transformed—transformed in the wink of history's eye, in one-ten-thousandth of one tick on the biological clock—by the hand of man. Humanity has surged into the megalopolis in such multitude that there is scant space or sustenance left for other creatures than those hardy few whose ancient way of life has fitted them, fortuitously, for man's close-quartered companionship—the likes of the robin, the roach, the occasional prowling raccoon. The rest is man and the man-made—rivers of asphalt, mountains of glass and steel, hybrid flowers in tidy rows, trees in holes in the sidewalk.

There is, to be sure, much good here; the privileges and pleasures of membership in the civilization of the late twentieth century hardly need cataloguing. But we must not forget that art and love and achievement and comfort and other of civilization's high glories all have their sources in nature, and from nature the modern city dweller is, as a rule, profoundly isolated. What do we see in our daily life? The television screen, the car just ahead, the perpetually perplexing faces of our fellow city dwellers; a squirrel, a tulip, a lawn? What do we smell? Exhaust, perfume, hot coffee? What do we hear? The radio, a jackhammer, the hiss of tires on pavement, a shout in the street; a barking dog, a chattering sparrow? Motion. Commotion. Noise.

Night falls on the small town in a shower of birdsong. Over the soybean field at the foot of the street the sun sets crimson above crimson maples. A south wind brings the scent of rain and a faint rumble of thunder. But John is underneath his truck, and Mary is watching the TV news. A kid or two may be out catching frogs, an old man may be out on his porch watching the nimbus-anvil rise from the horizon, but in the main the town today is as detached from the natural world, as turned in on itself and its consuming human affairs, as the city. That is the way we live now.

The clatter of quail wings is no longer heard in the high-plains wheat, gone with the coming of new pesticides; gone too are the butterflies that fed on now herbicide-killed weeds; gone are the rat snake's soft passage beneath and the eagle on the old oak snag above. An owl still roosts, this dawn, in the hayloft, and the geese still forage in the stubble; the wild mint still exhales sweet fragrance at the edge of a still clean spring; deer still glide among the shadows of the woodlot, and a fox still dens in the cow pasture hedge. Sometimes, just before dawn, coyotes still can be heard from the distant hills. But nature has been tamed on the farm: it is a resource, like a bank account, to be drawn on, fretted over, and, when convenient, ignored. The tractor is enclosed and air-conditioned now, and the shriek of a rabbit caught in the harrow goes unheard. The worst threat to the cows is that they will develop tolerance to their antibiotics.

And yet we may, from time to time, perhaps, in some lonely place, in one of those precious few patches of darkness in the megalopolitan constellation, stand on the snow in the middle of the night and feel stillness soaking into our grateful beings like rain into parched earth. And, then, we may sense, if only for a fugitive moment, how busy, how buffeted, how radically unpeaceful we have been all day . . . all week . . . all our lives. . . .

It has been in our interest as members of a technologically advancing society to forget that we are animals, not far removed from an environment much unlike the one we live in now. We are biological strangers to this life. The world which we as animals evolved for was one in which man functioned as only one of several relatively dominant animals, dependent on wild foods, subject to the vagaries of weather and natural catastrophe, fellow of the wolf and the grizzly bear: alert in ways we nearly have lost, perceiving the world more with our senses than with our minds.

Presumably unlike the perceived world of their fellow beasts, however, that of our uncivilized ancestors was also, to a now inconceivable extent, a spirit-world. Where their senses left off, their human imagination took over. Darkness was full of brooding menace, silence alive with numinous voices, a starry sky the realm of divinity. It was a world they could not dream of mastering as we have mastered ours, and that humility bred awe, an awe which our own not unjustified civilized pride has obscured.

But not quite extinguished. It is not just as make-believe primitive man and fellow beast that we come into the wilderness, but also in quest of that lost sacred awe. We come as a king might come disguised among his peasantry, trying to feel unalien in a world that seems more real than our daily busy noisy own—which, in terms of biological familiarity, the wilderness truly is. False though our atavistic incursion into an image of the distant racial past may feel, we also feel our pulse really slow down, the muscles in our social face really relax. We hear the rustlings and stirrings of the living creatures around us, so immitigably unintelligible. We peer into the darkness, and wonder. We listen into the silence for voices too still and small to be heard within ourselves in the deafening life we usually lead. In half-pretended faith, we feel our way back toward a love of nature not unmingled with dread; we are at once alone and at one with all; and an ancient awe steals over us.

Still, the ultimate awestruck peace must always elude us—a fitting reminder, perhaps, of the weakness inherent in being as strong a force as we are even when we least mean to do harm. To the most hidden and tranquil of wilderness places, the remote subalpine mountainsides where grizzly bears prepare their winter dens and, in pre-hibernation lethargy, are now at their most vulnerable, we can come only in imagination; for if we were really to go there, the grizzly bears would leave. This is the paradox of modern citizens thronging into the wilderness: our very presence may degrade what we come for.

The last bearberries and buffaloberries, wizened to raisins, have been plucked. The elk and deer and bighorn sheep have moved down to their winter range. Mouse and marmot and gopher and vole are all underground to stay. The roots and whitebark pine nut caches are locked in the hard-frozen soil. Even on the few windblown slopes where the meadows are free of snow, the last forbs and grasses have withered to straw.

The days are dark, the low clouds muttering as the last warm winds above clash against upwelling earthly chill. The ripple of a rill beneath the snow falls silent, frozen. The mother grizzly and her cub sleep such days away in snow beds near the den. They have nothing to do but wait. There is nothing to eat.

And then an auspicious mercy befalls them. The cub has been nursing a little, and has fallen deeply asleep. But a faint scent rouses the mother bear. As the cub still sleeps, she rises, moves downslope, stands up on her hind legs, and lifts her nose into a wisp of breeze. She returns to the cub and wakes him with a touch of her paw. They walk slowly into the trees.

An aging moose, his lungs and liver infested with worms, his teeth falling out from necrosis of the jaw, has wandered into the subalpine snows and died.

The bears eat until they can barely walk. They yawn and cannot stop yawning. Pacing dreamily back and forth on the porch of the den, they are already half insensate. You could probably walk right up and scratch them behind the ears.

And still they stagger to the moose carcass, half a dozen times a day for half a dozen days, grunting, belching, roly-poly and languorous as sultans. Their layers of fat grow thicker. Their coats are thick and oily-sleek.

At last their appetite fails them. When the blizzard comes, therefore, they are ready. They stretch, crawl in through the long dark tunnel, and snuggle up, the big bear curled around her curled-up cub.

Three days and nights of white tempest pass. The apron of spoil, their tracks, the den entrance, all signs of grizzly bear are gone.

The sun is a pale disc in the thinning silver overcast. All the windless afternoon, not a willow shoot quivers. All the windless night, the moon is a silver disc in a blackness pricked with stars. The aurora borealis shimmers over the far peaks. The stillness is complete.

AFTERWORD

Things have changed. Five years after publication of this book's first edition, the grizzly bear population of the Greater Yellowstone ecosystem seems actually to be increasing.

The age at which females first give birth is lower, and on average there are more cubs in each litter. The sex ratio and age structure of the population are much improved. Grizzlies are colonizing country where they haven't lived for generations.

The grizzly bear *habitat*, meanwhile, is headed the other way.

Grant Village is built, in return for which, you'll recall, the Fishing Bridge complex was to be dismantled. Thanks to brick-brained political meddling, however, the sprawl of development at Fishing Bridge continues to sit plop in the middle of some of the ecosystem's best habitat, and continues to attract bears, thus to habituate them, and thus, ultimately, to kill them. New national forest master plans lay out thousands of miles of new road—the most destructive single thing you can do to grizzly habitat. Oil and gas exploration is scheduled far and wide—so much of it that if full-scale development ensues, it could spell disaster for the grizzly population. Gigantic mining and smelting operations are gearing up, bringing hundreds of workers and their machinery into the heart of grizzly country.

Why then more bears? Partly good work, partly good luck.

The main accomplishment, modest enough in principle but in fact dramatic, has been improved sanitation—fewer grizzlies attracted to human foods, thus fewer habituated to human presence, thus fewer killed. Law enforcement still can't possibly cover the vast Yellowstone backcountry, but there is widespread perception that poachers are now more likely to get caught, and so illegal killing is down (probably; you can never know for sure). The Interagency Grizzly Bear Committee, made up of managers high-ranking enough to make major decisions, has brought forth a number of initiatives favoring survival of the all-important breeding-age female grizzlies. In congressional hearings in 1986, the Greater Yellowstone Coalition and other conservationists showed the agencies' claims of coordinated ecosystem management to be, to say the least, rather thin. After those hearings, and a devastating critique by the Congressional Research Service, the Greater Yellowstone Coordinating Committee, long an ineffectual and half-forgotten government body, started actually trying to do some coordinating—a first step toward integrated ecosystem management. As long as the national forests remain primarily devoted to commodity production, however, and timber quotas remain intolerably high, there are harsh limits on what the GYCC can hope to accomplish, but it does beat the poke in the eye that used to be grizzly bear policy.

Most of the sheep grazing allotments have been taken out of grizzly range on the Targhee Forest. Black bear hunting has been severely restricted in several national forests, thereby cutting the chances of mistaken identity. Food storage poles, bearproof caches, and detailed new rules (often, now, actually enforced) have sharply lessened the opportunities for bears to come into conflict with campers and outfitters. Large areas of Yellowstone Park are closed at the times of highest grizzly use. The agencies have undertaken a campaign to educate visitors in avoiding bear trouble. All, good work.

And the good luck? Burgeoning elk herds, the result of a long series of mild winters, have meant more calves in spring and more carrion. Many grizzlies, as Dick Knight predicted, have become better predators. The huge wildfires of 1988 burned a great deal of lodgepole pine forest, and it is widely believed that the fires were a bonanza for grizzlies. Lodgepole woods tend to be poor in grizzly foods, and most of the experts contend that the fires have created hundreds of thousands of acres of at least temporarily improved feeding sites, where grass, forbs, and berry bushes are replacing wood and pine needles. Where meadows and sagebrush steppes burned, they too have been enriched. The benefits of those vegetative changes, these scientists say, have accrued not only to bears but to many other animals that bears eat, from gophers to bison.

John Craighead, on the other hand, maintains that because vast tracts of old-growth lodgepole were destroyed, the maturing spruce-fir climax forest beneath the lodgepole canopy was set back to zero—a habitat type that would eventually have provided some of the best possible grizzly habitat. Craighead says that most of the burned areas will soon be overgrown by skinny, close-set "doghair" lodgepole, which is virtually worthless to bears. Park Service biologists disagree, asserting that even the best lodgepole forest was never very important to grizzlies. Craighead also insists that whole populations of small mammals were wiped out, and that it will be years until they are reestablished. The Park Service, again, disagrees. Craighead counters that they have no hard data to support their contention. The Park Service counter-counters that that may be true, but small mammals are an insignificant part of the grizzly's diet.

Park Service scientists, over and over, say the 1988 fires were almost entirely a good thing. Craighead calls them "an unprecedented catastrophe." The Park Service and the Craigheads can keep up these round-and-round disagreements till one's head spins. So far, in any case, there is no evidence of grizzly starvation or malnutrition.

The combination of the several-year drought and then the burning of some winter range and then a deep snowpack caused a massive die-off of elk in the winter of 1988–89. There were far more carcasses than the grizzly population could ever eat—indeed they became quite the gourmets, often dining on only the choicest morsels and then moving on to another. The heavy snow also meant a rich bounty of resurgent vegetation. Undoubtedly, after a tough 1988, the spring of 1989 was fat city. And then the summer produced a huge crop of whitebark pine nuts, the single most important food of Yellowstone grizzlies.

All this, sheer luck.

Increasing numbers, declining habitat: a paradox, in whose explication lies grounds for hope and grounds for despair, according to your inclination.

One aspect of the paradox is that in the near term, Yellowstone grizzly habitat will probably not be declining, because the fires have increased the proportion of high-quality feeding sites. (That, at least, is the majority view. John Craighead fiercely disagrees. Again, this can go around and around for whole volumes; indeed, the postfire production of scientific monographs and books will probably kill more trees than the fires did.) Meanwhile, the net acreage of habitat has indisputably increased, as grizzlies have colonized new range. In the Dunoir River country north of Dubois, Wyoming, for example, which is classified as Management Situation Five ("grizzlies do not occur, or occur only rarely"), there are in fact a number of grizzlies thriving. Whether the Forest Service will have the guts to reclassify that area as occupied habitat will be a telling test of its willingness to live up to its grizzly conservation guidelines—whose principal author, you will recall, was Steve Mealey.

Mealey is proud of his role in the improved situation—he has served as supervisor of the Shoshone National Forest, where he made major strides forward in grizzly conservation, and he is now among the top leaders of the Forest Service in Washington, the first wildlife biologist ever to rise so high in that agency—but he gives major credit to the bear: "What I feel these days is awe, wonder, and humility at the amazing adaptive power of that animal. We've spent so much time imagining living without them, and now we've got to learn how to live *with* them. I honestly believe that this population is at carrying capacity. That means that the next big question is how to deal with a recovered population. Nobody even thought about asking that question in 1982, but I think we're looking at recovery"— that is, official removal from the federal roster of threatened and endangered species, commonly called delisting—"maybe as soon as five years from now."

Chris Servheen is more cautious: "The big thing I've learned in the last five years is that good biology won't save the grizzly. What will is political savvy. I get very frustrated with the Forest Service— so many of the people there want to do the right thing, but they're continually short-circuited by politics. They're facing timber quotas out of Washington that are simply not sustainable. But all that aside, we're moving toward delisting in the Northern Continental Divide. It's for real. The bears are doing well. And recovery in Yellowstone may not be that far away."

Recovery, by the way, has been redefined. It used to be three hundred bears for the Yellowstone ecosystem. Now, the interagency grizzly committee figures first of all that an accurate total is beyond the reach of available research techniques, and second that three hundred may not have been realistic in the first place. The new recovery plan focuses on females with cubs-of-the-year: if family groups are well distributed throughout the available habitat, it is thought, then the population will have recovered. There's a new and somewhat controversial method for determining "well distributed," breaking the whole Yellowstone ecosystem down into eighteen Bear Management Units, fifteen of which must be occupied by mothers with cubs for three years running; no two adjacent BMUs can go three years without an observation of grizzly family groups in them. There have been objections—Dick Knight wanted not 15/18 but 18/18, for example—but even the critics concede that a full count is virtually impossible and that the new census system is essentially not a bad one. Other new recovery criteria are a maximum of seven man-caused mortalities per year, of which only two can be females, and "adequate regulatory mechanisms" for the period to follow delisting—when bear management will be back in the hands of the states.

It's hard not to share Mealey's and Servheen's excitement. But three things must be remembered. One, the habitat trend, once you factor out the recent lucky breaks, is lousy. Two, these are men for whom grizzly bear recovery amounts to professional success. And three, bad luck always, eventually, follows good.

What's going to happen when drought comes again? Bad pine nut years, maybe a trout disease, a population crash of ungulates, even a permanent greenhouse warming and drying? The managers' assumption is that they will always be able to intervene on the bears' behalf. Is that the best we can do? Or is it not still possible to preserve habitat with enough resilience that the grizzly population will survive its inevitable runs of bad luck?

Plans now on paper will make that impossible. The agencies seem to have the idea that grizzly habitat can be massively degraded—roaded, timbered, drilled, paved over—but that somehow the grizzly population can be forced to survive in spite of all that. How? Mitigation. Intervention. Well, who knows, maybe it *is* possible, but let's think about the world that that kind of management would bring into being.

At the Overton Park Zoo in Memphis, there is a gray fake-stone environment just to the right of the popcorn stand, and in that rather cramped "ecosystem" there has lived since the year 1930 what some observers might deem a viable population of grizzly bears (currently, three). Intensive management is necessary in a population like this— feeding with nonnatural foods, culling when carrying capacity is exceeded, segregation of adult males from cubs, segregation of human visitors from bears, veterinary care, periodic introductions of exogenous genetic material, aversive conditioning, intervention in the social hierarchy. For all that, and for all their years of habituation to humans, those yardbird bruins have retained one strong attribute in common with wild grizzlies: if a human being crowds them, they will try to kill him. As a matter of fact they'll try to kill any living being that gets within reach. Every year, they get a raccoon, a few pigeons, a peacock or two. Not to mention plenty of flying cheeseburgers.

It's a supremely depressing spectacle: all that brute power, all that adaptive brilliance—*grizzly bears*, for heaven's sake!—chasing hot dogs and pigeons, pacing back and forth in the "management situation" set aside for them. Is this a difference in kind from the grizzly sanctuaries of the future? Or is it only a difference in degree?

What's most depressing is that there may be no choice except to minimize the degree of likeness between zoos and nature reserves. Much has been made lately of the view that there is nothing left on this planet but "anthropic ecosystems"—that is, environments in which the dominant influence is human. At least, thank God, there do remain differences of degree. And it is no coincidence that the places where wild grizzly bears still live happen to be the places where human influence on natural forces has been least.

Nobody's dreaming that Greater Yellowstone can be simply left alone. What is to be hoped is that when it does become unavoidable, intervention will exercise the quickest and lightest of touches, always with the object of maintaining maximum possible naturalness, and emulating natural processes. The obvious example is reestablishing a gray wolf population and then letting them shift for themselves (at least in a central recovery zone; in the outlying ranching regions, there may have to be some control of depredating wolves).

Much more important than things you might do, though, are all the things you ought *not* to do. Like dirt-bike racing in spring grizzly range (not a joke: this was really happening on the Flathead National Forest, until the Swan View Coalition finally had to sue). Like Ski Yellowstone (defeated recently, after years of struggle). Like huge resort complexes on trout spawning streams (Grant Village). Like opening forty-six percent of your prime grizzly habitat to clear-cutting (as the Gallatin National Forest is now proposing). Like planting carrots, building a slaughterhouse, growing fruit trees, digging gigantic fallout shelters, and settling hundreds of people in grizzly country (this nightmare has come to life on the vast ranch of a bizarre sect known as the Church Universal and Triumphant, just north of Yellowstone Park).

For many land managers and even some biologists, the gospel remains *mitigation*—compensation, somehow, somewhere, for the damage done to grizzly habitat. These interventionists' basic assumption is that human influence is so ubiquitous and so strong that we ought to put behind us such antiquated notions as wildness. John Craighead has written: "Is wilderness in the traditional sense an illusion at the end of the twentieth century? . . . Should we be actively managing the Greater Yellowstone ecosystem to counteract the disruptive processes at work?" He goes on to make clear that he thinks we should.

The philosopher Holmes Rolston III writes what could be seen as a rebuttal: "There is also a relative sense of 'natural,' one consistent with human management. Some human interventions are more, others less natural, depending on the degree to which they fit in with, mimic, or restore spontaneous nature. . . . Biology and philosophy [in Yellowstone] ought to seek to appreciate, rather than to manipulate."

These points of view define two paths for survival of the grizzly in Greater Yellowstone: we can protect the wildness of the ecosystem, letting it fluctuate and evolve, and taking what comes, or we can constantly intervene and tinker to achieve specified goals such as a certain number of grizzlies. The bear himself might not even know the difference, but for the rest of us there's a big question, namely, which way will yield the kind of Yellowstone we want to leave to future generations.

Scientifically, the distinction is not quite that simple; it's generally agreed that even in what seems pristinely wild landscape there must be some adjustments to counteract negative human influences. Esthetically, it may not make that much difference either. An intensively managed environment can be made to *look* wild, or almost.

The distinction lies deeper, down in the darkness of nature's profoundest mysteries. Ecosystems have learned to work, energy and nutrients have found ways to interact to sustain life through whole eras of geological time, Yellowstone has defined itself—all—*without human guidance*. No more perfect exemplar of that sheer otherness can be imagined than the grizzly bear. If the wild, free-ranging grizzly and a living remnant of the world that gave birth to him can survive in the modern era, it will be proof that we have not made everything ours, that here, this once, we have subdued our passion to take possession. It will be proof that not every corner of the planet is an anthropic ecosystem. It will be proof that there is life here on earth that we have decided just to let be.

We could make Yellowstone into a fairly convincing simulacrum of wildness. Our management techniques—think hard on those cold words—our management techniques are quite effective. But, oh, how bleak an achievement! A wax museum, a Disneyland with mechanical dinosaurs, and finally a controlled environment with real live grizzly bears—

Thus we come to the moral, the philosophical question: Do we want the grizzly bear's world to be a zoo, or a wilderness?

Meanwhile the bear, in his still unspoiled world, continues to disclose astonishments. A remote zone of high peaks turns out to be dense with grizzlies in late summer gorging on (of all things) millions of army cutworm moths. Were the bears always here in such numbers, just undiscovered? Or did they only recently find these bugs and find out they were good to eat?

A Yellowstone Park physician, Steve French, and his wife, Marilynn, took a grizzly bear course at the Yellowstone Institute taught by Steve Mealey and soon became so engrossed in the systematic observation of grizzlies in the wild that they are now devoting themselves full time to it, through their newly established Yellowstone Grizzly Foundation. Theirs is the first truly independent grizzly study in the park since the Craigheads'. The Frenches have recorded hundreds of hours of grizzly behavior, much of it never before seen by a human being. They have filmed over a hundred episodes of grizzly predation on elk calves. They have shown that the bears depend much more heavily on spawning trout than anybody ever suspected (a finding with important implications for the continuing controversy over developments like Fishing Bridge and Grant Village). They have recorded dozens of courting and mating encounters, including many behaviors never before observed. Perhaps most important, they have validated the indispensability of a very old and low-tech research technique: getting out in the field and sitting and *watching*—a philosophical as well as a scientific validation. And all this they have learned to do without intruding on or in any way disturbing the bears' conduct of their daily lives.

A new member of the interagency study team, David Mattson, has also been turning up novel observations, which in composite yield a grizzly more complex than has hitherto been imagined. "I think bears are highly dependent on information lineages," says Mattson. "The knowledge of those moths may have been disrupted back when Wyoming was overhunting grizzlies, twenty-five or more years ago. All the killings that followed the closing of the dumps in the park undoubtedly severed a lot of information lineages, and naturally it takes time to build them back up again. I think that's what we're seeing now.

"This is above all an animal that has to be studied for a long time before you can conclude *anything*. In bad years for whitebark pine, the bears seem to turn to a different alternative every time. One year they'll go to yampah, one year to clover, the next year to sweet cicely. The whole population went crazy for sweet cicely in 1988, and it had never even shown up in scats before. So, you see, even fifteen or twenty years of data can't predict what they'll do next year. This, to me, is the most important quality of the grizzly bear—individualism. And it's that *information-intensive* aspect of their lives that makes such individualism possible.

"Of course, it's also what makes them so hard to deal with."

Mattson is skeptical about the spreading enthusiasm for delisting. "I'm confident that the population is growing," he says, "and expanding into new range, but even six million acres is a small piece of ground for grizzly bears. A lot of people are overoptimistic right now, who have political and maybe personal agendas. But when you consider the likelihood of survival over the span of a century, the only view that's fully warranted is pessimism. The reality is that this population will always be at risk."

Which will probably mean that we will go on studying the bear, and hence the bear will continue to speak to us, obscurely but perhaps less so as time goes by, from deep inside his otherness.

On August 3, 1988, Grizzly Bear Number One, whom everybody had given up for doomed seven years before, was caught yet again in an interagency study team trap in Sunlight Basin. He was in excellent condition.

In midsummer of 1989, he managed to shed his radio collar and so has not been heard from again. If he's still alive, old Number One turned twenty-six this year.

—T.M.
February 26, 1990

BIBLIOGRAPHY

THE following list includes all the publications and other documents which have informed the writing of this book, as well as a number of others which do not figure directly in the text but still warrant mention for having provided invaluable background.

Certain groups among the principal references have been so rich a source of information that I have drawn on them over and over again, to the point where their contents have become nearly second nature to me, and these deserve to be singled out, for without them I could not even have begun: the research of Frank and John Craighead and their associates; the work of Charles Jonkel and his colleagues and students in the Border Grizzly Project; and the reports of the Yellowstone Interagency Grizzly Bear Study Team.

Several references occur so frequently in the bibliography that I have abbreviated them; these are all marked with an asterisk. Citations of reports from within the Yellowstone Interagency Grizzly Bear Study Team's reports, for example, refer to *IGBST [year]*.* Full bibliographic information for these references will be found under Knight et al. Three collections of research papers by various authors are also referred to in abbreviated form. When you see *Bears, IUCN, 1972**, that is a reference to

HERRERO, STEPHEN, ed. 1972. *Bears—their biology and management:* a selection of papers and discussion from the Second International Conference on Bear Research and Management, held at the University of Calgary, Canada, 6 to 9 November 1970. Morges, Switzerland: International Union for Conservation of Nature and Natural Resources.

When you see *Bears, IUCN, 1976**, that is a reference to

PELTON, MICHAEL R., JACK W. LENTFER, AND G. EDGAR FOLK, eds. 1976. *Bears—their biology and management:* a selection of papers from the Third International Conference on Bear Research and Management, held at the 54th annual meeting of the American Society of Mammalogists, Binghamton, New York, USA, and First International Theriological Congress, Moscow, USSR, June 1974. Morges, Switzerland: International Union for Conservation of Nature and Natural Resources.

And when you see *Bears, BBA, 1980**, that is a reference to

MARTINKA, CLIFFORD J., AND KATHERINE L. McARTHUR, eds. 1980. *Bears—their biology and management:* a selection of papers from the Fourth International Conference on Bear Research and Management, held at Kalispell, Montana, USA, February 1977. Washington, D.C.: Bear Biology Association/Government Printing Office.

Readers who want to explore further in the scientific literature of bears may wish to consult two publications of the University of Alaska's Cooperative Park Studies Unit at Fairbanks—the *Brown Bear Bibliography* and *Black Bear Bibliography*—each of which lists over four thousand titles. Both of those compilations have mainly omitted hunting stories and other items in the popular press, which would probably have doubled the number of references. The great thing about these University of Alaska bibliographies is that they are kept in a computer and are being constantly updated, and you can request a search of the computer files for particular areas of interest.

ADERHOLD, MIKE. 1982. The grizzly bear: the animal, the symbol, the enigma. *Montana Outdoors*, May/June.

ALLEN, DURWARD A., E. RAYMOND HALL, WALTER M. SCHIRRA, AND LARRY ERICKSON. 1981. A review and recommendations on animal problems and related management needs in units of the National Park System. National Park System Advisory Board report to Secretary of the Interior James Watt.

ANDERSON, SYDNEY, AND J. KNOX JONES, JR. 1967. *Recent mammals of the world.* New York: Ronald Press.

APPLEGATE, ROGER D., LYNN L. ROGERS, DAVID A. CASTEEL, AND JAMES M. NOVAK. 1979. Germination of cowparsnip seeds from grizzly bear feces. *Journal of Mammalogy* 60(3).

Associated Press. 1980. Guide who says he slew grizzly with handheld arrow is disputed. *The New York Times*, 29 February.

———. 1980. Rancher kills two grizzlies. *Billings Gazette*, 16 May.

———. 1983. Man-killing grizzly trapped, put to death. *The New York Times*, 27 June.

———. 1983. Bear's killing of camper puzzles wildlife officials. *The New York Times*, 28 June.

———. 1983. National park tourists tangle with animals. *The New York Times*, 12 September.

ATWELL, GERRY, DANIEL L. BOONE, JACK GUSTAFSON, AND VERNON D. BERNS. 1977. Brown bear summer use of alpine habitat on the Kodiak National Wildlife Refuge. In *Bears, BBA, 1980.**

AUNE, KEITH. 1981. Rocky Mountain Front grizzly bear monitoring and investigation. Annual report.

AUNE, KEITH, AND TOM STIVERS. 1982. Rocky Mountain Front grizzly bear monitoring and investigation. Annual report.

———. 1983. Rocky Mountain Front grizzly bear monitoring and investigation. Annual report.

BACON, ELLIS S. 1977. Curiosity in the American black bear. In *Bears, BBA, 1980.**

BACON, ELLIS S., AND GORDON M. BURGHARDT. 1974. Ingestive behaviors of the American black bear. In *Bears, IUCN, 1976.**

———. 1974. Learning and color discrimination in the American black bear. In *Bears, IUCN, 1976.**

BEAL, MERRILL D. 1949. *The story of man in Yellowstone.* Caldwell, Ida.: Caxton Printers.

BEEBE, B. F., AND J. R. JOHNSON. 1965. *American bears.* New York: David McKay.

BEECHAM, JOHN. 1977. Some population characteristics of two black bear populations in Idaho. In *Bears, BBA, 1980.**

BERNS, VERNON D., GERRY C. ATWELL, AND DANIEL L. BOONE. 1977. Brown bear movements and habitat use at Karluk Lake, Kodiak Island. In *Bears, BBA, 1980.**

BJÄRVALL, ANDERS. 1977. The brown bear in Sweden—distribution, abundance, and management. In *Bears, BBA, 1980.**

BLANCHARD, BONNIE M. 1980. Grizzly bear–timber relationships in the Yellowstone area. In *IGBST 1978–79.**

BLANCHARD, BONNIE M., AND RICHARD R. KNIGHT. 1980. Movement of grizzly bears in the Yellowstone ecosystem during 1978 and 1979. In *IGBST 1978–79.**

BLANCHARD, BONNIE M., RICHARD R. KNIGHT, AND E. M. YOUNT. 1980. Mortality. In *IGBST 1978–79.**

BOURLIÈRE, FRANÇOIS. 1970. *The natural history of mammals.* New York: Knopf.

BOYD, RAYMOND J. 1978. American elk. In *Big game of North America.* Edited by John L. Schmidt and Douglas L. Gilbert. Harrisburg, Pa.: Stackpole.

BRANHAM, BUD, AND PAT SMITH. 1973. The most savage animal on earth. *Sports Afield,* June.

BRANNON, ROBERT D. 1983. Blood profile of grizzly bears in central and northern Alaska. Paper presented at the Sixth International Conference on Bear Research and Management, Grand Canyon, Ariz.

BRODY, JANE E. 1983. Scientists find complex causes of human appetite. *The New York Times,* 30 August.

BROWN, GARY. 1982. The Yellowstone perspective: where have all the Yellowstone bears gone? *Western Wildlands,* winter.

BUCHALCZYK, TADEUSZ. 1977. The brown bear in Poland. In *Bears, BBA, 1980.**

BUNNELL, F. L. 1983. Food habits of grizzly bears: synthesis, hypotheses, and tests. Paper presented at the Sixth International Conference on Bear Research and Management, Grand Canyon, Ariz.

BUNNELL, F. L., AND D. E. N. TAIT. 1980. Bears in models and in reality—implications to management. In *Bears, BBA, 1980.**

———. 1981. Populations dynamics of bears—implications. In *Dynamics of large mammal populations.* Edited by C. W. Fowler and T. D. Smith. New York: John Wiley & Sons.

BURGHARDT, GORDON M., AND LORRAINE S. BURGHARDT. 1970. Notes on behavioral development of two female black bear cubs: the first eight months. In *Bears, IUCN, 1972.**

BURNS, JOHN E. 1981. Targhee National Forest grizzly bear–grazing controversy. U.S. Forest Service.

BURTON, M. 1950. Kodiaks and other brown bears. *The Illustrated London News.* 18 February.

CARLTON, D. C. 1983. Analysis of U.S. Forest Service management of the threatened grizzly bear (*Ursus arctos horribilis*) in the border ecosystems of the Flathead, Kootenai, Idaho Panhandle, and Colville National Forests.

CARLTON, D. C., AND BOB SUMMERFIELD. 1982. Historical summary of grizzly bears (*Ursus arctos horribilis*) in the Selkirk Mountains of northern Idaho and northeastern Washington.

CARTMILL, MATT. 1983. "Four legs good, two legs bad": man's place (if any) in nature. *Natural History*, November.

CAYOT, LINDA, AND MARY ANN DOHN. Yellowstone grizzly controversy (malice in wonderland).

CBS NEWS. 1983. Transcripts of interviews with Christopher Servheen, Thomas McNamee, Clarence Johnson, Carrie Hunt, Charles Jonkel, Stephen Mealey, Frank Craighead, Donald Turner, Robert Barbee, Bart Schleyer, and Craig Rupp. Taped for broadcast on *Paradise Lost*, 2 September.

———. 1983. Transcript of hearing of U.S. Senate Committee on the Environment and Public Works, Cody, Wyo., 11 August.

CHASE, ALSTON. 1983. The last bears of Yellowstone. *The Atlantic*, February.

CHESTER, JAMES M. 1977. Factors influencing human-grizzly bear interactions in a backcountry setting. In *Bears, BBA, 1980.**

CHITTENDEN, HIRAM M. 1912. *The Yellowstone National Park*. Cincinnati: Stewart & Kidd.

CHRISTENSEN, ALAN G. 1982. Cumulative effects analysis process. Kootenai National Forest.

CLARK, KENNETH. 1977. *Animals and men*. New York: Morrow.

COLBERT, EDWIN H. 1980. *Evolution of the vertebrates*. New York: John Wiley & Sons.

COLE, GLEN F. 1972. Preservation and management of grizzly bears in Yellowstone National Park. In *Bears, IUCN, 1972.**

———. 1978. A naturally regulated elk population. Paper delivered at the symposium on natural regulation, The Wildlife Society, Vancouver, B.C.

COLINVAUX, PAUL. 1978. *Why big fierce animals are rare*. Princeton: Princeton University Press.

COLMENARES, F., AND H. RIVERO. 1983. Group formation studies in captive brown bears: socioecological implications. Paper presented at the Sixth International Conference on Bear Research and Management, Grand Canyon, Ariz.

COLMENARES, R., AND J. ORTEGA. 1983. Social dynamics in a captive group of brown bears: sociobiological aspects. Paper presented at the Sixth International Conference on Bear Research and Management, Grand Canyon, Ariz.

CONOVER, ADELE. 1983. Getting to know black bears—right on their home ground. *Smithsonian*, April.

COUTURIER, MARCEL A. J. 1954. *L'ours brun*. Grenoble: Couturier.

COWAN, IAN M. 1970. The status and conservation of bears (*Ursidae*) of the world—1970. In *Bears, IUCN, 1972.**

CRAIGHEAD, FRANK C., JR. 1974. Grizzly bear ranges and movement as determined by radiotracking. In *Bears, IUCN, 1976.**

———. 1979. *Track of the grizzly*. San Francisco: Sierra Club Books.

CRAIGHEAD, FRANK C., JR., AND JOHN J. CRAIGHEAD. 1970. Data on grizzly bear denning activities and behavior obtained by using wildlife telemetry. In *Bears, IUCN, 1972.**

———. 1972. Grizzly bear prehibernation and denning activities as determined by radiotracking. *Wildlife Monographs*, no. 32.

CRAIGHEAD, JOHN J. 1976. Studying grizzly habitat by satellite. *National Geographic* 150(1):148–58.

————. 1977. A proposed delineation of critical grizzly bear habitat in the Yellowstone region. In *Bears, BBA, 1980.**

————. 1982. Satellite imagery: an alternative future. *Western Wildlands*, winter.

CRAIGHEAD, JOHN J., AND FRANK C. CRAIGHEAD, JR. 1970. Grizzly bear–man relationships in Yellowstone National Park. In *Bears, BBA, 1980.**

CRAIGHEAD, JOHN J., FRANK C. CRAIGHEAD, JR., AND RAY J. DAVIS. 1963. *A field guide to Rocky Mountain wildflowers.* Boston: Houghton Mifflin.

CRAIGHEAD, JOHN J., FRANK C. CRAIGHEAD, JR., AND JAY SUMNER. 1974. Reproductive cycles and rates in the grizzly bear, *Ursus arctos horribilis*, of the Yellowstone ecosystem. In *Bears, IUCN, 1976.**

CRAIGHEAD, JOHN J., MAURICE HORNOCKER, AND FRANK C. CRAIGHEAD, JR. 1969. Reproductive biology of young female grizzly bears. *Journal of Reproduction and Fertility*, suppl. 6(1969):447–75.

CRAIGHEAD, JOHN J., J. S. SUMNER, AND G. B. SCAGGS. 1982. *A definitive system for analysis of grizzly bear habitat and other wilderness resources.* Missoula, Mont.: Wildlife-Wildlands Institute.

CRAIGHEAD, JOHN J., JOEL R. VARNEY, AND FRANK C. CRAIGHEAD, JR. 1974. A population analysis of the Yellowstone grizzly bears. Montana Forest and Conservation Experiment Station, University of Montana, bulletin no. 40.

CRAIGHEAD, JOHN J., JOEL R. VARNEY, FRANK C. CRAIGHEAD, JR., AND J. S. SUMNER. 1974. Telemetry experiments with a hibernating black bear. In *Bears, IUCN, 1976.**

CURRY-LINDAHL, KAI. 1970. The brown bear (*Ursus arctos* L.) in Europe: decline, present distribution, biology, and ecology. In *Bears, IUCN, 1972.**

CUSHING, BRUCE S. 1980. Responses of polar bears to human menstrual odors. In Meslow, E. Charles, ed. 1984. *Bears—their biology and management:* a selection of papers from the conference held at Madison, Wisconsin, U.S.A., February 1980. International Association for Bear Research and Management.

DASMANN, RAYMOND F. 1981. *Wildlife biology.* New York: John Wiley & Sons.

DEAN, FREDERICK C. 1974. Aspects of grizzly bear population ecology in Mount McKinley National Park. In *Bears, IUCN, 1976.**

————. 1975. A land use philosophy proposal for bear management. Paper presented at meeting of the Northwest Section of the Wildlife Society Anchorage.

DEMARCHI, RAY. 1981. Protecting female and juvenile grizzly bears from hunting mortality.

DESPAIN, DON D. 1975. *Field key to the flora of Yellowstone National Park.* Yellowstone Library and Museum Association.

DEVOTO, BERNARD, ed. 1953. *The journals of Lewis and Clark.* Boston: Houghton Mifflin.

DUFRESNE, FRANK. 1965. *No room for bears.* New York: Holt, Rinehart & Winston.

EAST, BEN. 1977. *Bears.* New York: Outdoor Life/Crown.

EGBERT, ALLEN L., AND ALLEN W. STOKES. 1974. The social behavior of brown bears on an Alaskan salmon stream. In *Bears, IUCN, 1976.**

ELGMORK, KÅRE. 1974. A remnant brown bear population in southern Norway and problems of its conservation. In *Bears, IUCN, 1976.**

ERDBRINK, D. P. 1953. *A review of fossil and recent bears of the Old World, with remarks upon their phylogeny based upon their dentition.* Deventer, The Netherlands: Jan de Lange.

EVANS, BROCK. 1983. Our national wood factories. *Audubon*, March.

EWER, R. F. 1968. *Ethology of mammals.* New York: Plenum Press.

FARROW, MOIRA. 1981. "Rape of wilderness" imperils wildlife in the East Kootenay. *Vancouver Sun,* 25 July.

FOLK, G. EDGAR, MARY A. FOLK, AND JUDY J. MINOR. 1970. Physiological condition of three species of bears in winter dens. In *Bears, IUCN, 1972.**

FOLK, G. EDGAR, JILL M. HUNT, AND MARY A. FOLK. 1977. Further evidence for hibernation of bears. In *Bears, BBA, 1980.**

FOLK, G. EDGAR, ANNA LARSON, AND MARY A. FOLK. 1974. Physiology of hibernating bears. In *Bears, IUCN, 1976.**

FOLLMANN, E. H., AND J. L. HECHTEL. 1983. Bears and pipeline construction in the far North. Paper presented at the Sixth International Conference on Bear Research and Management, Grand Canyon, Ariz.

FREE, STUART L., AND EUGENE MCCAFFERY. 1970. Reproductive synchrony in the female black bear. In *Bears, IUCN, 1972.**

FROME, MICHAEL. 1983. Losing balance. *Wilderness,* summer.

FRYE, STEPHEN J. 1982. Environmental assessment for the construction of a hiker's shelter at Granite Park. Glacier National Park.

GAINES, CHARLES. 1981. Griz. *Geo,* November.

GEBHARD, J. 1983. Annual activities and behavior of a grizzly bear family. Paper presented at the Sixth International Conference on Bear Research and Management, Grand Canyon, Ariz.

GEORGE, JEAN CRAIGHEAD. 1979. The kingdom of the grizzly. *Scene,* December.

GIANETTINO, SUSAN. 1981. The wildlife resource. In Flathead National Forest social and economic assessment. Draft.

GLENN, LELAND P., JACK W. LENTFER, JAMES B. FARO, AND LEO H. MILLER. 1974. Reproductive biology of female brown bears, *Ursus arctos,* McNeil River, Alaska. In *Bears, IUCN, 1976.**

GLENN, LELAND P., AND LEO H. MILLER. 1977. Seasonal movements of an Alaska Peninsula brown bear population. In *Bears, BBA, 1980.**

GRABER, D. M., AND M. WHITE. 1983. Parks and bears: the ecological consequences of recreation. Paper presented at the Sixth International Conference on Bear Research and Management, Grand Canyon, Ariz.

GRACHEV, Y. A. 1974. Distribution and quantity of brown bears in Kazakhstan. In *Bears, IUCN, 1976.**

GREAT BEAR FOUNDATION. 1983. Montana children choose grizzlies. *Bear News,* fall.

GREER, KENNETH R. 1970. Grizzly bear mortality and studies in Montana. In *Bears, IUCN, 1972.**

———. 1974. Managing Montana's grizzlies for the grizzlies. In *Bears, IUCN, 1976.**

GRIFFEL, DAVID E. 1978. Bear-livestock interaction study, 1978. Targhee National Forest.

GRIFFEL, DAVID E., AND JOSEPH V. BASILE. 1981. Identifying sheep killed by bears. U.S. Forest Intermountain Forest and Range Experiment Station, Ogden, Utah.

GRITMAN, JAMES C. 1980. Biological opinion in response to request for formal consultation regarding the proposed drilling of two exploratory oil/gas wells on the Bridger-Teton National Forest. U.S. Fish and Wildlife Service.

Grizzly fund earns interest. 1983. *Audubon Action,* June.

HAINES, AUBREY L. 1977. *The Yellowstone story.* 2 vols. Yellowstone Library and Museum Association/Colorado Associated University Press.

HALL, E. RAYMOND. 1981. *The mammals of North America.* New York: John Wiley & Sons.

HAMER, DAVID, STEPHEN HERRERO, AND LYNN L. ROGERS. 1981. Differentiating black and grizzly bear feces. *Wildlife Society Bulletin* 9(3):210–11.

HANSON, DENNIS. 1983. The aspect of the tally-sheet. *Wilderness,* summer.

HARDING, LEE, AND JOHN A. NAGY. 1977. Responses of grizzly bears to hydrocarbon exploration on Richards Island, Northwest Territories. In *Bears, BBA, 1980.**

HARMS, DALE R. 1977. Black bear management in Yosemite. In *Bears, BBA, 1980.**

HASTINGS, BRUCE C., BARRIE K. GILBERT, AND DAVID L. TURNER. 1981. Black bear behavior and human-bear relationships in Yosemite National Park.

HAYNES, BESSIE DOAK, AND EDGAR HAYNES, eds. 1966. *The grizzly bear: portraits from life.* Norman, Okla.: University of Oklahoma Press.

HENCKEL, MARK. 1983. *The great bear.* Billings, Mont.: *Billings Gazette.*

HERREID, CLYDE F., II. 1977. *Biology.* New York: Macmillan.

HERRERO, STEPHEN. 1970. Aspects of evolution and adaptation in American black bears (*Ursus americanus* Pallas) and brown and grizzly bears (*Ursus arctos* Linné) of North America. In *Bears, IUCN, 1972.**

———. 1970. Human injury inflicted by grizzly bears. *Science* 170:593–98.

———. 1970. Man and the grizzly bear (past, present, but future?) *BioScience* 20(21):1148–53.

———. 1974. Conflicts between man and grizzly bears in the national parks of North America. In *Bears, IUCN, 1976.**

———. 1978. A comparison of some features of the evolution, ecology, and behavior of black and grizzly/brown bears. *Carnivore* 1(1):7–17.

HERRERO, STEPHEN, AND D. HAMER. 1977. Courtship and copulation of a pair of grizzly bears, with comments on reproductive plasticity and strategy. *Journal of Mammalogy* 58(3):441–44.

HOAGLAND, EDWARD. 1976. *Red wolves and black bears.* New York: Random House.

HOLZWORTH, JOHN M. 1930. *The wild grizzlies of Alaska.* New York: Putnam's.

HOUSTON, DOUGLAS B. 1971. Ecosystems of national parks. *Science* 172:648–51.

———. 1971. Research on ungulates in northern Yellowstone National Park. Paper presented at AAAS symposium on research in national parks.

———. 1982. *The northern Yellowstone elk.* New York: Macmillan.

HUNT, CARRIE L. 1983. Tests of repellents and deterrents for bears: progress report: 1982 summary. Department of Wildlife, University of Montana, Missoula.

The importance of being handsome. 1983. *The Economist,* 30 July.

JACOBSON, ROBERT D. 1977. Legal aspects of critical habitat determinations. In *Bears, BBA, 1980.**

JONKEL, CHARLES. 1978. Border Grizzly Project annual report no. 3. School of Forestry, University of Montana, Missoula.

———. 1978. Grizzly bears and the mountain pine beetle. Border Grizzly Project special report no. 21.

———. 1979. Yellowstone grizzlies: management versus protection. Border Grizzly Project special report no. 24.

———. 1980. Grizzly bears and livestock. *Western Wildlands*, summer.

———. 1980. The North End Salvage Sale and grizzlies—an opinion. Border Grizzly Project special report no. 44.

———. 1980. The West Glacier area—a background sketch of bear/people conflicts. Border Grizzly Project special report no. 43.

———. 1980. Winter disturbance and grizzly bears. Border Grizzly Project special report no. 46.

———. 1981. The Border Grizzly Project. School of Forestry, University of Montana, Missoula.

———. 1982. The border grizzly. *Western Wildlands*, winter.

———. 1983. Bears of the world. Paper presented at the Sixth International Conference on Bear Research and Management, Grand Canyon, Ariz.

JONKEL, CHARLES, PETER HUSBY, RICHARD RUSSELL, AND JOHN BEECHAM. 1977. The reintroduction of orphaned grizzly bear cubs into the wild. In *Bears, BBA, 1980.**

JONKEL, CHARLES, AND RICHARD R. KNIGHT. 1979. Recommendations for the grizzly bear.

JONKEL, CHARLES, CHRISTOPHER SERVHEEN, AND L. LEE. Grizzly bears and the RARE II process, border grizzly area. Border Grizzly Project special report no. 20. School of Forestry, University of Montana, Missoula.

JOPE, K. L. McARTHUR. 1982. Interactions between grizzly bears and hikers in Glacier National Park, Montana. Cooperative Park Studies Unit, Oregon State University, Corvallis.

———. 1983. Implications of habituation for hikers in grizzly bear habitat. Paper presented at the Sixth International Conference on Bear Research and Management, Grand Canyon, Ariz.

JORDAN, ROBERT H. 1974. Threat behavior of the black bear, *Ursus americanus*. In *Bears, IUCN, 1976.**

JORGENSEN, CAROLE, AND ARTHUR ALLEN. 1975. Grizzly bear study, Targhee National Forest.

JOSLIN, GAYLE. 1971. The Great Bear Wilderness and its implications for grizzly bears. Border Grizzly Project special report no. 5.

JUDD, STEVEN L., AND RICHARD R. KNIGHT. 1977. Movements of radio-instrumented grizzly bears within the Yellowstone area. In *Bears, BBA, 1980.**

JUDD, STEVEN L., RICHARD R. KNIGHT, AND BONNIE M. BLANCHARD. 1983. Denning of grizzly bears in the Yellowstone area. Paper presented at the Sixth International Conference on Bear Research and Management, Grand Canyon, Ariz.

KAAL, MATI. 1976. Ecology, protection, and prospect of utilization of the brown bear in the Estonian SSR. In *Bears, IUCN, 1976.**

KEMP, GERALD A. 1974. The dynamics and regulation of black bear, *Ursus americanus*, populations in northern Alberta. In *Bears, IUCN, 1976.**

KENDALL, KATHERINE C. 1980. Bear–squirrel–pine nut interaction. In *IGBST 1978–79.**

———. 1980. Food habits of Yellowstone grizzly bears, 1978 and 1979. In *IGBST 1978–79.**

———. 1983. Trends in grizzly-human confrontations, Glacier National Park, Montana. Paper presented at the Sixth International Conference on Bear Research and Management, Grand Canyon, Ariz.

KERSHNER, JIM. 1977. Cody man fined $800 for grizzly bear killing. *Cody* (Wyo.) *Enterprise*, 14 September.

KILGORE, BRUCE M., CLYDE JONES, REID GOFORTH, JOHN BEECHAM, JOHN WEIGAND, AND DALE STRICKLAND. 1981. Technical review of the IGBST and recommendations for future research. National Park Service.

KISTCHINSKI, A. A. 1970. Life history of the brown bear (*Ursus arctos* L.) in northeast Siberia. In *Bears, IUCN, 1972.**

KNIGHT, RICHARD R. 1977. Biological considerations in the delineation of critical habitat. In *Bears, BBA, 1980.**

———. 1980. Population parameters of the Yellowstone grizzly. In *IGBST 1978–79.**

———. 1980. Status and suggestions for management of the grizzly bear.

KNIGHT, RICHARD R., JOSEPH V. BASILE, KENNETH R. GREER, STEVEN L. JUDD, LLOYD E. OLDENBURG, AND LARRY J. ROOP. 1976. *Yellowstone grizzly bear investigations: annual report of the interagency study team, 1975.*

———. 1978. *Yellowstone grizzly bear investigations: annual report of the interagency study team, 1977.*

KNIGHT, RICHARD R., AND STEVEN L. JUDD. 1980. Grizzly bears that kill livestock. In *IGBST 1978–79.**

KNIGHT, RICHARD R., BONNIE M. BLANCHARD, KATHERINE C. KENDALL, AND LLOYD E. OLDENBURG, eds. 1980. *Yellowstone grizzly bear investigations: annual report of the interagency study team, 1978–79.*

KNIGHT, RICHARD R., BONNIE M. BLANCHARD, KATHERINE C. KENDALL, LARRY J. ROOP, KENNETH R. GREER, AND LLOYD E. OLDENBURG. 1981. *Yellowstone grizzly bear investigations: report of the interagency study team, 1980.*

KNIGHT, RICHARD R., BONNIE M. BLANCHARD, KATHERINE C. KENDALL, KENNETH R. GREER, LLOYD E. OLDENBURG, AND LARRY J. ROOP. 1982. *Yellowstone grizzly bear investigations: annual report of the interagency study team, 1981.*

KNIGHT, RICHARD R., AND BONNIE M. BLANCHARD. 1983. *Yellowstone grizzly bear investigations: annual report of the interagency study team, 1982.*

KOFORD, C. B. 1969. The last of the Mexican grizzly bears. *IUCN* Bulletin New Service 2:95.

KRAKEL, DEANE, II. 1976. *Season of the elk.* Kansas City, Kans.: Lowell Press.

KURTÉN, BJÖRN. 1968. *Pleistocene mammals of Europe.* Chicago: Aldine.

———. 1976. *The cave bear story.* New York: Columbia University Press.

LANGFORD, N. P. 1870. *The discovery of Yellowstone Park.* St. Paul: J. E. Haynes (1905 edition).

LEASURE, BOB. 1973. The bear no man could kill. *Colorado Magazine*, September/October.

LEE, L., AND CHARLES JONKEL. 1981. Grizzlies and wetlands. *Western Wildlands*, winter.

LEE, LYNDON C., AND ROBERT D. PFISTER. 1978. *A training manual for Montana forest habitat types.* Montana Forest and Conservation Experiment Station, University of Montana, Missoula.

LEE, PHILIP. 1981. Biological evaluation: man/grizzly bear conflicts related to sheep grazing in essential grizzly bear habitat on the Targhee National Forest. U.S. Forest Service.

LEISTER, CLAUDE W. 1931. *Present day mammals.* New York: New York Zoological Society.

LENTFER, JACK W., RICHARD J. HENSEL, LEO H. MILLER, LELAND P. GLENN, AND VERNON D. BERNS. 1970. Remarks on denning habits of Alaska brown bears. In *Bears, IUCN, 1972.**

LEONARD, R. D. 1983. A review and correction of bear management practices in some Canadian national parks. Paper presented at the Sixth International Conference on Bear Research and Management, Grand Canyon, Ariz.

LEOPOLD, A. STARKER, STANLEY A. CAIN, IRA N. GABRIELSON, CLARENCE M. COTTAM, AND THOMAS L. KIMBALL. 1963. Wildlife management in the national parks. Report to Secretary of the Interior Stewart Udall.

LEWIN, ROGER. 1982. Food fuels reproductive success. *Science* 217:238–39.

———. 1982. Red deer data illuminate sexual selection. *Science* 218:1206–8.

———. 1983. Predators and hurricanes change ecology. *Science* 221:737–40.

———. 1983. Santa Rosalia was a goat. *Science* 221:636–39.

LOY, THOMAS H. 1983. Prehistoric blood residues: detection on tool surfaces and identification of species of origin. *Science* 220:1269–70.

LUCAS, ROBERT C. 1983. The role of regulations in recreation management. *Western Wildlands,* summer.

LUDLOW, JEANNE C. 1974. Observations on the breeding of captive black bears, *Ursus americanus.* In *Bears, IUCN, 1976.**

MACE, RICHARD D., AND CHARLES JONKEL. 1980. The effects of a logging activity on grizzly bear movements. Border Grizzly Project special report no. 38.

———. 1983. Regional food habits of the grizzly bear in Montana. Paper presented at the Sixth International Conference on Bear Research and Management, Grand Canyon, Ariz.

MADEL, MICHAEL J. 1982. Grizzly habitat component mapping. Kootenai National Forest.

MALLOY, MICHAEL T. 1973. Bear fight bares few bear facts. *National Observer,* 24 November.

MANNING, AUBREY. 1979. *An introduction to animal behavior.* Menlo Park, Calif.: Addison-Wesley.

MARKOV, GEORGIE. 1977. On the distribution of the brown bear in Bulgaria. In *Bears, BBA, 1980.**

MARSH, JOHN S. 1970. Bears and man in Glacier National Park, British Columbia, 1880–1980. In *Bears, IUCN, 1972.**

MARTINKA, CLIFFORD J. 1971. Status and management of grizzly bears in Glacier National Park, Montana. Transactions of the 36th North American Wildlife and Natural Resources Conference.

———. 1972. Habitat relationships of grizzly bears in Glacier National Park, Montana.

———. 1974. Ecological role and management of grizzly bears in Glacier National Park, Montana. In *Bears, IUCN, 1976.**

———. 1974. Population characteristics of grizzly bears in Glacier National Park, Montana. *Journal of Mammalogy* 55(1):21–29.

———. 1974. Preserving the natural status of grizzlies in Glacier National Park. *Wildlife Society Bulletin* 2(1):13–17.

———. 1982. Keeping people and bears apart: people management in Glacier Park. *Western Wildlands*, winter.

———. 1982. Rationale and options for management in grizzly bear sanctuaries. Transactions of the North American Wildlife and Natural Resources Conference.

McArthur, Katherine L. 1979. The behavior of grizzly bears in relation to people in Glacier National Park.

———. 1981. Factors contributing to effectiveness of black bear transplants. *Journal of Wildlife Management* 45(1):102–10.

McCool, Stephen F. 1983. The national parks in post-industrial America. *Western Wildlands*, summer.

McCracken, Harold. 1955. *The beast that walks like man: the story of the grizzly bear*. Garden City, N.Y.: Hanover House.

McCullough, Dale R. 1969. *The Tule elk*. Berkeley: University of California Press.

———. 1978. Population dynamics of the Yellowstone grizzly bear. Paper prepared for presentation at the international symposium on population dynamics of large mammals, Utah State University, Logan, Utah.

———. 1983. Interpretation of the Craigheads' data on Yellowstone grizzly bear populations and its relevance to current research and management. Paper presented at the Sixth International Conference on Bear Research and Management, Grand Canyon, Ariz.

McMillin, J. Michael, U. S. Seal, Lynn Rogers, and A. W. Erickson. 1976. Annual testosterone rhythm in the black bear (*Ursus americanus*). *Biology of Reproduction* 15:163–67.

McNamee, Thomas. 1982. Breath-holding in grizzly country. *Audubon*, November.

Meagher, Mary. 1973. *The bison of Yellowstone National Park*. National Park Service Scientific Monograph Series 1.

———. 1978. Evaluation of bear management in Yellowstone National Park, 1977. Research note no. 8, Yellowstone National Park.

Meagher, Mary, and Jerry R. Phillips. 1980. Restoration of natural populations of grizzly and black bears in Yellowstone National Park.

Mealey, Stephen P. 1975. The natural food habits of free ranging grizzly bears in Yellowstone National Park, 1973–1974. M.S. thesis, Montana State University.

———. 1977. Method for determining grizzly bear habitat quality and estimating consequences of impacts on grizzly bear habitat quality. In *Grizzly Bear Recovery Plan*, U.S. Department of the Interior, Fish and Wildlife Service, 1982.

———. 1982. Executive summary: status of the grizzly bear population in the Yellowstone grizzly bear ecosystem. U.S. Forest Service.

Mealey, Stephen P., and Charles Jonkel. 1975. Grizzly bear food habits and habitat use. Border Grizzly Project special report no. 1. School of Forestry, University of Montana, Missoula.

MEALEY, STEPHEN P., CHARLES JONKEL, AND RAY DEMARCHI. 1977. Habitat criteria for grizzly bear management. Proceedings of the International Conference of Game Biologists 13:276–89.

MECH, L. DAVID. 1975. Disproportionate sex ratios of wolf pups. *Journal of Wildlife Management* 39(4):737–40.

MILLER, JOAQUIN. 1949. *True bear stories*. Portland, Ore.: Binfords & Mort.

MITCHELL, JOHN G. 1982. *The hunt*. New York: Knopf.

MUNDY, K. R. D. 1973. Background for managing grizzly bears in the national parks of Canada. Canadian Wildlife Service report no. 22.

MURIE, OLAUS J. 1944. Progress report on the Yellowstone bear study. Yellowstone National Park.

———. 1951. *The elk of North America*. Jackson, Wyo.: Teton Bookshop (1979 reprint of Stackpole/Wildlife Management Institute edition).

MYSTERUD, IVAR. 1977. Bear management and sheep husbandry in Norway, with a discussion of predatory behavior significant for evaluation of livestock losses. In *Bears, BBA, 1980*.*

NAGY, J. A., AND R. H. RUSSELL. 1978. Ecological studies of the boreal forest grizzly bear (*Ursus arctos* L.)—annual report for 1977. Canadian Wildlife Service.

National Academy of Sciences, Division of Biological Sciences, Assembly of Life Sciences, National Research Council. 1974. Report of committee on the Yellowstone grizzlies. Washington, D.C.

NELSON, RALPH A. 1973. Winter sleep in the black bear—a physiologic and metabolic marvel. *Mayo Clinic Proceedings* 48:733–37.

———. 1979. Protein and fat metabolism in hibernating bears. *Federation Proceedings* 39(12):2955–58.

———. 1981. Polar bears—active yet hibernating? In *Spirit of Enterprise—the 1981 Rolex Awards*. San Francisco: W. H. Freeman.

NELSON, RALPH A., G. EDGAR FOLK, JR., EGBERT W. PFEIFFER, JOHN J. CRAIGHEAD, CHARLES J. JONKEL, AND DIANNE L. WELLIK. 1977. Behavior, biochemistry, and hibernation in black, grizzly, and polar bears. In *Bears, BBA, 1980*.*

NELSON, RALPH A., D. L. STEIGER, AND THOMAS D. I. BECK. 1982. Neuroendocrine and metabolic interactions in the hibernating black bear. Proceedings of the Third International Theriological Congress, Helsinki.

———. 1983. Physiology and biochemistry of hibernation in the bear. Paper presented at the Sixth International Conference on Bear Research and Management, Grand Canyon, Ariz.

The New York Times. 1981. Canadian mine held pollution threat to U.S. park. 15 October.

———. 1982. Yellowstone officials fear leases will harm grizzlies. *Denver Post*, 9 August.

———. 1982. Grizzlies seen as imperiled in Wyoming. 1 October.

———. 1983. Campsites may go to protect bears. 27 August.

O'GARA, GEOFFREY. 1980. The grizzly: how many? where? for how long? *High Country News* (Lander, Wyo.), 21 March.

O'HARRA, DOUG. 1982. What to do in grizzly country. *Western Wildlands*, winter.

OLSEN, JACK. 1969. *Night of the grizzlies*. New York: Putnam's.

PEARSON, A. M. (chairman). 1968. *Proceedings of the first bear workshop*.

Whitehorse, Yukon. International Association for Bear Research and Management reprint, 1983.

PEARSON, A. M. 1970. Population characteristics of the northern interior grizzly in the Yukon Territory, Canada. In *Bears, IUCN, 1972.**

———. 1974. Population characteristics of the Arctic mountain grizzly bear. In *Bears, IUCN, 1976.**

———. 1975. *The northern interior grizzly bear*, Ursus arctos L. Canadian Wildlife Service report series no. 34.

PERRY, RICHARD. 1970. *Bears*. London: Arthur Barker.

PETERSON, ROLF O. 1981. Wolf and moose studies on the Kenai Peninsula, Alaska, 1976–80.

PETITE, IRVING. 1963. *Mister B*. Garden City, N.Y.: Doubleday.

PICTON, HAROLD D. 1978. Climate and reproduction of grizzly bears in Yellowstone National Park. *Nature* 274(5674):888–89.

———. 1983. Grizzly link? Yellowstone and Glacier, its biology and dynamics. Paper presented at the Sixth International Conference on Bear Research and Management, Grand Canyon, Ariz.

———. 1983. Using climate data to predict grizzly bear litter size. Paper presented at the Sixth International Conference on Bear Research and Management, Grand Canyon, Ariz.

PICTON, HAROLD D., AND RICHARD R. KNIGHT. 1980. Obtaining biological information from grizzly bear (*Ursus arctos horribilis*) hair. Paper presented at meeting of the Northwest Section of the Wildlife Society, Banff, Alberta.

PRUITT, CHERYL H. 1974. Play and agonistic behavior in captive black bears. In *Bears, IUCN, 1976.**

RAMSAY, M., AND I. STIRLING. 1983. The effects of handling on free-ranging polar bears. Paper presented at the Sixth International Conference on Bear Research and Management, Grand Canyon, Ariz.

REYNOLDS, HARRY V., III, JAMES A. CURATOLO, AND ROLAND QUIMBY. 1974. Denning ecology of grizzly bears in northeastern Alaska. In *Bears, IUCN, 1976.**

REYNOLDS, HARRY V., III, AND G. W. GARNER. 1983. Factors affecting population biology of northern Alaska grizzly bears. Paper presented at the Sixth International Conference on Bear Research and Management, Grand Canyon, Ariz.

REYNOLDS, P. E., HARRY V. REYNOLDS, III, AND E. H. FOLLMANN. 1983. Effects of seismic surveys on denning grizzly bears in northern Alaska. Paper presented at the Sixth International Conference on Bear Research and Management, Grand Canyon, Ariz.

RÖBEN, PETER. 1977. Status of the brown bear in the Pyrenees. In *Bears, BBA, 1980.**

ROGERS, LYNN L. 1974. Shedding of foot pads by black bears during denning. *Journal of Mammalogy* 55(3):672–74.

———. 1975. Black bears of the Lake Superior region. *North Land* 3(1).

———. 1975. Parasites of black bears of the Lake Superior region. *Journal of Wildlife Diseases* 11:189–91.

———. 1976. Effects of mast and berry crop failures on survival, growth, and reproductive success of black bears. Transactions of the Forty-first

Annual North American Wildlife and Natural Resources Conference, Wildlife Management Institute.

———. 1977. Social relationships, movement, and population dynamics of black bears in northeastern Minnesota. Ph.D. diss., University of Minnesota.

———. 1977. The ubiquitous American black bear. In *North American Big Game*. Edited by William H. Nesbitt and Jack S. Parker. Washington: Boone and Crockett Club/National Rifle Association of America.

———. 1980. Inheritance of coat color and changes in pelage coloration in black bears in northeastern Minnesota. *Journal of Mammalogy* 61(2):324–27.

———. 1981. A bear in its lair. *Natural History*, October.

———. 1983. Effects of food supply, predation, cannibalism, parasites, and other health problems on black bear populations. In *Natural Regulation of Wildlife*. Edited by D. L. Eastman, F. Bunnell, and J. Peek. Moscow, Ida.: University of Idaho Press. In press.

ROGERS, LYNN L., DAVID W. KUEHN, ALBERT W. ERICKSON, ELSWORTH M. HARGER, LOUIS J. VERME, AND JOHN J. OZOGA. 1974. Characteristics and management of black bears that feed in garbage dumps, campgrounds, or residential areas. In *Bears, IUCN, 1976*.*

ROGERS, LYNN L., AND L. DAVID MECH. 1981. Interactions of wolves and black bears in northeastern Minnesota. *Journal of Mammalogy* 62(2):434–36.

ROGERS, LYNN L., AND SUSANNE M. ROGERS. 1974. Parasites of bears: a review. In *Bears, IUCN, 1976*.*

ROGERS, LYNN L., CLARENCE W. STOWE, AND ALBERT W. ERICKSON. 1974. Succinylcholine chloride immobilization of black bears. In *Bears, IUCN, 1976*.*

ROOP, LARRY J. 1976. Grizzly bear progress report. Wyoming Game and Fish Department.

———. 1977. Grizzly bear progress report. Wyoming Game and Fish Department.

———. 1978. Grizzly bear progress report. Wyoming Game and Fish Department.

———. 1979. Grizzly bear progress report. Wyoming Game and Fish Department.

———. 1980. Grizzly bear progress report. Wyoming Game and Fish Department.

———. 1980. The Yellowstone grizzly bear: a review of past and present population estimates. In *IGBST 1978–79*.*

———. 1981. Grizzly bear progress report. Wyoming Game and Fish Department.

———. 1981. A preliminary summary of grizzly bear problems, mortalities, and captures in Wyoming, 1981. Wyoming Game and Fish Department.

———. 1982. Grizzly bear progress report. Wyoming Game and Fish Department.

ROOSEVELT, THEODORE. 1893. An elk hunt at Two Ocean Pass. In *The wilderness hunter*. New York: Putnam's.

———. 1983. *American Bears*. Edited by Paul Schullery. Boulder: Colorado Associated University Press.

ROTH, HANS U. 1974. Status of the last brown bears of the Alps in the Trentino, Italy. Abstract. In *Bears, IUCN, 1976*.*

ROTH, HANS U., AND D. HUBER. 1983. Diel activity patterns of brown bears in Plitvice Lakes National Park, Yugoslavia. Paper presented at the Sixth International Conference on Bear Research and Management, Grand Canyon, Ariz.

RUEDIGER, WILLIAM, AND STEPHEN P. MEALEY. 1978. Coordination guidelines for timber harvesting in grizzly bear habitat in northwestern Montana. U.S. Forest Service.

RUSSAKOFF, DALE. 1982. Bad news bears: grizzly scarcer in Yellowstone. *Washington Post,* 31 August.

RUSSELL, ANDY. 1967. *Grizzly country.* New York: Knopf.

RUSSELL, R. H., J. W. NOLAN, N. G. WOODY, G. H. ANDERSON, AND A. M. PEARSON. 1978. A study of the grizzly bear (*Ursus arctos*) in Jasper National Park, 1976–77. Parks Canada, Canadian Wildlife Service.

SAX, JOSEPH L. 1980. *Mountains without handrails: reflections on the national parks.* Ann Arbor: University of Michigan Press.

———. 1983. Free enterprise in the woods. *Natural History,* June.

SCHALLENBERGER, ALLEN. 1977. Review of oil and gas exploitation impacts on grizzly bears. In *Bears, BBA, 1980.**

SCHALLENBERGER, ALLEN, AND CHARLES JONKEL. 1978. Critique of the U.S. Forest Service Rocky Mountain Front plan. Border Grizzly Project special report no. 13. School of Forestry, University of Montana, Missoula.

———. 1978. Rocky Mountain East Front grizzly studies, 1977: annual report. Border Grizzly Project.

SCHLEYER, BART O. 1980. Daily routine of grizzly bears in the Yellowstone ecosystem. In *IGBST 1978–79.**

———. 1983. Activity patterns of grizzly bears in the Yellowstone ecosystem and their reproductive behavior, predation, and the use of carrion. M.S. thesis, Montana State University.

SCHMIDT-NIELSEN, KNUT. 1979. *Animal physiology.* Cambridge: Cambridge University Press.

SCHNEIDER, BILL. 1977. *Where the grizzly walks.* Missoula, Mont.: Mountain Press.

———. 1977. Will this grizzly attack? *National Wildlife,* February/March.

———. 1978. Last fight for the grizzly. *Outdoor Life,* January.

SCHOEN, J. W. 1983. Differential distribution of brown bears on Admiralty Island, southeast Alaska: a preliminary assessment. Paper presented at the Sixth International Conference on Bear Research and Management, Grand Canyon, Ariz.

SCHOONMAKER, W. L. 1968. *The world of the grizzly bear.* Philadelphia: Lippincott.

SCHULLERY, PAUL. 1980. *The bears of Yellowstone.* Yellowstone Library and Museum Association.

SEGARTY, TERRY. 1981. "Present annual output of mines . . ." (no headline). *Kootenay* (B.C.) *Daily Townsman,* 16 June.

SERVHEEN, CHRISTOPHER. 1981. Grizzly bear ecology and management in the Mission Mountains, Montana. Ph.D. diss., University of Montana, Missoula.

———. 1982. A national plan of recovery. *Western Wildlands,* winter.

———. 1983. Grizzly bear food habits, movements, and habitat selection in the Mission Mountains, Montana. *Journal of Wildlife Management.* In Press.

————. 1983. The status of the grizzly bear in the lower 48 states: an outline of progress toward recovery. Paper presented at the Sixth International Conference on Bear Research and Management, Grand Canyon, Ariz.

SETON, ERNEST THOMPSON. 1899. *The biography of a grizzly.* New York: Grosset & Dunlap.

SHABECOFF, PHILIP. 1981. Measures to control coyotes are sought by U.S. officials. *The New York Times,* 20 November.

————. 1981. Poll finds strong support for environmental code. *The New York Times,* 4 October.

————. 1981. Townspeople join to fight drilling. *The New York Times,* 14 September.

SHAFFER, MARK L. 1980. Determining minimum viable population sizes for the grizzly bear. Ph.D. diss., Duke University.

SHARAFUTDINOV, I. V., AND A. M. KOROTKOV. 1974. On the ecology of brown bears in the southern Urals. In *Bears, IUCN, 1976.**

SHAW, RICHARD J. 1974. *Plants of Yellowstone and Grand Teton National Parks.* Salt Lake City: Wheelright.

SHAW, RICHARD J., AND DANNY ON. 1979. *Plants of Waterton-Glacier National Parks and the northern Rockies.* Missoula, Mont.: Mountain Press.

SIMPSON, GEORGE F. 1945. The principle of classification and a classification of mammals. *Bulletin of the American Museum of Natural History* 85.

SINGER, FRANCIS J. 1978. Seasonal concentrations of grizzly bears, North Fork of the Flathead River, Montana. *Canadian Field-Naturalist* 92(3):283–286.

SIZEMORE, DENNIS. 1980. Seasonal susceptibility of grizzly bears to rodent poisoning programs. Border Grizzly Project special report no. 40. School of Forestry, University of Montana, Missoula.

SIZEMORE, DENNIS, AND CHARLES JONKEL. 1979. Bioenergetics as a prerequisite for grizzly bear habitat improvement. Border Grizzly Project special report no. 26. School of Forestry, University of Montana, Missoula.

SKINNER, M. P. 1925. *Bears in the Yellowstone.* Chicago: McClurg.

SMITH, MARTIN E. 1983. Proposal for research on repellents and deterrents for bears. Department of Wildlife, University of Montana, Missoula.

STEBLER, A. M. 1970. Conservation of the grizzly—ecologic and cultural considerations. In *Bears, IUCN, 1972.**

STEELE, ROBERT, ROBERT D. PFISTER, RUSSELL A. RYKER, AND JAY A. KITTAMS. 1981. *Forest types of central Idaho.* U.S. Forest Service Intermountain Range and Experiment Station, Ogden, Utah.

STEINHART, PETER. 1978. Getting to know bruin better. *National Wildlife,* May.

STENHOUSE, GORDON B., AND PAUL A. GRAY. 1982. Northwest Territories: bear detection and deterrent program. In *Proceedings of the Second Western Black Bear Workshop, Logan, Utah.*

STEVENS, MONTAGUE. 1943. *Meet Mr. Grizzly: a saga on the passing of the grizzly.* Albuquerque: University of New Mexico Press.

STOKES, A. W. 1970. An ethologist's views on managing grizzly bears. *BioScience* 20(21):1154–57.

STONOROV, DEREK, AND ALLEN W. STOKES. 1970. Social behavior of the Alaska brown bear. In *Bears, IUCN, 1972.**

STORER, TRACY I., AND LLOYD P. TEVIS, JR. 1955. *California grizzly.* Lincoln: University of Nebraska Press.

STRAIN, PEGGY. 1981. Don't put blame on bear, mauling victim says. *Denver Post*, 8 July.

STRINGHAM, STEPHEN F. 1977. Possible impacts of hunting on the grizzly/brown bear, a threatened species. In *Bears, BBA, 1980.**

———. 1983. Factors governing reproduction and recruitment rates in grizzly populations. Paper presented at the Sixth International Conference on Bear Research and Management, Grand Canyon, Ariz.

STUART, THOMAS W. 1977. Exploration of optimal backcountry travel patterns in grizzly bear habitat. In *Bears, BBA, 1980.**

———. 1978. Management models for human use of grizzly bear habitat. In *Transactions of the Forty-third North American Wildlife and Natural Resources Conference* 43:434–41.

SUTTON, ANN, AND MYRON SUTTON. *Yellowstone.* New York: Bonanza/Yellowstone Library and Museum Association, n.d.

TATE, J. 1983. Behavioral patterns in human-bear interactions. Paper presented at the Sixth International Conference on Bear Research and Management, Grand Canyon, Ariz.

THIER, TIMOTHY J. 1981. Cabinet Mountains grizzly bear studies, 1979–80. Border Grizzly Project special report no. 50. School of Forestry, University of Montana, Missoula.

THOMAS, JACK W., AND DALE E. TOWEILL, eds. 1982. *Elk of North America: ecology and management.* Harrisburg, Pa.: Stackpole/Wildlife Management Institute/U.S. Forest Service.

THOMAS, KEITH. 1983. *Man and the natural world.* New York: Pantheon.

TITLOW, BUDD, AND DEBBY TITLOW. 1981. Where have all the bears gone? *National Parks*, May.

TRACY, D. M., F. C. DEAN, C. M. ANDERSON, AND T. M. JORDAN. 1982. *Brown bear bibliography.* Anchorage: Alaska Cooperative Park Studies Unit, University of Alaska.

TREVIÑO, J. C., AND CHARLES JONKEL. 1983. Do grizzlies still live in Mexico? Paper presented at the Sixth International Conference on Bear Research and Management, Grand Canyon, Ariz.

TURNER, FREDERICK. 1983. The language of the forest. *Wilderness*, summer.

TURNER, GEOFFREY. 1979. *Indians of North America.* Poole, Dorset, U.K.: Blandford.

United States. 1983. The Endangered Species Act as amended by public law 97-304 (The Endangered Species Act Amendments of 1982). Washington, D.C.: Government Printing Office.

U.S. Council on Environmental Quality, Executive Office of the President. 1978. Regulations for implementing the procedural provisions of the National Environmental Policy Act. Washington, D.C.: Government Printing Office.

U.S. Department of Agriculture, Forest Service. 1979. Mining in national forests. Current information report no. 14.

———. 1979. National Forest System land and resources management planning. *Federal Register*, 17 September.

———. 1981. Criteria for the analysis of the management situation: coefficients: Kootenai National Forest: vol. 4, appendix 6: procedure for identification of grizzly habitat and development of grizzly management goals.

———. 1981. Grizzly bear habitat management guidelines, Kootenai National Forest. Draft.

———. 1981. Procedure for evaluating the effects of alternative forest plan prescriptions on five Flathead National Forest grizzly bear productivity areas.

———. 1982. Draft environmental impact statement, Kootenai National Forest land and resource management plan.

———. 1982. Habitat management program, threatened and endangered plants and animals, Bridger-Teton National Forest.

———. 1982. Lewis and Clark National Forest draft environmental impact statement; Middle Fork Judith and Big Snowies wilderness study report.

———. 1982. Proposed Lewis and Clark National Forest plan.

———. 1983. Guidelines for managing grizzly bear habitat in northern Idaho. Idaho Panhandle National Forests.

———. 1983. Information initiative: "grizzlies—bear us in mind." Greater Yellowstone U.S. Forest Service administrators.

———. 1983. Kootenai National Forest plan.

U.S. Department of Agriculture, Forest Service, and U.S. Department of the Interior, National Park Service, 1978. Grizzly grizzly grizzly. Washington: Government Printing Office.

———. 1979. Guidelines for management involving grizzly bears in the greater Yellowstone area.

U.S. Department of the Interior, Bureau of Land Management. 1981. Oil and gas: environmental assessment of BLM leasing program, Butte District.

———. 1983. Headwaters Resource Area resource management plan: environmental impact statement. Draft.

U.S. Department of the Interior, Fish and Wildlife Service. 1980. Biological opinion of Asarco exploratory drilling in the Chicago Peak area of the Cabinet Mountains.

———. 1981. Consultation re sheep grazing in essential grizzly bear habitat. Targhee National Forest.

———. 1982. Grizzly bear recovery plan.

U.S. Department of the Interior, Minerals Management Service. 1982. Grizzly/wolf technical workshop: administration of oil and gas activity.

U.S. Department of the Interior, National Park Service. 1973. Master plan, Yellowstone National Park.

———. 1978. Yellowstone operating procedure: policy statements: bear policy.

———. 1979. Environmental assessment for the development concept plan for Grant Village, Yellowstone National Park.

———. 1980. State of the parks, 1980. Office of Science and Technology.

———. 1982. Final environmental impact statement, grizzly bear management program, Yellowstone National Park.

———. 1982. Information for cooperating researchers, Yellowstone National Park.

———. 1983. Bear management plan, Glacier National Park.

USTINOV, S. K. 1974. The brown bear on Baikal: a few features of vital activities. In Bears, IUCN, 1976.*

VERESCHAGIN, N. K. 1974. The brown bear in Eurasia, particularly the Soviet Union. In Bears, IUCN, 1976.*

VROOM, G. W., S. HERRERO, AND R. T. OGILVIE. 1977. The ecology of winter den sites of grizzly bears in Banff National Park, Alberta.

WALKER, ERNEST P. 1975. Mammals of the world. Third ed., rev. John L. Paradiso.

Baltimore: Johns Hopkins University Press.

WALKER, STEPHEN. 1983. *Animal thought*. London: Routledge & Kegan Paul.

WASHBURN, WILCOMB E. 1975. *The Indian in America*. New York: Harper & Row.

WEAVER, JOHN. 1978. The wolves of Yellowstone. National Park Service.

————. 1979. Biological assessment of two proposed oil/gas well drilling sites on the Bridger-Teton National Forest. U.S. Forest Service.

————. 1982. Wolf management guidelines and control plan for the northern Rocky Mountains. Draft.

WIENS, JOHN A. 1983. Competition or peaceful coexistence? *Natural History*, March.

The Wilderness Society. 1983. Toward the twenty-first century. *Wilderness*, summer.

WILSON, EDWARD O., AND WILLIAM H. BOSSERT. 1971. *A primer of population biology*. Stamford, Conn.: Sinauer.

WILTSE, ERIC. 1981. Grizzly can't stay away from Cooke City. *Bozeman Daily Chronicle*, 15 September.

WOOLDRIDGE, DONALD R. 1977. Chemical aversion conditioning of polar and black bears. In *Bears, BBA, 1980.**

WORLEY, DAVID E., J. CARL FOX, JOHN B. WINTERS, RICHARD H. JACOBSON, AND KENNETH R. GREER. 1974. Helminth and arthropod parasites of grizzly and black bears in Montana and adjacent areas. In *Bears, IUCN, 1976.**

WRIGHT, WILLIAM H. 1909. *The grizzly bear*. New York: Scribner's. Reprint, 1977. Lincoln: University of Nebraska Press.

ZAGER, PETER, CHARLES JONKEL, AND RICHARD MACE. 1980. Grizzly bear habitat terminology. Border Grizzly Project special report no. 41. School of Forestry, University of Montana, Missoula.

ZAVADSKI, B. P. 1977. Ecology of the brown bear in the Enisei taiga. In *Bears, BBA, 1980.**

INDEX